Darkness at Heart

Recent Titles in
Contributions to the Study of World Literature

DARKNESS AT HEART

Fathers and Sons in Conrad

CATHARINE RISING

Contributions to the Study of World Literature, Number 37

GREENWOOD PRESS
New York • Westport, Connecticut • London

26084

Library of Congress Cataloging-in-Publication Data

Rising, Catharine.
    Darkness at heart : fathers and sons in Conrad / Catharine Rising.
      p. cm.—(Contributions to the study of world literature,
  ISSN 0738-9345 ; no. 37)
    Includes bibliographical references.
    ISBN 0-313-26880-0 (alk. paper)
    1. Conrad, Joseph, 1857-1924—Characters—Fathers. 2. Fathers and
sons in literature. 3. Fathers in literature. 4. Sons in
literature. I. Title. II. Series.
PR6005.04Z7878 1990
823'.912—dc20   89-29432

British Library Cataloguing in Publication Data is available.

Copyright © 1990 by Catharine Rising

Library of Congress Catalog Card Number: 89-29432
ISBN: 0-313-26880-0
ISSN: 0738-9345

First published in 1990

Greenwood Press, Inc.
88 Post Road West, Westport, Connecticut 06881

Printed in the United States of America

The paper used in this book complies with the
Permanent Paper Standard issued by the National
Information Standards Organization (Z39.48-1984).

10 9 8 7 6 5 4 3 2 1

To Beez, without whose unfailing support and encouragement this work would not have been possible.

Contents

Acknowledgments

I am indebted to the San Francisco Psychoanalytic Institute, which generously admitted to its seminars a newcomer from another discipline; to the late Shakespearean Joel Fineman, who made available a wealth of psychoanalytic papers, in a collection he had aptly titled Sourcebook; and to Alex Zwerdling, Gerald Mendelsohn, and Andrew Griffin, who offered constructive criticisms of the resulting text.

List of Abbreviations

Except as noted, page numbers for quotations from Conrad refer to his <u>Works</u>, Uniform Edition, 22 vols. (London: J. M. Dent & Sons, Ltd., 1923-28).

		Vol.
<u>AF</u>	Almayer's Folly	1
<u>ET</u>	The End of the Tether	20
<u>F</u>	"Falk"	7
<u>HD</u>	Heart of Darkness	20
<u>I</u>	"The Idiots"	1
<u>LJ</u>	Lord Jim	5
<u>MS</u>	The Mirror of the Sea	6
<u>NLL</u>	Notes on Life and Letters	9
<u>NN</u>	The Nigger of the "Narcissus"	7
<u>OI</u>	An Outcast of the Islands	10
<u>OP</u>	"An Outpost of Progress"	1
<u>PR</u>	A Personal Record	6
<u>R</u>	The Rover	13
<u>S</u>	Suspense	21
<u>SA</u>	The Secret Agent	14
<u>SL</u>	The Shadow-Line	16
<u>SS</u>	"The Secret Sharer"	17
<u>T</u>	"Typhoon"	7
<u>UWE</u>	Under Western Eyes	18
<u>V</u>	Victory	19
<u>Y</u>	"Youth"	20

<u>LE</u>   <u>Last Essays</u> (New York: Doubleday, Page & Co., 1926).

Darkness at Heart

1

Introduction

Despite the attention that has been given to Conrad's works as psychological studies, the theme of ambivalence in the relations of father and son appears to have been relatively neglected, whether at the family level or at the level of social authority and institutions. Jungian critics have emphasized the roles of the shadow--the dark self, and the anima--the woman within. Freudian critics have repeatedly stressed maternal themes--in particular, the role of the preoedipal mother, who combines traits of both parents; she antedates the hero's relation to any father figure. Yet the wide variety of fathers and father substitutes in Conrad's work might be taken to signify an obsessive concern with paternity, as an object either of fear and hatred or of longing: that is, in the two ways that characterize the Oedipus complex. Freud concluded that in its complete form the complex

> is twofold, positive and negative, and is due to
> the bisexuality originally present in children:
> that is to say, a boy has not merely an ambivalent
> attitude towards his father and an affectionate
> object-choice towards his mother, but at the same
> time he also behaves like a girl and displays an
> affectionate feminine attitude to his father and
> a corresponding jealousy and hostility towards
> his mother.[1]

In Conrad's fiction these emotions can become attached to any father figure--that is, as the term is used in this work, to any older male who has power or influence over a younger one.

The attitudes of the child to his father become trans-

lated into adult postures of social rebellion and conform-
ity. Conrad himself was an uneasy blend of the dutiful
seaman-son and the rebel. Irving Howe has commented that
under his conscious ethic of control and order lies a
repressed impulse to anarchy, a lava breaking through
the surface of the fiction as a "radical skepticism that
corrodes the underside of everything he values."[2] But
his official philosophy stresses the need for the father's
authority, and particularly at the social level. Sons
must come to terms with an older generation of employers,
captains, and politicians, and their representatives.
In this undertaking the price of failure is isolation,
which for Conrad meant the failure to attain full mascu-
line selfhood or identity. He would have rejected
any notion of the person as what Thomas Parkinson, in
another context, has called "pre-existent"--a unique
soul that could be discovered or revealed through experience, and whose value did not depend on social function.[3]
In 1892 Conrad wrote to Marguerite Poradowska: ". . . by
oneself, one is nothing . . . man is worth neither more
nor less than the work he accomplishes."[4] By this cri-
terion, identity could not exist against or without
social organization. We "must fight in the ranks or our
lives don't count," says the "privileged man" of Lord Jim
(LJ, 337, 339). Conrad himself, having entered the rigid
hierarchy of men at sea, wrote that he "had elected to be
one of them very deliberately, very completely. . . . if
I wasn't one of them I was nothing at all."[5]

From his stated beliefs, and particularly from his
sense of fidelity as the cardinal human virtue,[6] it might
appear that his fiction would offer a large sphere of
conflict-free parent-child relations, like that envisioned
by Erik Erikson and other ego psychologists. For Erikson
the principal task of the older generation is the rendering
of protective assistance to the younger one. Moreover,
only by such activity do the elders escape isolation,
self-absorption, and despair in their own lives; each
generation needs the other.[7] One can glimpse something
resembling an Eriksonian parent in a seaman-mentor like
Solomon Rout of "Typhoon." But the fiction more often
presents another model, an Oedipal and Freudian struggle
in which no peaceful accession of the son to the father's
prerogatives is possible. In this second model the relation is one of mutual betrayal, in a competition at once
social, political, economic, and sexual.[8]

Although Conrad seems until nearly the end of his life
to have been unacquainted with the work of Freud, his
contemporary, Lord Jim was published in 1900, the same year
as The Interpretation of Dreams. Conrad came out of the

intellectual milieu that produced psychoanalysis. His
fiction accords with Freud's "most fundamental discov-
ery--that the unconscious never ceases to challenge our
apparent identity as subjects."[9] As one character
remarks in <u>Nostromo</u>, to be sure of oneself is to be "sure
of nothing. . . . It is the last thing a man ought to be
sure of" (<u>N</u>, 310). Conrad, like Freud, had encountered the
notion of a human unconscious in Schopenhauer's <u>The World
as Will and Idea</u>.[10] And if John Saveson is correct in
assuming he absorbed whatever his friend H. G. Wells had
read, he also knew it from the German psychologist Edward
von Hartmann's <u>Philosophy of the Unconscious</u>.[11] A third
source is reflected in the many explicit references to a
divided self in "The Secret Sharer." From his reading in
German romanticism, and perhaps from Dostoevsky, Conrad was
familiar with the literary use of the double to represent
the unconscious. But although his insights or borrowings
often paralleled Freud's, he evidently did not wish to know
Freud, or the depth of his own psychology. The French
writer H. R. Lenormand tells of having met him in Corsica
in 1921, and of having lent him Brill's translations of the
dream book and <u>Wit and Its Relation to the Unconscious</u>;
Conrad returned them unopened. Lenormand, noting in particular Almayer's incestuous passion for his daughter in
Conrad's first novel, remarks, "I dared sometimes to wonder
if he hadn't managed to deceive himself, voluntarily or
not, on the true motives of his heroes"--for the author
"protested against the existence of such an emotion" in
Almayer. "I don't want to get to the bottom," he said. "I
want to look on reality as something rough and coarse over
which I pass my fingers. Nothing more."[12]
     Two advantages he might have seen in an art of the
surface were an escape from his own emotions, and an
increase in sales to the public. But despite this disavowal of psychological complexity, he uses in his fiction an array of fathers and paternal types to achieve a
constantly shifting perspective on filial relationships.
Furthermore, the possibility of conflict is kept always
before us by the existence of one or more Oedipal triangles
in his novels not concerned exclusively with men and the
sea, and in such shorter works as "Amy Foster," "A Smile of
Fortune," and "Freya of the Seven Isles." Whereas it is
rarely stressed in the plot, the characteristic aim of the
Conradian older man is to kill a younger rival for the
affection of a wife, daughter, or desired mistress. Often
he succeeds; less often, the father himself dies. In
reading Conrad it is, I think, impossible to forget Freud's
"primitive fragment of Greek mythology which tells how
Kronos, the old Father God, swallowed his children and

sought to swallow his youngest son Zeus like the rest, and how Zeus was saved by the craft of his mother and later on castrated his father."[13]

In a panorama of conflict, potential or actual, I attempt here to give portraits of Conrad's father and son, and to show what chance of accommodation he offers. In the process he may emerge as a writer more Oedipally motivated than has usually been supposed, and more aware than Freud that the son's hostility to the father can be matched, as in the story of Kronos, by the father's to the son. Although in the last novels, The Rover and Suspense, he appears to have sought new avenues of reconciliation, the father-son antagonism is, as I try to demonstrate, never fully resolved in his fiction.

Norman Holland, among others, has offered the simplified formula that the content of fiction represents instinctual drives of the artist, whereas the form represents the ego's defenses against the id.[14] If so, one technique, little noticed by critics, by which Conrad could have defended himself against possible Oedipal conflict is the practice of splitting the father figure, which can isolate those traits seen by the son as desirable from those he despises or fears. The multiple fathers of Conrad's works suggest Ernest Jones's famous critique of Hamlet. According to Jones, the elder Hamlet, Claudius, and Polonius represent aspects of a composite Shakespearean parent: the good, idealized father, the pillar of the state; the bad, sexual father, its subverter; and the prating bore.[15] Similarly, if Prince Hamlet, Laertes, and Fortinbras, all three bearing the burden of revenge for a father, represent aspects of the Shakespearean son,[16] Conrad also splits the son figure in its response to authority. But his fragmentation of the father is wider and more frequent, even obtrusive. In its simplest form of duality, the device reminds us of what Freud has called the traditional ambivalence of all religions toward God.[17] Either God's combination of benevolence and egotism, or love and wrath, has been derived from earthly fathers, or they derive from Him. In either case, splitting relieves the son or worshipper of the pain of mixed feelings toward a single parental figure. The pious man can love God and hate the devil, although these two were for Freud merely doubles.[18]

At the risk of undue stress on works usually taken as minor Conrad, I should like to suggest that his pro- totypal, and complete, father figure is the ambiguous Captain Tom Lingard of the first two novels--Rajah Laut and the self-appointed god of the River Pantai. This red-faced deity decides what is good for the people on his river and boasts of the size of his alligators in

the same watercourse. He brings peace and prosperity to
the region, yet his "infernal charity" (OI, 161) leads
directly or indirectly to the deaths of two white protégés,
and an indefinite number of natives. In Almayer's indictment of the father's beneficence:

> Cat, dog, anything that can scratch or bite;
> as long as it is harmful enough and mangy enough.
> A sick tiger would make you happy. . . . A half-
> dead tiger that you could weep over and palm upon
> some poor devil in your power, to tend and nurse
> for you. Never mind the consequences--to the
> poor devil. (OI, 161)
>
> You have no morality. (OI, 162)

Both Almayer and Willems betray their benefactor, Willems
for a woman and Almayer for gold. But in the circumstances
in which he had placed them in his fief of Sambir, both
younger men were likely to destroy themselves. Almayer's
brain is weak; Willems, rusticated and idle, had little to
do but fall in love with his nemesis Aïssa. The demise of
the sons occurs as if Lingard had consciously intended
infanticide; Almayer drowns himself in opium; Willems is
exiled by Lingard to the care of Aïssa, who shoots him when
he tries to escape her. The Rajah Laut establishes a
pattern in which no authority figure in Conrad's work is
wholly to be trusted by his sons or subordinates.
   Subsequent Conradian novels may add intellectual power
or artistic sophistication to the basic Lingard model, but
the paradigm retains its three essential attributes: the
father is protective, deadly, and comic. In the end we
have something like Shakespeare's King Hamlet, Claudius,
and Polonius. These aspects of paternity appear somewhere
in the cast of every novel Conrad wrote. But as an indication of his wish to escape the stress of ambivalent
response, after Lingard he avoided combining all three in a
single character, or he avoided the realistic balance in
which they appear in his prototype. A lifelike figure is
sometimes averted, as in the creation of Captain MacWhirr
of "Typhoon" and Giles of The Shadow-Line, by comedy that
extends to caricature. In his insistence on a comic view
of paternity, Conrad aligns himself with two contem-
poraries, Samuel Butler and James Joyce. For all three,
however, the laughter has a defensive ring. Like Ernest
Pontifex and Stephen Dedalus, Conrad's younger heroes
never attain the full status and prerogatives--social,
political, economic, and sexual--of the prior generation.
Most of them die early, and quite a few die willingly.

I have tried to delineate a Conradian father figure who is, from the son's standpoint, incalculable, possibly unknowable, and never without some aura of danger. But if the father is an uncertain combination of protection, menace, and comedy, the Conradian son is a simpler figure. Like Kafka's son-protagonist, he has one dominant trait: guilt. Critics have noted the high death rate among Conrad's heroes, whether the destructive impulse is ascribed to a character or emanates directly from the author. The fate of Conrad's young men suggests that he construed any act of filial self-assertion as an attempt to supplant the father, and hence a punishable impulse. Although such rebels as Almayer and Willems are guilty of overt crimes against the father and his codes, death is also the fate of young men far less obviously culpable. Any involvement of the son with women may be treated by Conrad as a capital offense. He sometimes relaxes his severity for youths who are nonwhite; in Almayer's Folly, for example, the Malay Dain Maroola is allowed to marry Almayer's daughter and father a child. And even the hero of the short story "Falk," though white, slips by on the ground of primitivism. Lacking full human consciousness in his hunger for a woman, as in the hunger that drove him to murder and cannibalism on a stricken ship, he has not been held humanly responsible by his creator. Toward young men resembling himself, however, Conrad regularly reacts as a punitive superego to any filial encroachment on a droit du seigneur made permanent.

Freud has written in The Ego and the Id that in the resolution of the boy's normal Oedipus complex, his hostility toward the father is replaced by an identification with him, and that this identification effects a modification of the child's ego that henceforth constitutes an ego ideal or superego. The relation of the superego to the ego "is not exhausted by the precept: 'You ought to be like this (like your father).' It also comprises the prohibition: 'You may not be like this (like your father)-- that is, you may not do all that he does; some things are his prerogative.'"[19] The statement refers specifically to the ban laid by the infantile superego on the mother as a sexual object. However, according to Freud's primal-horde theory of human prehistory, the Oedipus complex of a number of sons led at some immemorial time to the killing of a primal father to whom all women belonged by right.[20] Conrad's fiction often reads as if this myth were operative for European man in the nineteenth and twentieth centuries. As a rule, only older men are able to love and marry with impunity.

The method by which Conradian sons reach an accom-

modation with the fathers, or with an author acting on
their behalf, is readily apparent. A precedent is set by a
minor character in the early Malaysian fiction--the wealthy
Arab trader Abdulla, the victorious rival of Lingard on the
Pantai. He foreshadows a line of surviving heroes--most
notably, Marlow--who share with him, besides a measure of
power, asceticism. All thrive in some area of the fathers'
domain but have paid a price by the renunciation of
another. Whereas asceticism might be thought to reflect a
Conradian abhorrence of sex--possibly grounded in the
Victorian ethos that sexual indulgence was a dangerous
waste of energy[21]--the fact remains that it is not a
requisite for the Conradian father. I therefore consider
it relevant to the problem of Oedipal guilt.

The concept of renunciation as a solution to the
Oedipal problem was set forth by Freud in a note to "The
Psychogenesis of a Case of Homosexuality in a Woman"; a
son's flight from both women and work was motivated by fear
of the father, to whom these pursuits seemed rightfully to
belong.[22] Freud's insight was developed by Jule Nydes in
"The Paranoid-Masochistic Character." Nydes regarded both
the paranoid and the masochist--two personality types
Conrad knew well--as living in the grip of unresolved
Oedipal conflict. For either:

> . . . self-assertion--even when it is not
> competitive--and reality success--even when it
> excites little or no hostile enviousness--are
> unconsciously construed . . . as defiance of, and
> transgression against a supreme authority figure.
> Success equals incest with the parent of the
> opposite sex. Success means murder of the parent
> of the same sex. Such murder, since it is
> perpetrated by a little boy (let us say) against
> his gigantic father, implies great power. The
> fantasy exercise of such power leads to intolerable
> guilt and dread of retaliation from the introjected
> parental superego, which in turn is projected onto
> surrogates in the world of contemporary adults.
> For the most part, the sense of guilt is repressed
> and remains unconscious. . . . It is the attempt to
> defend against guilt that is openly demonstrated.

One such defense is what Nydes called the "private
compromise"; success "may be tolerated in one area, if
defeat is endured in another."[23] The defeat to which
Conrad's heroes regularly submit is the loss of women.

As long as the sexual mode of replacing the father is
abjured, Conrad--at least in the fiction up to 1910

--excuses a striking display of other parricidal
impulses, including the attempted murder of a captain in
The Nigger of the "Narcissus." But in Under Western Eyes
(1910), in which the Freudian primal crime, the father's
murder by the son, is actually reenacted, Conrad is less
forgiving. The "private compromise" of his fiction
collapses; celibacy is no longer a defense against the
author. For Haldin's killing of the czar's minister, both
the assassin and Razumov, a secret double[24] in parricide,
are doomed. During the writing of his Russian novel,
Conrad suffered a mental breakdown in which he babbled
deliriously in Polish and, in the words of his wife, held
"converse with the characters"[25] he had created. Biographers have usually concluded that the work came too
near his own past as a victim of Russian autocracy;
however, Oedipal guilt may also have played a part.

Under Western Eyes marks a turning point in the degree
of self-assertion he allows his fictional sons, and in the
quality of his work. Thomas Moser and Albert Guerard, two
members of the achievement-and-decline school of Conrad
criticism, have concluded that after 1910 he simplified his
moral universe by placing evil, or the cause of suffering,
wholly outside a set of passive and spiritless younger
heroes.[26] Bernard Meyer, a psychoanalyst, corroborates
their theory of the innocent protagonist.[27] His assent
is a curious one, since Oedipal sexual rivalry continues in
the later work and draws a condign (for Conrad) punishment
in various kinds of emotional and physical death. But as I
try to indicate, a notable change can be found after 1910
in the sphere of nonsexual rivalry; later men in competition with the father for wealth or position pale beside
the interesting rebels of an earlier day.

Conrad's biography offers ample possibility of both
kinds of Oedipal contest. A sexual rivalry with the father
has been inferred by Richard Sterba and Frederick Crews
from his boyhood wish, transferred to the Marlow of Heart
of Darkness, to penetrate an unknown area on the map of
Africa: "When I grow up I shall go there" (PR, 13); ". . .
When I grow up I will go there" (HD, 52).[28] The
character of his adult relationships with women might also
be mentioned as symptomatic of sexual conflict. The story
of a liaison in Marseilles with the mistress of the
Pretender to the Spanish throne has been discredited; there
remains, however, a distant love affair with an older woman
novelist, Marie Poradowska, whom he called "Aunt" and whose
husband died two days after Conrad had sought her aid in
gaining a command on the Congo. In addition, one might
note a marriage outside his country and social class, as if
an "element of exogamy"[29] were needed to avert incest;

his wish to remain childless; and at the time of his
proposal to Jessie George, his expectation of an early
death. How he himself construed his sexual attitudes is
unknown. But another kind of Oedipal rivalry almost
certainly entered his consciousness. Of Freud's two
spheres outside the family in which the father imago is
decisive, one's "attitude towards the authority of the
State and towards belief in God,"[30] Conrad was ambivalent
toward the first and hostile to the second. In evaluating
his relations with his actual father, no one, so far as I
know, has seriously undermined Gustav Morf's theory that
his art reflects the conflicts surrounding his desertion of
Poland, at sixteen, to go to sea.[31] Although his decision was opposed by a substitute parent, his uncle and
guardian Tadeusz Bobrowski, these conflicts revolved
chiefly around Apollo Korzeniowski--poet, playwright,
translator, and revolutionary--who represented an artistic
and patriotic ideal, yet whose politics had left his son an
orphan. Ewa Korzeniowska had died in 1865 of tuberculosis
contracted in exile in Russia; her husband followed her
within four years. Dedicated by his father to the
apparently hopeless cause of Polish liberation, Conrad's
reply was, in effect, that of Stephen Dedalus in another
occupied country: non serviam. In this resolve he may have
been strengthened by the rational Bobrowski's criticism of
Apollo's impracticality and emotionalism as a fatal inher-
itance--to be, if possible, refused.[32]

   Guilt and exaltation in the betrayal of Poland--and in
a second piece of defiance, the decision to supplant his
father as a writer--might have provided part of the
instinctual base of his literary career. Zdzisław Najder
has said that Conrad in youth declared his ambition to
become "a great writer"[33]; Apollo was a minor one.
Biographers have noted Conrad's difficulties in becoming
any sort of writer and his frequent experience of blockage.
That the source of his affliction was Oedipal is suggested
by a childhood incident in which, having invaded his
father's library, he was caught reading the manuscript of
Apollo's translation of The Two Gentlemen of Verona.
Although his father only directed him to read the page
aloud, he had expected punishment for his "impulsive
audacity" (PR, 72). The threat to supersede a Polish man
of letters is less apparent in Conrad's career as an
officer in the British merchant navy; nevertheless, as
Robert Armstrong has suggested, he seems to have regarded
even this calling as an encroachment on the father.
Armstrong ascribes his psychological barrier to the
captaincy of the Otago--his only command and one he
resigned after only fourteen months--to a war of active and
passive impulses toward Apollo.[34]

But however Oedipally motivated Conrad may appear, recent research into ego psychology and the creative process has demonstrated the need for caution in attempting to derive an author's fiction from his life. The literary work, which requires a complex achievement of sublimation, is now seen as more than what Freud emphasized in it, the fantasy gratification of the artist's frustrated ambitions or erotic wishes: "oppressed by excessively powerful instinctual needs" he lacks the means to satisfy, he turns from reality to "wishful constructions."[35] Of greater interest to post-Freudians has been the ego's role in imposing form on the content dictated by the id. "The artist has created a world and not indulged in a daydream," warns Ernst Kris, and also: success or failure in creativity "depends, among other factors . . . on the extent to which the activity itself has for any particular individual become autonomous, i.e., detached from the original conflict which may have turned interest and proclivity into the specified direction."[36]

One use of Kris's formulation, however, is surely to indicate where and why an author may have faltered. An artistic failure may signify a failure of detachment. In the Familiar Preface to A Personal Record, Conrad appears less than confident of sufficient ego strength to master the products of the id: ". . . I have a positive horror of losing even for one moving moment that full possession of myself which is the first condition of good service" (PR, xix). A possible indication that ego control was precarious throughout his literary career is the existence of an ambiguous line of youthful suicides. Precisely what opportunity, for example, is represented by Jim's veiled "Eastern bride" (LJ, 244, 416)? In the same novel, why should the thriving Captain Brierly drown himself? In Under Western Eyes, why should Razumov, having declared himself "washed clean" (UWE, 357) by his confession to Natalia Haldin, condemn himself by a further confession to the revolutionaries? In Victory, why should Heyst burn himself up for a woman who could not overcome his "infernal mistrust of all life" (V, 406)? These men and others die for reasons that their creator does not fully explain, or cannot. To the vaguely motivated deaths of Conrad's fiction, much of T. S. Eliot's analysis of the absence of an objective correlative for the hero's emotions in Hamlet is applicable. Conrad's work also apparently contains "some stuff that the writer could not drag to light, contemplate, or manipulate into art."[37]

The presence of buried material, inaccessible to other critical methods, invites the use of psychoanalytic theory, as in Ernest Jones's attribution of an unresolved Oedipal constraint to both Hamlet and his creator.

Psychoanalytic critics have, however, disagreed in their
identification of the most significant level of psycho-
sexual development for Conrad. Bernard Meyer's biography, which brilliantly describes the terror and fascination of the preoedipal mother in his life and art,
posits a phallic woman who draws author and heroes alike
toward reunion with her in death. As Freud has said,
". . . in mental life nothing which has once been formed
can perish"[38]; one could scarcely deny that the survival
of an earlier psychic stage underlies the depiction of
Oedipal conflict in Conrad's fiction. The question is one
of relative weight. Meyer discounts the Oedipal problem for
this author: neither the fiction nor the life seems to
project a "hard core" of father-son rivalry; indeed, one
might ask "whether powerful and aggressive heterosexual
strivings could have played an important role in the life
of this man whose childhood was characterized by such
profound maternal deprivation." Meyer considers Conrad's
dominant aggressive impulse to have been not genital but
oral--an "insatiable" appetite expressed, for example, in
the overt cannibalism of "Falk" or the "devouring" quest
for ivory in <u>Heart of Darkness</u>.[39] From this point of
view, love in much of Conrad's fiction represents, at
bottom, "the re-establishment of a blissful intimacy
between mother and child . . . like superimposed pictures,
the pale outlines of adult sexuality are barely visible
against the brighter background of the child at his
mother's breast."[40] Meyer's approach, however,
inevitably stresses such later and weaker works as <u>Chance</u>,
"The Planter of Malata," and <u>The Arrow of Gold</u>, in which
love--for many critics, Conrad's "uncongenial subject"[41]
--has become the dominant issue. A second medical analyst,
Robert Armstrong, has made the necessary point that
"although the pregenital mother may be discerned behind
Conrad's attachment to his father, it seems . . . crucial
that the active struggle with the father figure is at the
heart of Conrad's most successful fiction."[42]
     A hypothesis of Oedipal conflict prolonged into adult-
hood may explain the formal gaps in Conrad's seemingly
arbitrary and abrupt suicides--those in which the emotion
of the victim, as T. S. Eliot said of Hamlet's, is "in
<u>excess</u> of the facts as they appear."[43] Even though
Conrad could not quite manipulate self-destruction into
art, he displays a subliminal insight--not surprising in
a man who once tried to kill himself[44]--into its
motivation. In varying proportions, consciously or
unconsciously, the successful suicide, as defined by Karl
Menninger in <u>Man against Himself</u>, unites the wish to kill,
the wish to be killed, and the wish to die.[45] Additional

terms for the first impulse are "aggression, accusation, blame, eliminating, driving away, disposing of, annihilating, and revenge"; for the second, "submission, masochism, self-blame, and self-accusation"; for the third, "hopelessness, fear, fatigue, and despair."[46] Whether death is self-inflicted or pursued so closely that it becomes inevitable, the three wishes are implicit or explicit in the histories of a majority of Conrad's self-destructive sons. The third was derived by Menninger from Freud's controversial theory, first advanced in <u>Beyond the Pleasure Principle</u> (1920), of a biological death instinct, Thanatos, in conflict with the life instinct, Eros, and finally, invariably, triumphant: ". . . <u>the aim of all life is death</u>."[47] The wish to die comes closest to Meyer's paradigm of the blissful return of the Conradian hero to the peace and safety of the womb. But the other two wishes can be related quite specifically to Oedipal tension. The affinity of suicide with murder Freud recognized before Menninger:

> . . . probably no one finds the mental energy required to kill himself unless, in the first place, in doing so he is at the same time killing an object with whom he has identified himself, and, in the second place, is turning against himself a death-wish which had been directed against someone else. . . . the unconscious of all human beings is full enough of such death-wishes, even against those they love.[48]

The suppressed aggression of an ambivalent relationship can be directed against an internalized person. In Conrad this target is likely to be an actual or substitute father in the manifest content, especially one who has bequeathed to the son an unattainable standard of conduct. Conrad's work parallels Freud's theory that the superego, or conscience, "retains the character of the father."[49] Even Bernard Meyer, who focused on the imprint of the mother, noted a legacy of Apollo's disastrous idealism and egotism in every story Conrad wrote; the son presumably regretted that the poet-patriot had remained for him an ego ideal, the "fixed star in the firmament of [his] aspirations."[50] But if the aim of the Conradian hero is to kill the father within himself, he also loves the father; the guilt of his hostility contributes to the second suicidal motive, the wish to be killed. The omniscient Freudian superego makes no distinction between the murderous thought and the murderous act; guilt for aggression fantasied is equal to guilt for aggression carried out.[51]

Besides a failure, more or less continuous throughout his work, to bring suicide under artistic control, Conrad in his later fiction generally failed to create heroes of sufficient interest to sustain his narratives. Again, a lapse of authorial detachment may be conjectured. Other factors were doubtless present: in particular, his own exhaustion from years of overwork, financial stress, and the torments of gout may have helped to drain his protagonists of energy. But the coincidence in 1910 of a parricidal novel, a mental breakdown, and a literary shift toward male passivity may indicate a reactivation or intensification of Oedipal conflict. If so, his career supports the inference of Clarence Oberndorf, from the biographies of De Quincey, Coleridge, Poe, Baudelaire, and Hawthorne, that "confessional writing" rarely entails a cathartic benefit to the writer. If he has sought through his art a liberation from neurotic conflicts, "in most cases . . . the attempt of the author to free himself of the neurosis by writing it out is unsuccessful."[52]

Indeed, if any therapeutic reaction could be inferred from Conrad's case, a negative one might be argued from his collapse in the midst of writing a parricidal novel. This crisis was perhaps foreshadowed at the beginning of his literary career. His most courageous portrayal of the father occurs, as will be seen, in his first two novels; here he dared to present his paternal prototype realistically, as a complex figure likely to elicit conflicting responses from both reader and author. No such balanced and complete father was ever to appear in his fiction again; in the creation of Lingard, Conrad appears to have frightened himself.

2

The Prototype of the Father:
Lingard in *Almayer's Folly*
and *An Outcast of the Islands*

In the Lingard of his first two novels,[1] Conrad created
as his prototypal father a man whose supposed benevolence
achieves the ruin of two adoptive sons and who acquires
control of all the women in whom they have been known to
show an interest. The portrait of the autocratic Lingard
owes something to the late-nineteenth-century preoccupation
with the god-man, the mere human being who in the absence
of transcendent moral sanctions is obliged to make his own
laws.[2] In paternalistic colonial relationships or in
paternal ones within a family, he could be equally characterized by a lack of external restraint. But Lingard's
role as a sexual and financial monopolist relates him
also to Freud's concept (taken, Freud said, from Charles
Darwin) of the primal horde--a group headed by a jealous
father who kept all the power and all the women for
himself.[3] In a similar refusal to yield any of his
prerogatives to men of the next generation, Lingard
embodies what John Munder Ross has recently called a
"heart of darkness," a regressive potential for harm, in
all fatherhood.[4]

     It may be significant that Conrad approached this
formidable patriarch of his fiction only by indirection.[5]
He wrote a first novel, Almayer's Folly, in which the
Rajah Laut is distanced as an absent father, or a deity
who--like the god of the deists--has withdrawn from his
creation, the little world of Sambir, leaving his followers
to make of it what they can. Conrad attributes the decline
and fall of Almayer to a combination of forces, including
his own folly and the machinations of colonial and native
rulers. The British Borneo Company, on whose future in
island development he has heavily gambled, inexplicably

cedes to the Dutch its claim to the Pantai region. Later,
in a complex intrigue with the young Malay Dain Maroola,
Almayer agrees to furnish gunpowder to native rebels
against the Dutch, in return for Maroola's support in an
expedition to tap an Eldorado that Lingard claimed to have
found in the interior of Borneo. But the wreck of
Maroola's brig removes his value as an ally; and the
Malay's love for Nina Almayer, a half-caste who has elected
native identity instead of white, breaks a father's
incestuous tie to his daughter. Nina's marriage to
Maroola, which affronts not only Almayer's jealous
affection but his racial pride, is the immediate cause of
his death. After the birth of Nina's son—a source of joy
for Maroola's father, the old Rajah of Bali, but not for
the child's white grandfather—Almayer becomes addicted to
opium and expires in middle age.

The title of the novel affirms a Bovaryish dreamer's
weaknesses of mind and will. It is apparent, for example,
that Almayer has no need to renounce his daughter and
Maroola, to whom a wiser father-in-law might have assumed a
paternal role as an interpreter of the dominant white
culture. Instead he feebly tries to kill Maroola, then
banishes the pair from Sambir as a personal shame no other
white man can be permitted to see; he carefully erases
Nina's very footprints from the sand she crossed to reach
her boat to the outer world. But whatever Almayer's
errors—and they are many—the environment that has enabled
him to assist materially in his own downfall has been
imposed on him by Lingard. That seemingly benevolent
despot lured a young Dutch clerk to Sambir with the promise
to make his fortune if he would marry Lingard's Malay
foster daughter, whom the old man had orphaned in a fight
with Sulu pirates. "And don't you kick because you're
white!" he thunders. "Call me father, my boy. . . . I
always get my way" (AF, 10, 11). In the thought she may
die and leave him rich, Almayer agrees to marry a savage
largely untouched by the brief exposure to a Christian
convent Lingard has arranged for her. A reluctant Galatea,
who had hoped to wed and rule Lingard as his captive,
instead finds herself despised by the man he has bought for
her. Reverting to native betel-chewing and stupor, she
signifies for Almayer the threat of poison and the fact of
intrigue with the native ruler Lakamba, as well as an
influence that helps to estrange Nina from the white race.

The money that was to have been Almayer's compensation
for domestic misery has never been forthcoming, nor would
Lingard's psychology have left a rational basis for great
expectations. The schemes of an adventurer "ragged,

dishevelled, enthusiastic" (AF, 26) crash like the house of cards he built for Nina as a child in part 3, chapter 3 of An Outcast; but even as a man of some wealth, in the best years of the Sambir trade, he does not allow his son-in-law to batten noticeably. And after Willems's betrayal of the river channel to Sambir has brought in Arab competition and the Dutch flag, what meager profits might have been left to Almayer are drained away to finance Lingard's mysterious gold enterprise in Dyak country. Finally, under circumstances left vague, Lingard vanishes with the available capital of both men; in Almayer's Folly he may be dead, he may not. A letter from Singapore has announced his departure for Europe to raise money for the great venture.

> There would be no difficulties, he wrote. People
> would rush in with their money. Evidently they
> did not, for there was only one letter more from
> him saying he was ill, had found no relation
> living, but little else besides. Then came a
> complete silence. Europe had swallowed up the
> Rajah Laut. (AF, 27-28)

Almayer's eventual betrayal of what purports to be Lingard's way to the gold is not without extenuation. Like Jim after the abandonment of the Patna, a ruined junior partner might have asserted, "There was not the thickness of a sheet of paper between the right and wrong of this affair" (LJ, 130).

An Outcast, the inverse sequel to Almayer's Folly, carries Sambir back fifteen or twenty years to the events of Willems's betrayal. The lucky and successful Lingard, seen at his zenith, is a simple man to whom all things are simple.

> He seldom read. Books were not much in his way,
> and he had to work hard navigating, trading, and
> also, in obedience to his benevolent instincts,
> shaping stray lives he found here and there under
> his busy hand. He remembered the Sunday-school
> teachings of his native village and the discourses
> of the black-coated gentleman connected with the
> Mission to Fishermen and Seamen.

This "clever . . . sky-pilot" (OI, 198) of his childhood is a formative influence on Lingard's future largesse. Ignorant of books, knowing nothing of Arcadia, he dreams without interference of "Arcadian happiness for that little

corner of the world which he loved to think all his own.
. . . only he . . . knew what was good for them. . . . He
would make them happy whether or no" (OI, 200). A long set
piece identifies him as Conrad's ironically limited "man of
purpose," who walks "the road of life . . . generally
honest, invariably stupid, and . . . proud of never losing
[his] way" (OI, 197). He

> knows where he is going and what he wants.
> Travelling on, he achieves great length
> without any breadth, and battered, besmirched,
> and weary, he touches the goal at last; he
> grasps the reward of his perseverance . . . an
> untruthful tombstone over a dark and soon
> forgotten grave.
>   Lingard had never hesitated in his life.
> Why should he? (OI, 197)

He does not hesitate to trust Willems, whose treachery
would appear--except to Lingard--entirely predictable.
Willems first surfaces in An Outcast as a bright lad of
seventeen who has jumped ship, deserting a friendly Dutch
captain, in order to get more money. Not finding it on
Lingard's brig, he deserts this second benefactor also--to
become, in time, the confidential clerk of the Macassar
merchant Hudig. When he embezzles from Hudig, he commits
his third betrayal of an authority figure within fourteen
years. Reproachfully, Lingard prevents the suicide of the
disgraced clerk and takes him in hand once more--in deference, it is said, to his own "absurd conscience." "We
are responsible for one another" (OI, 40), he explains the
fatal decision to show Willems the way into Sambir by
taking him there for a refuge.
    Lingard's sentiment of responsibility turns out, as we
shall see, to mask an unconscious bid for power; but the
conscious motive refers back to a familiar dichotomy in
Conrad's fiction: the opposition of innocence at sea to
corruption on land. Perhaps the clearest statement of a
faith he strove to preserve appears, ironically, in the
story of a near mutiny--The Nigger of the "Narcissus"
(1897). Once the ship has left the last vestige of "the
sordid earth," a tug's "unclean" patch of soot on the
swell, we are told that "the true peace of God begins at
any spot a thousand miles from the nearest land" (NN, 27,
31, 165). At this distance, sailors' "simple hearts" are
said to "beat undisturbed by envy or greed" (NN, 31).
Conrad obviously intended to depict the Rajah Laut as a
naif made vulnerable by the element on which he has spent

his life: "The sea took him young, fashioned him body and soul; gave him . . . his stupidly guileless heart. [It made] his absurd faith in himself, his universal love of creation . . . his straightforward simplicity of motive and honesty of aim" (OI, 13). But when Willems is fired by Hudig for theft, Lingard recognizes the baleful influence of the land upon this fallen protégé: ". . . you got yourself so crooked amongst those 'longshore quill-drivers that you could not run clear in any way. . . . there's only one place for an honest man. The sea, my boy, the sea! But you never would; didn't think there was enough money in it" (OI, 41-42). Thus if the sea has rendered Lingard simple, it has also equipped him to detect one who is not. Willems, a precursor of the execrable Donkin in The Nigger of the "Narcissus," has failed Lingard's and Conrad's test of character: a preference for sea over land. The question remains, then, of the basis for Lingard's trust in Willems.

Despite his attempt to idealize seamen, Conrad concedes that no one is "so simple as not to feel and suffer from the shock of warring impulses" (OI, 129). R. A. Gekoski has found an explanation for Lingard's self-betrayal in the power drive underlying his apparently disinterested actions. In the urge to dominate, inci-dentally, he closely resembles Willems. Just as the younger man exults in his role as provider for his wife and her swarm of relatives--"They lived now by the grace of his will. This was power. Willems loved it"--so Lingard relishes the dependence of Sambir: ". . . I brought prosperity to that place"; ". . . I have them all in my pocket. . . . My word is law--and I am the only trader" (OI, 5, 43, 45).[6] By a natural association Lingard moves from his power over Sambir to his apparent power over Willems--now that the confidential clerk has been deposed--and then again to Sambir.

> You will live quietly there till I come back
> from my next cruise. . . . We shall see then
> what can be done for you. . . . I have no doubt
> my secret will be safe with you. Keep mum about
> my river. . . . that's where I get all my guttah
> and rattans. Simply inexhaustible, my boy.
> (OI, 43)

For Gekoski, these are "the words of a . . . man deeply convinced of his own omnipotence"[7]--even over one he apparently considers his mental superior: "A smart fellow. He had brought him up. The smartest fellow in the islands" (OI, 262). Lingard can never quite forget that he once

picked Willems up "in a ditch . . . like a starved cat"
(OI, 17).

In Conrad's fiction the exercise of power gratifies a
primitive appetite, best described in the first two novels
in terms of subject peoples. Babalatchi, the wily old
Malay politician of Sambir, links Lingard's charity to the
theme of European colonialism: all white men prattle of the
common good while they load their guns and sharpen their
swords. ". . . and when you are ready, then to those who
are weak you say: 'Obey me and be happy, or die!' You are
strange, you white men. . . . A black tiger knows when he
is not hungry--you do not" (OI, 226). Babalatchi's
accusation of European insatiability foreshadows Conrad's
celebrated image of colonialism in Heart of Darkness. As
Marlow describes Kurtz, the fallen "emissary of pity, and
science, and progress": "I saw him open his mouth wide--it
gave him a weirdly voracious aspect, as though he had
wanted to swallow all the air, all the earth, all the men
before him"; "everything belonged to him" (HD, 79, 116,
134). But in both the novel and the novella, the colonial
European is despotic as well as ravenous. In Freud's
terms, the Conradian Wille zur Macht combines two distinct
infantile impulses, the oral and the anal-sadistic: the
urge to devour and the urge to master. The first is
consistent with the abrogation of the object's "separate
existence," the second with "injury or annihilation of the
object [as] a matter of indifference"; only when the
genital organization has been established does love become
distinguishable from hate in its attitude to the object.[8]
The survival of infantile sexuality in an adult European
constitutes a danger to his subject or inferior. For Freud
the oral stage referred simply to incorporation, without
intent to harm; however, Karl Abraham, who came nearer
Conrad's view of colonialism, divided this first stage of
human development into two, an oral-incorporative and an
oral-sadistic, corresponding to the infant's sucking and
biting. The first phase Abraham considered "pre-
ambivalent," i.e., free of the wish to destroy the
object ("The child is not yet able to distinguish between
its own self and the external object."); the second,
corresponding to the teething period, did entail this
wish.[9] In proposing an angry and destructive phase of
orality, Abraham added a third infantile motive to the
urges to devour and master. Conrad knew them all from
imperialism; if Kurtz's open maw symbolizes the desire for
acquisition of native peoples, their land, and their ivory,
his European armory symbolizes the desire for mastery and
his final solution--"Exterminate all the brutes!" (HD,
118)--the impulse to destroy.

Conrad's insertion of the encounter with Babalatchi
just before Lingard's judgment of the traitor Willems
suggests an intended parallel between the Rajah Laut's
paternalistic relation to Malays and his paternal relation
to adoptive sons. In either inequality, apparently, the
lesser will must be destroyed. Conrad himself would have
explained the link between parental and political tyranny
in terms not of infantile sexuality but of what Allan
McIntyre has called a "Calvinistic view of human evil."
Although Conrad, a secular novelist, had discarded the
concept of original sin, men were, for him, nevertheless
doomed to become "<u>fourbes, lâches, menteurs, voleurs,
cruels</u>." Inevitably, "into the noblest cause, men manage
to put something of their baseness. . . . Every cause is
tainted: and you reject this one, espouse that other one as
if one were evil and the other good, while the same evil
you hate is in both, but disguised in different words."[10]
As the source of this evil--since original sin does not
figure--Royal Roussel has postulated a darkness, a chaos or
irrationality, at the heart of the Conradian universe, a
flaw that negates all human effort for order, progress, and
morality. The evolution of the cosmos itself has been an
absurdity, as Conrad viewed it:

> There is a--let us say--a machine. It evolved
> itself . . . out of a chaos of scraps of iron and
> behold!--it knits. . . . And the most withering
> thought is that the infamous thing has made itself;
> made itself without thought, without conscience,
> without foresight, without eyes, without heart.
> It is a tragic accident--and it has happened.
> You can't interfere with it. The last drop of
> bitterness is the suspicion that you can't even
> smash it.[11]

Roussel's metaphysical explanation might be taken as
primary. But whether the origin of evil is considered to
be moral, metaphysical, or psychological, the result is the
same for Conrad's fiction: no exercise of power can be
ultimately beneficent.

Willems--whose inexorable decline, like that of
Almayer, dates from his first meeting with his benefactor[12]--has some appreciation of Lingard as a foe.
On the point of giving away the secret of the old man's
prosperity, he remarks to Abdulla, "Injustice destroys
fidelity" (<u>OI</u>, 131). Although Willems is nothing if not
self-serving, the sudden charge, like an irruption from the
unconcious, may reveal a piece of knowledge he has

preferred to suppress. His exile to Sambir, ruinous to
Lingard, Almayer, and himself, had perhaps only the excuse
of an exercise of Lingard's power. Outside Hudig's family
and business, Willems's theft--largely repaid by himself
and fully made good by Lingard--was unknown even in
Macassar. A ship or any port within reach might have
sufficed as a refuge. Unlike Jim and Leggatt in later
works, Willems, who was not involved in a <u>cause célèbre</u>,
had no particular need to hide in what even the docile
Almayer calls a hole, and where Almayer shuns him as a
sibling rival for Lingard's money.[13] The justification
for the narrator's description of Willems as "crucified"
(<u>OI</u>, 256) is possibly that he was not an outcast until
Lingard made him one. Willems's brash summons to the man
he has sold--"Come and see me. I am not afraid. Are you?
W." (<u>OI</u>, 203)--implies some accusation of the victim. The
charge of Lingard's responsibility for the affair with
Aïssa--and hence for the betrayal required to keep her--is
Willems's first point in his own defense: ". . . you came
and dumped me here like a load of rubbish; dumped me here
and left me with nothing to do. . . . Months passed. I
thought I would die of sheer weariness. . . . And then
. . ." (<u>OI</u>, 267). Like Almayer, he has an ego ideal of
racial superiority. The surrender to a passion for Aïssa--
half Arab, half Malay, to Willems a mongrel--imbues him
with a sense of self-alienation and degradation.

> You don't know . . . I wanted to pass the time--
> to do something--to have something to think about.
> . . . she took me as if I did not belong to myself.
> . . . I did not know there was something in me she
> could get hold of. She, a savage. I, a civilized
> European, and clever! . . . Well, she found out
> something in me. She found it out, and I was lost.
> (<u>OI</u>, 269)
>
> I am white! I swear to you I can't stand this!
> Take me away. I am white! All white! (<u>OI</u>, 271)

But Lingard, in sentencing Willems to Aïssa for life,
chooses to make his degradation permanent: ". . . I leave
him his life not in mercy but in punishment" (<u>OI</u>, 255).
    Conrad observes that a man "does not live for years
beyond the pale of civilized laws without evolving for
himself some queer notions of justice" (<u>OI</u>, 235). It might
be noted also that Lingard has scant knowledge of his own
motives. Having persuaded himself that he is about to
execute on Willems, out of "sacred duty" (<u>OI</u>, 234), a white

man's "great justice that knows not anger" (<u>OI</u>, 229),[14]
he attacks the culprit with his bare hands.

> His grip on the revolver relaxed gradually. As
> the transport of his rage increased, so also his
> contempt for the instruments that pierce and stab,
> that interpose themselves between the hand and the
> object of hate. He wanted another kind of satisfac-
> tion. Naked hands, by heaven! No firearms. Hands
> that could take him by the throat, beat down his
> defence, batter his face into shapeless flesh; hands
> that could feel all the desperation of his resistance
> and overpower it in the violent delight of a contact
> lingering and furious, intimate and brutal.
> . . . everything passed from his sight. (<u>OI</u>, 259)

Only the lack of the expected resistance prevents an
immediate murder, in what appears to be sexual transport.
"Amazed and aggrieved" by Willems's passivity, Lingard
feels "the immense and blank desolation of a small child
robbed of a toy" (<u>OI</u>, 260). But his penchant for cru-
elty--hinted in an earlier description of his "little
red eyes . . . like a pair of frightened wild beasts" (<u>OI</u>,
188)--is well served in the aftermath, especially by his
neglect to furnish Willems any quinine in exile (<u>OI</u>, 341).
When Aïssa shoots her lover, her bullet ends the suffering
of a fever-racked skeleton. Almayer, at times a wise fool,
recites for a European visitor the inscription Lingard has
placed on an expensive tombstone for Willems, on a hill
overlooking the Pantai: "'Peter Willems, Delivered by the
Mercy of God from his Enemy.' What enemy--unless Captain
Lingard himself? . . . He was a great man--father was--but
strange" (<u>OI</u>, 364-65). In his thoughts Almayer has
rendered a plainer verdict on Lingard's sadistic treatment
of Willems: "You may kill a man, but you mustn't torture
him" (<u>OI</u>, 304).

In Conrad's proliferation of male authority figures,
Lingard's European concept of justice has been weighed
against Babalatchi's Malay standard. The counselor of
Sambir had assumed that Lingard's disposal of Willems would
consist of his briefly shooting the traitor on sight. In
Lingard's counterassertion of a white man's superior mercy,
Babalatchi was made to appear savage. But in the sentence
actually passed on Willems, it is the European who appears
the greater savage.

Lingard's revenge reflects a powerful alloy of oral
and anal-sadistic impulses in his parental love. In the
urge to make Willems and Almayer parts of himself, thus

cancelling their separate existences, to destroy them, or
to assert his mastery by the infliction of pain, there is
nothing specific to an Oedipal phase of parent-child
relations. However, in Almayer's Folly and An Outcast
these motives for parental hate appear to be reinforced by
another Freudian source of hostility: the instinct for
self-preservation. "Hate, as a relation to objects, is
older than love. It derives from the narcissistic ego's
primordial repudiation of the external world with its
outpouring of stimuli"; "the ego hates, abhors and pursues
with intent to destroy all objects which are a source of
unpleasurable feelings for it."[15] Paternal unpleasure
results from the Oedipal son's two normal wishes: the
murder of the father--here, by the sale of his secrets--and
the enjoyment of the mother--here, any of four maternal
women over whom, as I shall try to show, some father-son
rivalry is implied. The imputation of hostility to the
Oedipal father differentiates Conrad's view from that of
classical Freudian theory, which held that at least in the
modern civilized family, the child's view of the father as
a monster could be traced entirely to the projection of his
own murderous impulses, and to unconscious fantasies
derived from his phylogenetic inheritance; the father was
thus absolved of all blame for the child's attitude to him.
However, a few analysts have conceded the existence of a
paternal complement, sometimes called the Laius complex, to
the child's Oedipus complex. To John Munder Ross, for
example, the relation of Laius and Oedipus in the Greek
myth is a metaphor for the tragic "dialogue of the
unconscious" that can take place between any father and
son.[16] In Ross's reading, the Greek oracle has only
predicted the natural course of events: Oedipus will kill
his father in the sense of outliving and replacing him.
Unfortunately,

> Laius reacts to the prediction of his inevitable
> death as if he could, in fact, defy nature and
> live forever. . . .
>   It is a biological truism that physical life
> requires death. Moreover, psychological parricide
> is also inevitable. In assuming more and more
> their independent responsibility, their "paternality
> of self," children are fated to usurp parental
> functions and eventually to do away with their
> parents. . . .
>   . . . the castration implicit in this accession
> may be . . . too much for some men to bear. For
> them, the blush and promise, the inevitable
> brashness of youth are excruciating reminders of

their own frailty and finitude. Then, as now, men
made magical and often tyrannous efforts to undo
the passing of the generations by attempting to
create an illusion of personal immortality, by
acting to render of the young subservient
reflections or "clones" of the self, or by simply
oppressing or destroying them. Laius does all of
this.[17]

Freud's acquittal of the father in case histories and
in his account of the Oedipus myth has been ascribed by
Ross to a universal impulse to idealization. "Need and
guilt conspire in the exoneration of the father--the need
for his protection, guilt as his internal proxy."[18]
Toward himself as a parent, however, Freud was more
critical. In a note appended to the dream book in 1919 he
revealed his wish fulfillment in a dream that his son had
been wounded at the front in the first World War. The
parental emotion apparently gratified was "the envy which
is felt for the young by those who have grown old, but
which they believe they have completely stifled."[19] Ross
expressed regret that this insight was not incorporated
into general Oedipal theory, which "remained essentially a
psychology of sons and their filial conflicts."[20]

Laius's narcissism, hubris, and violence toward
Oedipus exemplified for Ross a potential "heart of
darkness" in fatherhood. I would submit that his analysis
is applicable to the kind of control that Lingard maintains
over his adoptive sons, who in effect die of their
dependence on him. Doom is banishment to his province of
Sambir, whose name recalls the Siberia of the czar's
political prisoners in Conrad's youth. Lingard's
gratuitous cruelty to Willems suggests the reaction of
Laius when **his** power threatened to be incomplete. The
child destined to replace him is not only exposed but
pinioned by the ankles--an apparently needless precaution
to keep a neonate from crawling, and one that gives Oedipus
his name: swollen foot.

One difference between Laius and Lingard, however, is
that whereas the first acts in what he takes to be self-
interest, the second believes his motives to be wholly
altruistic. "You are buried here" (OI, 277), he tells
Willems.

You are not fit to go amongst people. Who could
suspect . . . what's in you? I couldn't! You
are my mistake. I shall hide you here. If I let
you out you would go amongst unsuspecting men, and
lie, and steal, and cheat for a little money or for

some woman. . . . Do not expect me to forgive you.
To forgive one must have been angry and become
contemptuous, and there is nothing in me now--no
anger, no contempt, no disappointment. To me you
are not Willems, the man I befriended and helped
through thick and thin, and thought much of . . .
You are not a human being. (OI, 275)

As far as the rest of the world is concerned . . .
your life is finished. Nobody will be able to
throw any of your villainies in my teeth; nobody
will be able to point at you and say, "Here
goes a scoundrel of Lingard's up-bringing." (OI,
277)

Lingard's conscious altruism is undercut by the shift of
focus from society to self, in a concern for what he still
has left to lose--his reputation. Moreover, the style of
these tirades, the piling of imputed future misdeeds on
past malfeasance and the climactic denial of Willems's
humanity, effectively belie Lingard's assertion that he
feels neither anger nor contempt, two symptoms of personal
involvement.

 Of the two wishes attributed by psychoanalysts to the
normal Oedipal son, the murder of the father and the
possession of the mother, John Munder Ross's proposal of a
parental complement to the first has been noted. A possible complement to the second has been described by Neil
Friedman and Richard Jones in an article suggestively
titled "On the Mutuality of the Oedipus Complex." What the
authors see as the child's uncontrolled sexuality is
considered both a model and a potential threat to his
parents, who in their own development have long since
become subject to taboos of "basic repression (the oedipal
superego) and of surplus repression (education, religion,
morality, etc.)." As the child becomes more and more
disturbing to adult equanimity, the parental wish
"symbiotic with the child's incestuous wish" is that of
infanticide.[21] The Friedman-Jones theory of parental
repression resembles Lingard's view of himself in middle or
late age; consciously a celibate, he makes a standard
Conradian substitution of ship for woman, to the advantage
of the brig that now lies wrecked on a reef: "Wasn't she a
sweet craft? Could make her do anything but talk. She was
better than a wife to me. Never scolded" (OI, 173). By
contrast, Lingard's unconscious reality appears to be a
sexuality of which he himself has at least one glimpse in
An Outcast. When Aïssa, pleading for Willems's life, adds

an erotic reinforcement to her appeal--"You have been young. Look at me. Look, Rajah Laut!"--he blurts, "You shall have his life." Lingard has unexpectedly found a human being--"a woman at that"--with the power to make him disclose his will before its time. It is only at this point, when he has learned that Aïssa can attract him as well as Willems, that Lingard decides what to do with Willems. There must be a death, but a slow one: "Understand . . . that I leave him his life not in mercy but in punishment" (OI, 251, 255).

What this scene appears to represent, through several veils--a woman who is motherly yet not a mother, a woman of a different race, a man who is an adoptive rather than a natural parent--is the revenge of the Oedipal father on the son whom the mother has preferred to himself. A protective Aïssa has once told Willems, the son-lover-husband reclining on her breast, "I shall watch your sleep, O child!" (OI, 145); she then defended him against her father, the ruined Arab chieftain Omar. Later, when she kills Willems, the voice of this parent as a ghost impels her to shoot; hence her decision would eventually appear to be for the father--some father but not Lingard--against the son. Yet Omar the Arab wanderer can be interpreted as an alter ego of Lingard the white wanderer, who succeeds Omar as Aïssa's guardian. She comes to live at Sambir, where, in an interesting suggestion of maternal age, she is soon metamorphosed into a "doubled-up crone" (OI, 366).[22]

I have analyzed the connections between Aïssa, Willems, Omar, and Lingard in some detail as an example of Conrad's circuitous method of obtruding Lingard, invariably, as a possible rival for any woman in whom either of his foster sons happens to be interested. Bernard Meyer has described the frequent, explicit, and unsubtle father-daughter ties in Conrad's fiction, such as that between Aïssa and the possessive Omar, as a screen for their opposite: the incest of a mother with her actual son, a relation that the novelist entirely avoided.[23] Meyer seems to be correct if one adds to his mother-son dyad the figure of the son's father--since it is there, in actuality or in the form of a substitute. The complete relationship with which Conrad eschewed any direct engagement then becomes the competition of father and son for the mother. The fictional omission is compatible with Conrad's avoidance of mother-son incest in reality, by his marriage to a woman much younger than himself, and one outside his class and country.

In depicting what Oedipal relationships he has chosen to show, Conrad employs a technique of emphasis by

repetition. <u>Almayer's Folly</u> has one triangle in which
Lingard's adopted daughter hopes to become his wife instead
of Almayer's; a second involves the intrusion of Lingard
into Almayer's incestuous relation with <u>his</u> daughter, "upon
whom the old seaman seemed to have transferred all his
former affection for the mother" (<u>AF</u>, 26). Lingard insists
on taking Nina at the age of six to be "brought up
decently" by his "good friends in Singapore"; Almayer is
thus deprived of "the only human being he loved" (<u>AF</u>,
26).[24] <u>An Outcast</u> adds two more triangles, which bring
Lingard into sexual opposition with Willems as well. In
the Oedipal tangles of the second novel, not only has
Almayer been compelled to marry Lingard's Malay foster
child, but Willems under equal duress has taken the
illegitimate half-caste daughter of Lingard's alter ego
Hudig (the two fathers, matched in age, money, power, and
temper, employ at times the same two protégés). Each
husband scorns his wife as racially inferior[25]; and at
least one of the victims, Mrs. Almayer, looks down on
whites. Although the fathers would appear to have given
women away to younger men, it might be more accurate to
say that each has sought to retain his daughter, or his
paternal influence, by effecting a misalliance. If so,
Hudig, an "old sinner" (<u>OI</u>, 188) with women, is the more
forthright of the pair. He breaks with Joanna when she
proves loyal to her exiled husband; her protector then
becomes Lingard. In taking charge of Aïssa as well, after
she has killed Willems, Lingard succeeds a second overtly
jealous father--Omar, who once tried to murder Aïssa's
lover himself, and whose ghost speeds her fatal bullet with
the injunction, "Kill! Kill!" (<u>OI</u>, 359). That Lingard
does not object to murder may be inferred from Almayer's
summary of the Lingard-Aïssa relationship: "Father thought
a lot of her" (<u>OI</u>, 365).

A hypothesis that Lingard is a Freudian primal father,
successfully competing with his sons for women, might help
to explain the sexual aspects of his last interview with
Willems. We are told that Lingard treats Willems's message
as a piece of defiance, like the traitor's continued
presence around Sambir after he has brought in the Arabs
and the Dutch flag. In Lingard's ruminations: "He ought
to have cut Almayer's throat and burnt the place to
ashes--then cleared out. Got out of his way; of him,
Lingard! Yet he didn't. Was it impudence, contempt--or
what? He felt hurt at the implied disrespect of his power"
(<u>OI</u>, 202-3). However, when they meet, a motive for revenge
appears beyond the injury to Lingard's pride of territory.
Just before he goes blind with rage, the old man sees a

bone, "sharp and triangular like the head of a snake, dart up and down" (OI, 258) under the skin of his adversary's throat--that part of Willems that is to be Lingard's target. Only gradually he becomes aware of his grip on something: "Ah! the thing like a snake's head that darts up and down" (OI, 260). If the reptile has its conventional symbolism, one source of Lingard's fury is sexual; appropriately, Willems's defense includes the plea that having yielded to Aïssa, he now abhors all women.

> . . . I have always led a virtuous life. More
> so than Hudig--than you. Yes, than you. I drank
> a little, I played cards a little. Who doesn't?
> But I had principles from a boy. . . . I kept clear
> of women. It's forbidden--I had no time--and I
> despised them. Now I hate them. (OI, 266)

This renunciation (which disregards Lingard's professed aim to reunite him with Joanna) would grant an exclusive paternal right to the women of the novel, and would leave as his own sole erotic tie the negative, or homosexual, Oedipal link to Lingard, his source of love and protection: "In the whole world there was only one man that had ever cared for me. Only one white man. You!" (OI, 274). The negative Oedipal tie would be consistent with Willems's passivity before Lingard's attack, including the blow that closes one eye and might be taken to symbolize castration.

As shown by Lingard's prediction (OI, 275) that Willems, if he were freed, might betray again for a woman, the son's renunciation has left him unconvinced. Yet it has gone further than might have been expected. When Aïssa tries to revive his love, for the only erotic object left to him, he stiffens from her in "repulsion," "horror," and "revolt" (OI, 285). In a last effort, when Lingard has been gone several days:

> He took her in his arms and waited for the
> transport, for the madness, for the sensations
> remembered and lost; and while she sobbed gently
> on his breast he held her and felt cold, sick,
> tired, exasperated with his failure--and ended by
> cursing himself. . . .
> . . . She, wild with delight, whispered on
> rapidly, of love, of light, of peace, of long
> years. . . . He looked drearily above her head
> down into the deeper gloom of the courtyard.
> And, all at once, it seemed to him that he was
> peering into a sombre hollow, into a deep black
> hole full of decay and of whitened bones; into

an immense and inevitable grave full of corruption
where sooner or later he must, unavoidably, fall.
(OI, 338-39)

If the deep hole is read as a female symbol, one
possible meaning of this passage is sociological. A
renewed surrender to Aïssa would signify death to any
vestige of Willems's original concept of himself as a
clever and civilized European, part of a Victorian male
world of order, discipline, and achievement; he has
celebrated a male civilization when he linked "good men who
would rescue him" to "trade . . . houses . . . proper food,
and money . . . beds, knives, forks, carriages, brass
bands, cool drinks, churches with well-dressed people
praying in them" and the chance to "be virtuous, correct,
do business . . . become rich" (OI, 329-30). Besides
the sociological interpretation, however, at least two
psychological readings might be admitted. Early in the
novel, when Willems saw himself "surrendering to a wild
creature the unstained purity of his life," Aïssa was
linked with death: "With a faint cry and an upward throw of
his arms he gave up as a tired swimmer gives up . . .
because death is better than strife" (OI, 80, 81). Both
drowning and the black hole into which Willems must fall
suggest that return to the preoedipal mother which Bernard
Meyer saw as the aim and bane of the typical Conradian
protagonist. But the association of woman and death also,
on an Oedipal level, connotes the fear of castration by the
father as a penalty for the enjoyment of the mother.
Indeed, the narrator has repeated the symbolism of castration in describing Willems: ". . . since Lingard had
gone, the time seemed to roll on in profound darkness. All
was night within him. All was gone from his sight. He
walked about blindly in the deserted courtyards" (OI, 327).
     A comment by Bernard Meyer on An Outcast resembles the
conclusions of Richard Sterba and Frederick Crews regarding
Heart of Darkness: the latent content is a fantasy of
Oedipal usurpation.[26] In a note that contrasts with
Meyer's usual stress on preoedipal elements, he has written
of Lingard's loss of the secret route: "Viewed symbolically, Willems's betrayal of his benefactor has the
unmistakable stamp of an 'Oedipal' crime, which is
compounded by his piloting the Arab chieftain's ship
through the opening which heretofore had been known only to
Lingard."[27] The geography of the manifest content is the
same in An Outcast as in Heart of Darkness: Willems going
up the narrows of Lingard's river anticipates Marlow as a
son preempting the father's right, invading via the Congo a

terra incognita identified as female. Kurtz's African
mistress is the image of the "tenebrous and passionate
soul" (HD, 136) of a fecund wilderness; Aïssa in Borneo is
"the very spirit of that land of mysterious forests" (OI,
70). Meyer's interpretation of An Outcast is compatible
with an erotic element in Lingard's charity to Aïssa, with
the ferocity of his revenge on Willems, and with his
amorous reputation in Macassar, which has perhaps honored
him equally for "his smart business transactions, his
loves, and . . . his desperate fights with the Sulu
pirates" (AF, 7).

In structuring Willems's betrayal of Lingard as a
choice between a man and a woman, Conrad has set up a
conflict of positive and negative Oedipal urges. In the
hero's passion for Aïssa, as well as his ambition to become
Hudig's partner, he displays a positive attitude. It will
be recalled also that when he learns Hudig has married him
to an illegitimate daughter, his first impulse is to kill
this treacherous benefactor. In addition to tricking him,
Hudig is a father figure, the donor of his house and other
favors, who has become another Oedipal rival. But the end
of the novel shows the unexpected triumph of the negative
attitude, which is to say, the victory of the father.
Sudden passivity in Willems amounts to self-destruction;
like Lord Jim in Patusan, he will neither fight nor run.
Once he lets himself become Lingard's prisoner, only the
manner of his death remains to be determined. In the
reader's inadequate preparation for this outcome, Willems
foreshadows a male line of enigmatic Conradian suicides,
eluding explanation by conscious motives, and thus inviting
psychoanalytic inquiry. Willems's strong impulses to
parricide have been noticeable in his several betrayals,
all adverse to the father's power and privileges. Yet by
the end of An Outcast, defiance has almost entirely yielded
to its opposite: an urge to submission, castration, and
death, which both horrifies and fascinates him. In
captivity he sees "death looking at him from everywhere"
(OI, 330) and longs to hold on to a world full of life, yet
fixes on the stages in which ants will eat his corpse:
". . . little shining monsters . . . with horns, with claws,
with pincers, would swarm in . . . eager struggle . . .
till there would remain nothing but the white gleam of
bleaching bones in the long grass . . . that would shoot
its feathery heads between the bare and polished ribs"
(OI, 332).

It would be difficult to draw any meaningful line
between Conrad's actual or legal suicides and his virtual
suicides. The first group, which conforms to the
definition of suicide in Webster's Third New International

Dictionary, the "act or an instance of taking one's own life voluntarily and intentionally," includes Kayerts in "An Outpost of Progress," Brierly in Lord Jim, Captain Whalley in The End of the Tether, Decoud in Nostromo, De Barral in Chance, Renouard in "The Planter of Malata," and, presumably, Heyst and Jones in Victory. The second group, which merely hastens its own demise, includes Almayer and Willems, Kurtz, Lord Jim, the hero of "Il Conde," Razumov in Under Western Eyes, and Peyrol in The Rover. The virtual suicides form a continuum of intentionality with the actual suicides; thus Jim, who expects to be killed by Doramin, is closer to the dictionary definition than Willems, who believes Aïssa will miss. Yet Willems meets all three criteria of the actual suicide, as outlined by Karl Menninger in Man against Himself. In order for the death instinct to prevail over the forces of life, the victim must unite the wish to kill (as shown by Willems's accusation of Lingard), the wish to be killed (as shown by his submission to Lingard), and the wish to die (as evidenced by his despair at what Aïssa has taught him about himself--"I did not know there was something in me she could get hold of"--OI, 269).[28]

Since any psychic act has been thought to require a convergence of ego, id, and superego wishes,[29] it is worth noting what kinds of gratification might be available from a decision not to resist Lingard's justice, and even to provoke it by a summons. According to Willems, he sent for Lingard to end his isolation from the rest of the white race. After the betrayal he had found himself "alone in that infernal savage crowd," "delivered into their hands" (OI, 274). What he sought from a former protector was some form of rescue: "Hate is better than being alone! Death is better! I expected . . . anything. Something to expect. Something to take me out of this. Out of her sight!" (OI, 274). Evidently his sense of white identity required the message to Lingard, and it may also have prevented him from fighting another white man. But the same behavior would gratify as well a masochistic and homosexual id impulse, one which could accept punishment as a perverse expression of parental love. Finally, the superego, with its imposed burden of guilt, would be assuaged by submission, since Willems would at last have obeyed its ban on the unconscious wish to replace the father.

The question of guilt becomes interesting, however, because Willems has seemed remarkably free of this sensation in the past, and in the judgment scene his defense excludes it. He dismisses embezzlement as "an error of judgment" (OI, 266). He makes the betrayal of

Lingard's route and trade monopoly a mere hastening of the
inevitable, and, besides, an act outside his control: "I
had to do it. As far as you are concerned, the change here
had to happen sooner or later; you couldn't be master here
for ever. It isn't what I have done that torments me. It
is the why. It's the madness that drove me to it" (OI,
269-70). So thoroughly has he seemed to exonerate himself,
at least on a conscious level, that one might be surprised
at his willingness to take punishment. The text implies a
sense of guilt coupled with a protest of innocence, or else
unconscious guilt--for the ruin of Lingard and for an
infringement on the father's sexual prerogative--as the
cause of Willems's submission.

In one sense An Outcast is a novel of education, in
which Willems painfully learns the traits of the Conradian
father. At the beginning, from the "safe elevation" of his
own commercial success, his attitude to Lingard is one of
patronizing affection, "not unmixed with some disdain for
the crude directness of the old fellow's methods of conduct." At best the protégé achieves an early "qualified
respect" for Lingard's wealth and his ability to keep to
himself, for a time, the source of his india rubber and
rattans; this secret, which Willems has vainly sought to
extract for the benefit of himself and Hudig, is revealed
only at Lingard's pleasure, when Willems no longer works
for Hudig. That it was revealed at all would corroborate
Willems's initial impression of Lingard as a "lucky old
fool" (OI, 18). Even Lingard, when his charity misfires,
concludes, "I am an old fool" (OI, 273). Much of the
novel--for example, his inordinate delight in the
possession of Sambir--would tend to bear out his self-
estimate. "He loved everything there, animated or
inanimated; the very mud of the riverside; the very
alligators. . . . 'Immense fellows! Make two of them
Palembang reptiles!'" (OI, 201). But when Lingard in
revenge for the loss of his river maroons Willems for life,
the comedy of the father has ended. Stripped of motley, he
becomes the protector whom the protégé for half a lifetime
has felt "behind his back, a reassuring presence ready with
help, with commendation, with advice . . . a man inspiring
confidence by his strength. . . . And now that man was
going away. He must call him back. . . . He wanted to call
back his very life that was going away from him" (OI, 281).

This second view yields almost immediately to a third
and final perspective, that of a disobedient child in
terror of a parent. Willems has had an earlier glimmer of
fear, in his inability to clap Lingard on the shoulder: "He
had no idea that the man would turn out to be so tall, so

big and so unapproachable. It seemed to him that he had
never, never in his life, seen Lingard" (OI, 257). But
full knowledge of the father comes only after Lingard has
passed sentence on him and moved to depart. The perception
of an outsized human being modulates into a kind of apotheosis. Lingard's white figure lying in a chair in the
middle of a receding boat strikes Willems as "very terrible, heartless and astonishing, with its unnatural
appearance of running over the water in an attitude of
languid repose" (OI, 282). It leaves a jungle scene
reminiscent of Genesis 3, in which a supernatural visitant
also comes to pass judgment on a fallen son in a garden.
Willems's state of awe is soon externalized in a gathering
storm: ". . . the voice of the thunder was heard . . . like
a wrathful and threatening discourse of an angry god" (OI,
283). Then rain gleams red with lightning, "as if fire and
water were falling together . . . upon the stunned earth."
Willems and Aïssa resemble "two wandering ghosts of the
drowned that, condemned to haunt the water for ever, had
come up from the river to look at the world under a deluge"
(OI, 284). For Willems it is perhaps as if a second flood,
which Jehovah covenanted to spare the world, had been sent
by Lingard. With the perception of a god of wrath,
Willems's education in Conradian paternity is complete. Of
three attributes of the father--comedy, protection, and
menace--it is the last that finally predominates. Lingard,
the onetime Sunday-school pupil, has--in an Oedipal usurpation of his own--locally replaced the Christian god with
a quite different deity of his own devising.

Although Willems's self-protective impulse to renounce
women does not secure Lingard's forgiveness, it does, I
think, indicate the direction in which Conrad's imagination
was moving in 1896, as he approached his marriage--for him,
despite its avoidance of incest, an anxious union from
which he desired no children, and which, for no known
reason, he expected to end in his early death. His novel
of 1896, like his novel of 1895, suggests a preference for
celibacy in his young white protagonists, combined with
what Robert Hodges has called deep fellowship and male
bonding.[30] Even the ill-fated Willems and Almayer, as
long as they exist as partial celibates--the bought hus-
bands of unwanted women, who have been assigned them by
older men--are permitted to live. The doom of each appears
to date from the advent of a desirable woman: a grown-up
and beautiful Nina returns to her father from Singapore;
Aïssa on a forest path darts at Willems a look "silent and
penetrating like an inspiration" (OI, 69), and he awakens
to the flight of his old self. For a Malay youth there

would have been no sexual difficulty. Dain Maroola, the
future Rajah of Bali, is, like Lakamba, the new Rajah of
Sambir, destined to thrive as the master of a harem. But
in **Almayer's Folly** and **An Outcast** Conrad had not evolved a
formula by which he could allow white youths, whose Oedipal
guilt may have been his own, to survive the ends of his
novels.

Or one might say that he had evolved the formula, but
was as yet hesitant to apply it to whites. According to
Nydes's principle of Oedipal compromise, success may be
tolerated in one area of the father's realm if defeat is
endured in another. This prospective status for white sons
is first approached through a nonwhite, from whom Conrad
may have felt comfortably distanced--the Arab Abdulla, who
nevertheless resembles Europeans as a shipowner and trader.
Lingard's successor on the Pantai, he is the chief magnate
in a fictional Malaysia, and also its most conspicuous
model of filial duty. Before, or after, his earthly father
he defers to a heavenly one, that Most High who still
exists for Conrad's Moslems, though not for the majority of
his white men.

> For upwards of forty years Abdulla had walked
> in the way of his Lord. Son of the rich Syed
> Selim bin Sali, the great Mohammedan trader of
> the Straits, he went forth at the age of seventeen
> on his first commercial expedition, as his father's
> representative on board a pilgrim ship chartered by
> the wealthy Arab to convey a crowd of pious Malays
> to the Holy Shrine. . . . Allah had made it his fate
> to become a pilgrim very early in life. This was
> a great favour of Heaven, and it could not have
> been bestowed upon a man who prized it more, or who
> made himself more worthy of it by the unswerving
> piety of his heart and by the religious solemnity
> of his demeanour. . . . [When he was twenty-seven]
> the writing on his forehead decreed that the time
> had come for him to return to the Straits and take
> from his dying father's hands the many threads of
> a business that was spread over all the Archipelago.
> . . . Very soon his ability, his will--strong to
> obstinacy--his wisdom beyond his years, caused him
> to be recognized as the head of a family whose
> members and connections were found in every part
> of those seas. . . . they all paid great deference
> to Abdulla, listened to his advice . . . because
> he was wise, pious, and fortunate.
> He bore himself with the humility becoming a
> Believer, who never forgets, even for one moment

of his waking life, that he is the servant of the
Most High. (OI, 109-10)

If Freud is correct in supposing that the adult's image of
God derives from his childhood image of his father,
Abdulla's diligent service to Allah would imply a like
piety to Syed Selim bin Sali; however, in replacing him as
head of a business, and equalling or surpassing him in
influence over an extended family, the son might be said to
manifest a culpable vein of Oedipal self-assertion. In
Nydes's theory, for some sufferers from Oedipal guilt:

> . . . self-assertion--even when it is not
> competitive--and reality success--even when it
> excites little or no hostile enviousness--are
> unconsciously construed . . . as defiance of, and
> transgression against a supreme authority figure.
> Success equals incest with the parent of the
> opposite sex. Success means murder of the parent
> of the same sex.[31]

Nydes's thought seems to parallel Conrad's novel, which
leaves the domain of Syed Selim bin Sali in one respect
inviolate: Abdulla, attended in old age by his nephew and
heir Reshid, has never married.

This compromise suggests a discreet form of human
sacrifice to an angry father-god, like that of Willems's
jungle epiphany. Yet the Conradian father, under proper
conditions, could also be both comic and benevolent, albeit
"infernal" (OI, 161) in his charity. The Lingard of the
first two novels is the most balanced parental portrait
that Conrad ever created. Perhaps because it imposed in
unusual degree the stress of ambivalent response, he
quickly moved away from it. In subsequent works he
generally divided its traits among a number of characters.
In another kind of split, also conceivably defensive, he
divided the fictional land environment from the sea. In
the latter milieu the father is more easily dealt with;
until the land invades the sea in Chance, the absence of
attractive women on board a ship insures that the terms of
the son's submission are met automatically.

3

The Jeopardy of the Son on Land: From "The Idiots" to *Lord Jim*

In 1896, with the publication of a second novel, <u>An Outcast of the Islands</u>, Conrad became a professional writer, the successor to his father in a literary career. In that year he also, at the age of thirty-eight, married Jessie George, a woman of twenty-three; the ages of his parents at their wedding had been thirty-six and twenty-three. Guilt in following the father, both sexually and professionally, may have prompted Conrad's two warnings to his bride, that there were to be no children of the marriage and that he had not long to live.[1] His survival for the next twenty-eight years, through the birth of two sons, afforded him a much longer life span than he generally granted the married white protagonists of his fiction. But his work from <u>Tales of Unrest</u>, collected in 1898, through <u>Typhoon and Other Stories</u> (1903) shows a willingness to experiment with a formula that would allow the survival of literary characters like himself. In the sea stories of this period he readily adopted for Europeans the solution reached for an Arab, Abdulla, in the first two novels: celibacy combined with economic or professional achievement. As in the Oedipal compromise described by Jule Nydes, the son renounces one part of the father's domain in order to occupy, and succeed in, another. But in the land tales, this balance is struck only in <u>Heart of Darkness</u> and then lost in <u>Lord Jim</u>; thus from the standpoint of Conrad's adherence to his solution, the works from <u>Tales of Unrest</u> through <u>Typhoon</u> fall naturally into two groups. Reserving the sea fiction of this period for a later chapter, I deal for the present with a land group including "The Idiots" (1896), "An Outpost of Progress" (1897), <u>Heart of Darkness</u> (1899), and <u>Lord Jim</u> (1900).

Conrad's first new creative impulse after his marriage[2] produced the short story "The Idiots," the record of an Oedipal and marital disaster. The French peasant hero, Jean-Pierre Bacadou, returns from military service to challenge three anachronisms of his village: the local curé and marquis are threatened by his atheistic republicanism, and his father by a demand for control of the family farm. In Jean-Pierre's estimate, the father "had not the energy of old days. The hands did not feel over them the eye of the master" (I, 59). The elder Bacadou yields to his son with the Oedipal insight: "Do what you like. It's the mother that will be pleased"; the narrator remarks, "The world is to the young" (I, 59, 60). To support his new station, Jean-Pierre marries and begets two boys whom he imagines "striding over the land from patch to patch, wringing tribute from the earth beloved and fruitful" (I, 61). One woman, then, for whom successive generations of Bacadou men vie is the farm itself. But any successor to Jean-Pierre must be "a man that would think as he thought, that would feel as he felt; a man who would be part of himself, and yet remain to trample masterfully on that earth when he was gone" (I, 71). He is thus both an Oedipus and, in John Munder Ross's terms, a Laius, a father unwilling to relinquish his place. Unfortunately, however, the twins, a third son, and a daughter all prove to be idiots. Jean-Pierre's nemesis is evidently heredity; his father-in-law M. Levaille is described as "'deranged in his head' for a few years before he died," and Susan Levaille Bacadou, it is said, "always resembled" this parent (I, 74, 76). Jean-Pierre's renewed attempt to produce a normal child leads to his fatal stabbing by Susan, who foresees the birth of a fifth idiot: "Do you think I would . . . have my house full of those things—that are worse than animals who know the hand that feeds them? . . . And he would come. . . . I had my long scissors" (I, 75-76).

Hallucinating before her own death by drowning, she relates to imaginary judges that the elder Bacadou, who was present at his son's murder, "never turned his head. He is deaf and childish, gentlemen" (I, 82). It is not clear whether Conrad meant to convey senile incomprehension or the satisfaction of a Laius who voluntarily conceded nothing to a successor. At the end of "The Idiots," the royalist marquis intends to make Susan's energetic mother guardian of the children and administrator of the farm, thus superseding the entire Bacadou line. "It would be much better," reasons the marquis, "than having here one of those other Bacadous, probably a red republican, corrupting my commune" (I, 85).[3] But of the original proprietors,

it is Jean-Pierre's father who remains physically on the
land, in a Pyrrhic victory over the son whose sexuality has
proved fatal.

Since the dead man viewed marriage in practical
terms, as a source of farm laborers and heirs, sexual and
occupational usurpation are not entirely separable in "The
Idiots"; the protagonist would have been hard put to
renounce one for the other, in the Oedipal solution
envisioned by Nydes. The two forms of possible aggression
against the father are also linked in "An Outpost of
Progress," which depicts the destruction by older men
of two white agents of a Belgian trading company in the
Congo. Kayerts, the head of an isolated station, and his
subordinate Carlier exist at the mercy of two paternal
figures, the friendly native chief called Father Gobila and
the ruthless director of their company. Gobila, who seems
to love all white men as children, sends over part of
their food; the rest arrives in occasional visits of the
director's steamer. But when the agents allow natives to
be enslaved in a lucrative trade for ivory, Gobila breaks
off his support; and when the steamer, unaccountably
delayed, also fails to supply them, Kayerts kills Carlier
in a dispute over the sugar ration. He then hangs himself,
on the cross over the grave of the station's founder.
This gallows is the same structure that Carlier once
straightened up and tested for soundness: ". . . solid, I
promise you! I suspended myself with both hands to the
cross-piece. Not a move" (OP, 95). All three Europeans
might be regarded as sacrifices to their imperialistic
civilization, their own greed, and their profiteering
director, who has considered them undeserving of much
attention. Of the recent victims he has said: "Look at
those two imbeciles. . . . I always thought the station on
this river useless, and they just fit the station!" (OP,
88). The dead Kayerts, a parodic Christ who may have
lacked the resignation of the original, is found "irrev-
erently . . . putting out a swollen tongue" (OP, 117)
at his god, the company official he might have asked, "Why
hast thou forsaken me?"

The fine ivory that he and Carlier bought with slaves
redounds to the credit of a director who has used his
subordinates. The surface rivalry of father and son
figures in "An Outpost of Progress" is a competition for
prestige and profit. But Conrad may also have included an
undercurrent of Oedipal sexual rivalry. Neither Kayerts
nor Carlier appears to have a wife or mistress; as a
colonial alternative the two men, strolling arm in arm,
keeping house, and reading novels come "to feel something

resembling affection for one another" (OP, 92). However,
Kayerts is a widower; his motive for relinquishing the
dull comfort of a European post in the Administration of
Telegraphs was the hope that an African fortune would
supply a dowry for his daughter Melie. Conrad's distaste
for this family tie is evident in the description of a
perverse father who has "mooned" for hours over the
portrait of "a little girl with long bleached tresses and
a rather sour face" (OP, 108). On the other hand, Makola,
the native who does the work of the station, is a Conradian
embodiment of healthy African sexuality: "His wife was a
negress from Loanda, very large and very noisy. Three
children rolled about in sunshine"; Makola "spent the day
playing with his children. He lay full-length on a mat
. . . and the youngsters sat on his chest and clambered all
over him" (OP, 86, 105). By the contrast of etiolated
white with robust native, Conrad implies that sex and
marriage are not the proper preserve of European youth.
Both Kayerts and Carlier may have died for the Oedipal
presumption of one in having fathered a daughter. But
since her needs prompted Kayerts's hunger for percentages
on African ivory, sexual and economic usurpation (or what
Conrad treats as usurpation) tend, as in "The Idiots,"
to merge. Together, marriage and economic competition
constitute for a son forbidden territory, properly belong-
ing to his own father or a substitute.

    A separation of the forms of rivalry is finally
attained in Heart of Darkness, and a white son survives
after making a choice. At first glance the novella may not
appear to be concerned with father-son rivalry: Marlow, a
steamboat captain, is sent upriver to relieve Kurtz, a
rapacious ivory collector dying in the depths of the Congo;
after the man has been buried, the rescuer assumes the role
of protector of his reputation, even to the telling of a
lie to Kurtz's Intended in Europe. But Marlow's primitive
river journey, "back to the earliest beginnings of the
world," is also a personal regression: "There were moments
when one's past came back to one . . . in the shape of an
unrestful and noisy dream" (HD, 92, 93). The dream's
content may relate to the fact that Kurtz has been
anticipated by the dead founder of Kayerts's station:
". . . under a tall cross much out of the perpendicular,
slept the man who . . . had planned and had watched the
construction of this outpost of progress. He had been, at
home, an unsuccessful painter who, weary of pursuing fame
on an empty stomach, had gone out there through high
protections" (OP, 87). The Congo short story stands in the
same relation to the Congo novella as Almayer's Folly to An

Outcast of the Islands. In the first work of each pair,
Conrad establishes a powerful father figure as absent--
dead or missing; in the second, he moves back in time to
confront paternal and paternalistic relationships from what
seems to be, for him, a necessary position of psychic
safety.

Each father has attributes of both god and devil.
Lingard swells into an angry deity in Willems's jungle
epiphany; Kurtz, a "pitiful Jupiter" (HD, 134) whose
thunderbolts come from ordinary European weapons, is
worshipped by natives. According to his report to the
"International Society for the Suppression of Savage
Customs," whites "must necessarily" appear to savages "in
the nature of supernatural beings--we approach them with
the might as of a deity" (HD, 117-18). Lingard's "infernal
charity" (OI, 161) anticipates Marlow's journey to "the
centre of the earth"--in Dante, the abode of Satan--to meet
a Kurtz of lofty principles and "a high seat amongst the
devils of the land" (HD, 60, 116). Lingard's "queer
notions" of justice to Willems--ideas evolved "beyond the
pale of civilized laws" (OI, 235)--adumbrate Kurtz's
genocidal postscript to the report: "Exterminate all the
brutes!" (HD, 118). The difference between the two whites
in extent of savagery is probably a matter of circumstance:
Lingard has a partial lack of social restraint, Kurtz, in
"utter solitude without a policeman" (HD, 116), a total
one. Having dissuaded him from further attendance at his
"unspeakable" (HD, 118), possibly cannibal, rites,[4]
Marlow observes: ". . . I had to deal with a being to whom
I could not appeal in the name of anything high or low.
. . . He had kicked himself loose of the earth" (HD, 144).

Both Lingard and Kurtz fill paternal and paternalistic
roles; however, for Kurtz the sociopolitical father role,
in a novella whose surface concerns imperialism and
colonialism, is more obvious than the personal one. But
the personal relationship does appear, even in the manifest content, with a Russian disciple, the much-patched
harlequin; and three critics, Richard Sterba, Frederick
Crews, and Joseph Dobrinsky, have endeavored to show that
in latent content it exists with Marlow as well. By their
interpretations, the latent content is a fantasy of filial
usurpation--sexual, professional, or both; that is, Heart
of Darkness derives from a dream of one or more of the
Oedipal aggressions that Conrad might have ascribed to
himself in 1896.

Before attempting to assign priority to either the
sexual or the professional interpretation, it may be well
to examine each in some detail. On the assumption that the

river journey is a descent into the primitive unconscious ("inner station") of Marlow the protagonist, Richard Sterba and Frederick Crews have described sexual usurpation as the latent content of the novella. These critics read his penetration of the Congo by its narrow, snaky river as a reenactment of a small boy's horrified and fascinated intrusion into a primal scene (the "unspeakable rites"). For Sterba and Crews, much of the imagery--for example, the following passage from Marlow's travels--captures a memory or fantasy of intercourse between the parents: ". . . I made out, deep in the tangled gloom, naked breasts, arms, legs, glaring eyes,--the bush was swarming with human limbs in movement" (HD, 110). As further evidence of latent sexual content, Crews cites references to "a black and incomprehensible frenzy," "a great human passion let loose," the "inconceivable ceremonies of some devilish initiation" (HD, 96, 107, 115), and so on.

In what follows, I summarize his analysis, which is the second and fuller of the two.[5] The blank, or unknown, area of the map that Marlow, like Conrad, intended as a boy to explore when he grew up (HD, 52)[6] is the female genitalia; the father who possesses this terra incognita is Kurtz-Apollo. As an adult Marlow-Conrad feels irrationally compelled to probe a mysterious continent of which he has heard, ". . . Mr. Kurtz was in there" (HD, 81). In the bushy wilderness personified by Kurtz's African mistress, he becomes a voyeuristic and incestuous son traveling up an Oedipal river (an "immense snake uncoiled"--HD, 52) into the maternal body, which is the father's realm; understandably, he is confronted at the inner station by a volley of arrows, in an attack Kurtz has ordered, and by emblems of castration, the severed heads staked around the chieftain's house as a warning of the father's revenge on a filial usurper.[7] The outcome of the journey is the son's disillusionment on learning that an idealized mother, represented by Kurtz's Intended in Europe, has a dark alter ego, a sexual self, in Kurtz's African mistress.[8] Despite this similarity, however, the son is largely able to restrict feminine sexuality to the African woman; she symbolizes for him a "colossal body of . . . fecund and mysterious life" (HD, 136). By this split he reconstructs a sufficiently "pure" mother-son dyad to escape the threat of castration by the father as punishment for incestuous desires. "Only one complaint against the sainted mother is allowed to reach expression: the son tells her with devious truthfulness that the dying [father's] last word ('horror!') was 'your name'" (HD, 161).[9]

Equally well documented from manifest content is
Joseph Dobrinsky's parallel reading, in which Heart of
Darkness masks a latent fantasy of professional supersession. For this critic, ivory, which the trading
company's manager disparages as "mostly fossil" (HD, 115),
i.e., dug up, represents the "buried private ore,"[10] the
potentially creative hoard of emotional experience on
which art must draw; the symbolism accords with Conrad's
"imagings of the artist's endeavor or his own process of
writing as the snatching of a 'rescued fragment,' as
'rescue work,' or in terms of 'working like a miner in his
pit.'"[11] Dobrinsky retains the infantile sexual content
proposed by Sterba and Crews, but adds a second level of
meaning, from a later phase of authorial development. To
summarize his findings, the manifest episode, showing the
last stages of a great man's illness, in which he has
"enlarged" the mind of a "disciple" (HD, 125, 132), must
have drawn partly on Conrad's memories of his adolescent
years with his dying father. The period was marked by an
incipient literary rivalry with Apollo, the dilemma of an
artist's son who is heir to a creative gift. In the first
of two phases of a disguised autobiography, the boyish
harlequin at the inner station, who has relinquished at
gunpoint his small stock of ivory to Kurtz, is a younger
Conrad reduced to silence by his worship of, and dependence
on, a silver-tongued parent: "You don't talk with that
man--you listen to him," the harlequin exclaims with
"severe exaltation"; "'I am a simple man. I have no great
thoughts. I want nothing from anybody. How can you
compare me to . . . ?' His feelings were too much for
speech" (HD, 123, 132). Appropriately, the harlequin in
English pantomime is a mute character; Conrad's bepatched
young sailor looks "as though he had absconded from a
troupe of mimes" (HD, 126).[12] Marlow, on the other hand,
represents an older Conrad who refuses to share in the
Russian disciple's adulation: ". . . Mr. Kurtz was no idol
of mine" (HD, 132). Marlow's refusal to efface himself
enables him to become an artist in his own right.[13]

Ultimately he surpasses the father, although Kurtz-
Apollo himself moves from the slickness of journalistic
utterance in Europe to a genuine artistry, one that
requires the participation of the unconscious. That
he has made contact with an inner depth would appear from
his dying whisper of self-knowledge: "The horror! The
horror!" (HD, 149). But he lacks ego control over the
products of the unconscious (he is "hollow at the core");
thus his psychic descent, in which the wilderness has
whispered "things about himself which he did not know" (HD,

131), has ended in insanity; ego has been overwhelmed by
id.   Conrad has anticipated Freud's discovery that the
regression required of the artist must be closely
controlled in order not to become final. Marlow with
firmer ego control, derived from an "inborn strength" (HD,
97), adds to Kurtz's gift of expression the artistic
essentials of self-discipline and craftsmanship.
Responsive, like Kurtz, to the appeal of the unconscious,
symbolized by the passionate uproar of the savages, he is
saved from going ashore "for a howl and a dance"--that is,
from losing control of himself--by his devotion to duty.
As captain of the steamboat in the manifest content, he
"had to watch the steering"; as artist in the latent
content, he can tread the path back from fantasy to
reality, from the id to the ego. Proudly he asserts his
ego mastery: ". . . I have a voice, too, and for good or
evil mine is the speech that cannot be silenced" (HD,
97).[14]

To indicate the lure and the danger that Apollo
represented for his son, Dobrinsky has borrowed Crews's
chilling list of similarities--if a subjugated Poland
replaces a subjugated Congo--between Apollo and Kurtz:

> Both Kurtz and Korzeniowski--the names are alike--
> are intellectuals and versifiers; neither can be
> properly said to have a profession; both have
> dabbled in journalism and written pamphlets; both
> have messianic political ambitions and a mixture
> of refinement and demagoguery; both are accused of
> disrupting the orderly domination of a victimized
> territory; both die far from home, maintaining
> almost until the end a grandiloquent intention
> to return and prevail; both are remembered as
> prematurely withered and helpless, yet oppressive;
> both are famous for their arresting voices and
> their ability to persuade; both seem addicted to
> self-pity; both refuse an offer of rescue; both
> leave literary remains; both profess a high-minded
> Christianity.[15]

The derogatory view of Apollo's sanity and artistic
attainment that the Dobrinsky reading offers is consonant
with Conrad's lifelong ambivalence toward an admired but
destructive parent, for whom, as Zdzisław Najder has said,
he retained a mixture of "admiration and contemptuous
pity."[16] The last trait this father shares with Kurtz--
the profession of a "high-minded Christianity"--may
be the most damning, since for Conrad the Christian

religion entailed inevitable hypocrisy: "Great, improving, softening, compassionate it may be but it has lent itself with amazing facility to cruel distortion and is the only religion which, with its impossible standards, has brought an infinity of anguish to innumerable souls--on this earth."[17] He did not detail his objections to the faith in which he had been born. But an assumption of cant in the Christian demand for altruism pervades the Nigger of the "Narcissus," in which "tenderness to suffering" is possible only because it gratifies a "latent egoism" (NN, 138); the view is compatible with Freud's dictum that the fulfillment of the command to love one's neighbor cannot, on the latter's own merits, generally be "recommended as reasonable." A further objection may have been raised in both men by Christianity's demand for sexual repression. "Experience teaches us," wrote Freud in a Europe nominally Christian, "that for most people there is a limit beyond which their constitution cannot comply with the demands of civilization."[18] The more reticent Conrad, in the same letter as his indictment of Christianity, admitted an aversion to Tolstoy, whose "anti-sensualism" he considered "suspect."[19]

The writing of fiction is commonly regarded as a means of instinctual release. Hypotheses of latent Oedipal content in Heart of Darkness accord with Freud's most famous view of art, that it represents a fantasy gratification of frustrated ambitious or erotic wishes, and hence an improvement on unsatisfactory reality.[20] The artist's present wish, seeking fulfillment, reactivates a repressed infantile wish, and both find their satisfaction in the work of art. Imaginative creation, "like a daydream, is a continuation of, and a substitute for, what was once the play of childhood"[21]--a search for pleasure through magic.

The Oedipal character of the specific infantile wish behind Heart of Darkness might be deduced from post-Freudian theories of art, which have taken into account the defenses raised by the ego against instinctual wishes unacceptable to the superego. The usual opinion has been that the content of the work of art represents, in whatever disguise, the yearnings of the id, and that form represents the artist's defense against them.[22] With the proviso that the separation of content, or thematic material, from the techniques for presenting it must be incomplete, one might note some aspects, chiefly formal, of Heart of Darkness which resemble psychological defenses--isolation, undoing, and denial--and which are employed in ways suited to the relief of guilt or anxiety arising from a fantasy of Oedipal usurpation.

The first defense, isolation, involves the splitting of the father figure. Unlike Lingard, who dispenses a form of charity (however questionable), Kurtz has a paternal protective role confined to rhetoric, as in his "splendid monologues" to the harlequin on "love, justice, conduct of life" (HD, 132), or the peroration of his report, which gives Marlow "the notion of an exotic Immensity ruled by an august Benevolence" (HD, 118). In Heart of Darkness the father's actual protective traits are assigned to a character not only minor but absent, and yet a presence: the workmanlike author--"Tower, Towson--some such name" (HD, 99)--of An Inquiry into Some Points of Seamanship, a nautical bible carried by Kurtz's disciple through the jungle. As Jan Verleun has pointed out, the juxtaposition of the two authorial names suggests "a long line of decent students of the craft," in which Towson, "a tower of strength" in his profession, is "the 'son' of those who dutifully 'towed' before him" and, as an influential older man, a father to the readers of his manual.[23]   The advantage to Conrad, and perhaps to the reader, of the creation of such a splinter figure may have been stated by Otto Fenichel: isolation, or mentally "keeping apart that which actually belongs together," can be used to resolve conflicts produced by ambivalence. The good-bad object is split into one person unequivocally loved and another unequivocally hated--for example, "the good mother and the wicked stepmother in fairy tales."[24]

A second defense mechanism, undoing, comes into play, according to Fenichel, when something "is done which, actually or magically, is the opposite of something which, again actually or in imagination, was done before."[25] In Heart of Darkness the relief expedition looks like an intended counterweight to fantasies of Oedipal replacement of the father; Marlow pilots the steamer to the aid of the stricken Kurtz. However, the dream of such a mission may itself signify hostility. Freud has indicated that the Oedipal son, rejecting his debt for life to his father, longs to be independent of him. Often the rebel creates a fantasy--in which feelings of defiance far outweigh those of tenderness--of plucking his father (or king, or emperor) from danger and saving his life; by this rescue he "puts his account square with him."[26]   Richard Sterba adds that for anyone to be rescued, he must first have been put in danger; thus any rescue fantasy is the product of an aggressive wish, the crime of which is undone by the fantasied release.[27]   Sterba's view may illuminate Conrad's text, in which Kurtz does not wish to be saved: "Save me!--save the ivory, you mean. . . . Sick! Sick!

Not so sick as you would like to believe. . . . I'll carry
my ideas out yet--I will return. . . . you are interfering
with me. I will return. I. . . ." (HD, 137). Kurtz's
reluctance is vindicated by the conduct of Marlow, on whose
steamer he dies and by whom he goes unmourned--despite
Marlow's sense of an "unconscious loyalty" to "a remarkable
man" (HD, 151, 155). On the news, "'Mistah Kurtz--he
dead,' all the pilgrims rushed out to see. I remained,
and went on with my dinner. I believe I was considered
brutally callous" (HD, 150).

A paradoxical defense against the hated father is the
denial that he exists. In Heart of Darkness the company's
hierarchy contains powerful men, but no patriarch with the
sway of a Lingard in his own business. The baldheaded,
sonorous Kurtz, a father-god to Africans but a man of no
definite calling at home, has much the same status as
Marlow, a captain in Africa but a job applicant in Europe.
Kurtz, who was not rich enough to marry his Intended, may
have been a dependent and "a pauper all his life" (HD,
159). He is variously classified as a poet, a "great
musician," "a painter who wrote for the papers, or else
. . . a journalist who could paint," a "universal genius,"
and a budding "leader of an extreme party," any party; he
"had the faith. He could get himself to believe anything--
anything" (HD, 153-54). Somewhat ambiguous in Africa
as well, he is subordinate to the manager and yet, as
a prodigious ivory collector and member of "the new
gang--the gang of virtue" (HD, 79), an Oedipal rival for
the manager's job. He ends as a victim of what C. T. Watts
has termed the "covert murder-plot" of Heart of Darkness,
in which the manager delays the relief of a sick man until
he is past hope of recovery.[28] However, the victor in
this contest remains perilously dependent on the advice of
an uncle and on the uncle's influence in Europe, where "the
danger" is (HD, 91). The danger, presumably, lies in a
division of power between a liberal and philanthropic
Council and the "great man" of the trading company, with
his "grip on the handle-end of ever so many millions" (HD,
56). On the surface of the novella Conrad captures the
diffusion of power in a bureaucracy; at a deeper level he
may have sought to prove that since there is no father
whose authority is unmistakable, no Oedipal crime, whether
of sexual or of professional usurpation, can have been
committed.

An inadequacy in the defenses so far discussed--
isolation by splitting of the father, undoing, and
denial--may account for the use of isolation a second
time, to divide the son. The existence of both Marlow and

the Russian in the novella suggests Fenichel's analysis of
splitting in childhood: many children assert their division
into good and bad selves, often with different names, and
deny "the good one's responsibility for the bad one's
deeds."[29]   Kurtz's protégé, a "brother seaman" (HD, 138)
to Marlow, is an alter ego paradigmatically acceptable to
the father.   In the latent content, as seen by Sterba,
Crews, and Dobrinsky, he is guilty of neither sexual nor
literary usurpation.   In the manifest content this youth,
whose face, appropriately, contains "no features to speak
of" (HD, 122), has conciliated three different fathers:
Kurtz; an old storekeeper, Van Shuyten, who stocked him for
the wilderness; and his biological parent, the archpriest
he deserted for the sea.   He even carries with him, as a
kind of paternal emblem, Tower/Towson.   Once, for a reason
easily supplied from The Psychopathology of Everyday Life,
he does misplace this book: the apparently accidental loss
of an object often vents "a secret antipathy towards it
or towards the person that it came from; or else the
inclination to lose the object has been transferred to it
from other more important objects by a symbolic association
of thoughts."[30]   What the Russian unconsciously desires
to lose is very likely a father, actual or surrogate.
However, when Marlow restores the book to its owner, the
youth's ecstasy provides a model of filial subjection: "He
made as though he would kiss me" (HD, 124).   Not without
contempt, Marlow concludes, "Sometimes I ask myself whether
I had ever really seen him--whether it was possible to meet
such a phenomenon!" (HD, 140).

Like Conrad a Russian citizen in adolescence and a
runaway to sea, the harlequin, bewitched by Kurtz, attains
a degree of submission that is unlike Conrad.   Also unlike
Conrad, he has an immunity to the ordinary diseases, fever
and dysentery, of white men in their "fantastic invasion"
(HD, 76) of the Congo.   Marlow's statement that "glamour,"
or "the absolutely pure, uncalculating, unpractical spirit
of adventure," "kept him unscathed" (HD, 126) seems at
first glance a mere effusion, or the expression of a
dubious belief in psychosomatic medicine.   Marlow's view is
logical, however, as an intrusion of Conrad's psychology.
The harlequin has escaped disease--that is, authorial
retribution--by abjuring Oedipal rivalry.   His thirst for
pure adventure makes him a collector neither of ivory nor
of women.   "He surely wanted nothing from the wilderness
but space to breathe in and to push on through.   His need
was to exist, and to move onwards at the greatest possible
risk, and with a maximum of privation" (HD, 126).   Unlike
Almayer, Willems, Jean-Pierre Bacadou, or Kayerts, this

white son whom Conrad permits to survive with impunity on
land is an ascetic, a sailor ashore who carries with him
the sea life that Conrad likened to the regimen of a
"Carthusian monastery" (PR, 42).

By the standard of the three monastic vows (poverty,
chastity, and obedience), which would logically preclude
the literary rivalry of the Dobrinsky reading and the
sexual rivalry detected by Sterba and Crews, Marlow is an
imperfect seaman. Even in the manifest content he differs
from the exemplary harlequin. To the latter, Kurtz's
attachment to a glittering native mistress hung with brass
and glass to "the value of several elephant tusks" is an
enigma: "I don't understand. . . . Ah, well, it's all over
now" (HD, 135, 137). But Marlow sees her as "a wild and
gorgeous apparition of a woman," "treading the earth
proudly"; "she was savage and superb, wild-eyed and
magnificent," the image of the "tenebrous and passionate
soul" of the wilderness (HD, 135-36). For this attraction
Marlow apparently pays a penalty in disease, which he
describes in erotic terms; crime and punishment merge.
When he tells how he nearly followed Kurtz into death, he
seems to follow him sexually: ". . . the pilgrims buried
something in a muddy hole. And then they very nearly
buried me" (HD, 150).

It may be this climax of supersession to which he
refers when he designates Kurtz's inner station as "the
farthest point of navigation and the culminating point of
my experience. It seemed somehow to throw a kind of light"
(HD, 51). After the symbolic death of his bout with fever,
he is evidently reborn as the Buddha seen by the first
narrator: "He had sunken cheeks, a yellow complexion, a
straight back, an ascetic aspect, and, with his arms
dropped, the palms of hands outwards, resembled an idol";
". . . with his legs folded before him, he had the pose of
a Buddha preaching in European clothes and without a
lotus-flower" (HD, 46, 50). What the Buddha posture could
mean, for a man still actively engaged with the world, is a
renunciation of some of its amenities. When Kurtz's
Intended demands of him her idol's last words, Marlow's
lie, "your name" (HD, 161), preserves her deluded love for
the dead. To suppress Kurtz's actual words--"The horror!
The horror!"--signifies not only Marlow's compassion but
his resignation of a woman who strikes him as beautiful,
and in whom--despite his scorn for her woman's world, "out
of touch with truth"--he lauds "a mature capacity for
fidelity, for belief, for suffering" (HD, 59, 149, 157).
Hers is the soul "neither rudimentary nor tainted with
self-seeking" (HD, 119), which Kurtz conquered but which

Marlow forgoes. His tale ends with the memory of his
self-denying lie, and with the frame narrator's final
reference to Buddhism: "'I could not tell her. It would
have been too dark--too dark altogether. . . .' Marlow
ceased, and sat apart, indistinct and silent, in the pose
of a meditating Buddha" (HD, 162).

In "Youth" (1898), Lord Jim (1900), and Chance (1913),
Marlow displays the Oedipal compromise developed in Heart
of Darkness: he is depicted as an artist, a teller of
tales, but not as a lover of women. Conrad has separated
the two forms of filial usurpation and made his choice
between them. On the evidence of Marlow's celibacy, and
his survival as a literary character, it would appear that
Conrad was more disturbed by sexual than by professional
replacement of the father, so that the Sterba-Crews reading
of latent content in Heart of Darkness reflects his deeper
anxiety. The same conclusion might be reached from his
difficulty in realizing an adolescent ambition to become a
great writer.[31] At the age of thirty-eight he was
groaning to Edward Garnett: "I sit down . . . for eight
hours every day--and the sitting down is all. In the
course of that working day of 8 hours I write 3 sentences
which I erase before leaving the table in despair."[32] A
persistent literary paralysis has been ascribed by Robert
Armstrong to Oedipal conflict, in which ". . . the function
of writing itself was endangered."[33] However, a chronic
block became acute with the novel he abandoned, The
Sisters, and with The Rescue, which took him twenty-three
years to complete. Thomas Moser has argued that both works
foundered on the (for Conrad) rocky theme of love, which
elicited "only bad writing" from him and which remained
throughout a long literary career his "uncongenial
subject."[34]

Love is nevertheless prominent in the second half of
Lord Jim, the novel he interrupted to write Heart of
Darkness. The career of the protagonist may represent
an effort to solve the problem of Oedipal guilt by a
compromise more life-sustaining than the one imposed on
Marlow. In creating Jim, Conrad temporarily abandoned the
requirement for celibacy in European youth but endowed his
hero with a remarkable submissiveness in nonsexual areas of
potential conflict with the father. In a novel structured
as an almost unbroken series of capitulations to paternal
figures, Jim shows much of the harlequin's round-eyed
naiveté and docility. The son of a clergyman, he chooses a
career in the merchant marine in response to an ideal taken
from "the sea-life of light literature," and perhaps from
his father's sermons as well.

> He saw himself saving people from sinking
> ships, cutting away masts in a hurricane,
> swimming through a surf with a line. . . .
> He confronted savages on tropical shores,
> quelled mutinies on the high seas, and in a
> small boat upon the ocean kept up the hearts of
> despairing men--always an example of devotion
> to duty, and as unflinching as a hero in a
> book. (LJ, 6)

Yet in an unconscious urge to self-preservation--"I had
jumped. . . . It seems" (LJ, 111)--he abandons the old
steamer Patna, near sinking with 800 passengers and only
five boats. A second motive for the jump may have been
that to remain as the last living officer would have put
him in command. According to Robert Armstrong, he "obeyed
the superego prohibition against the unconscious wish to
replace father"[35]; this reading is consistent with his
passivity in other situations. When the ship makes port
after all, at the end of a tow rope, he alone of four
deserting officers submits to a court of inquiry. Away
from the courtroom he feels compelled to "make a clean
breast" of the affair "to an elder man" (LJ, 128)--Marlow,
a middle-aged captain--as his priest. "Didn't I tell you
he confessed himself before me as though I had the power to
bind and to loose? He burrowed deep, deep, in the hope of
my absolution, which would have been of no good to him"
(LJ, 97). When the verdict, which Marlow describes
as "infinitely worse than a beheading" (LJ, 158)--in
psychoanalytic terms, a castration[36]--goes against him,
he refrains from communicating with the father he
idealizes. Marlow gets the impression

> that the good old rural dean was about the
> finest man that ever had been worried by the
> cares of a large family since the beginning of
> the world. . . . "He has seen it all in the
> home papers by this time," said Jim. "I can
> never face the poor old chap. . . . I could
> never explain. He wouldn't understand."
> (LJ, 79)

Stripped of his certificate but befriended by Marlow,
Jim goes through a succession of shore jobs, leaving each
when the "irrepressible" (LJ, 151) Patna case surfaces
again. At a rice mill he ingratiates himself so thoroughly
with Marlow's friend Denver as to become the man's foster
son and projected heir, but flees when the second engineer

of the Patna turns up. Denver, he says, was "like a
father. . . . I would have had to tell him" (LJ, 191).
Instead he throws away Denver's fortune to become an
absurdly daring water clerk--"a yelling fiend at the
tiller" (LJ, 194)--to a string of delighted ship chandlers.
      Still later in his flight eastward from the Patna, he
is taken on by Marlow's friend Stein, an elderly trader and
entomologist who was himself in youth adopted by a Scotsman
named M'Neil. This patriarch introduced Stein in the
islands with the formula: "Look, queen, and you rajahs,
this is my son. . . . I have traded with your fathers, and
when I die he shall trade with you and your sons" (LJ,
206); Jim is to be Stein's foster son, the recipient of a
house and a stock of trade goods--if he lives. Consigned
to a defunct station in wartorn Patusan, a wilderness from
which he (like Willems in Sambir) is unlikely to return, he
lets Marlow convince him that burial is tantamount to
opportunity. "He had shown a desire, I continued inflexibly, to go out and shut the door after him. . . . 'Did
I?' he interrupted in a strange access of gloom. . . .
'You can't say I made much noise about it'" (LJ, 231-32).
Yet quite soon, in a romantic ardor abetted by what John
Munder Ross has called the need for "exoneration of the
father,"[37] Patusan becomes for Jim his "magnificent
chance" (LJ, 241). It remains so even when a half-caste
captain, willing to take him only as far as the mouth of
Patusan's river, comments that "the gentleman [is] already
'in the similitude of a corpse'" (LJ, 240). Typically,
Jim embarks on his new duties with a revolver but no
cartridges--an omission that would have struck Freud as
purposive; it resigns to older men--specifically, to
Doramin, a Malay chief loyal to Stein--the phallic power
symbolized by loaded pistols. Jim establishes himself as
"virtual ruler" (LJ, 273) of Patusan only under the aegis
of this substitute father, who oversees his most audacious
act, the storming of a rival chieftain's fort. Assuming
with unexpected success the Rajah Brooke role of white god
to natives, he subdues warring factions to establish the
order requisite for Stein's trade. By doing his duty to
"his people" (LJ, 377) he seeks to expiate the Patna,
thereby satisfying Marlow and, in a vague way, the parson
and others connoted by the term "home." At a last meeting
he tells Marlow, who is bound for England, that he will
never leave the natives entrusted to his care because "I
must stick to their belief in me to feel safe" and to
maintain contact "with those whom, perhaps, I shall never
see any more. With--with--you, for instance" (LJ, 334).
      In the white god's personal Arcadia, every man can

feel "sure of to-morrow" (LJ, 373) until Jim, against all
advice, allows a piratical white invader named Brown and
his gang to leave Patusan in arms. Allying himself with
Rajah Tunku Allang and Stein's former agent Cornelius,
Brown massacres a native force including Jim's friend Dain
Waris, the son of Doramin. Jim, who had staked his life on
the safety of all Patusan if his fellow whites were allowed
to go free, redeems his pledge by letting Doramin shoot him
with one of M'Neil's pistols. The gun was a token of
"eternal friendship" (LJ, 233) from Stein to an old war
comrade; Doramin's gift to Stein, a silver ring, rolls
against Jim's foot to identify him as the victim of a
convergence of fathers.

His death with "proud and unflinching glance" asserts
the courage that failed him on the Patna; he has finally
married, in place of Jewel, "a shadowy ideal of conduct"
(LJ, 416). In the psychologically convincing suicide
Conrad has given him, death would also gratify his passive,
masochistic, and homosexual impulses toward the father; as
Robert Armstrong suggests, ". . . deepest and most secret
of all perhaps . . . the passive longings to be penetrated
by father are gratified"[38] by Doramin's bullet. But
despite a predominance of negative Oedipal impulses, toward
submission, castration, and death, Jim is not devoid of
positive or parricidal ones, the guilt for which would
supply an additional motive for suicide. Armstrong has
traced his indulgence toward Brown to an identification
with the id of this freebooter, who once ran off with the
dying wife of a missionary; as the seducer of a clergyman's
wife, he has done what Jim, a parson's son, would have
liked to do.[39] Marlow hints at an unexplained complicity: through the "rough talk" of the pair runs
"a vein of subtle reference to their common blood, an
assumption of common experience; a sickening suggestion of
common guilt, of secret knowledge that was like a bond of
their minds and of their hearts" (LJ, 387).

Conrad has also depicted Jim as a parricidal threat to
fathers nearer at hand. Like Willems in An Outcast of the
Islands and Marlow in Heart of Darkness, he is an Oedipal
son who ascends a narrow, snaky river, this one possessing
the "shining sinuosity" of "an immense letter S of beaten
silver" (LJ, 260); like the Congo, it leads into a feminized wilderness. The moonlit landscape of Patusan,
dominated by Jewel and the grave of her mother, is arranged
above the level of the forests into "two steep hills very
close together, and separated by what looks like a deep
fissure. . . . the appearance from the settlement is of
one irregularly conical hill split in two, and with the two

halves leaning slightly apart" (LJ, 220). In this milieu
Jim becomes the implied rival of Doramin, Cornelius, and
Stein. As a fugitive from the Rajah's stockade he is
adopted by Doramin's motherly wife; exhausted from a
struggle with the Patusan mud, he lies in "an immense
bed--her state bed" (LJ, 255) as a son-lover. For this
youth the difference between mother and mistress is slight,
as the "vigilant affection" (LJ, 283) of his "wife" Jewel
later makes clear: "I watched your sleep. . . . You think I
watched on this night only!" (LJ, 298-99). The protective
Jewel is, moreover, a double of her own mother, whom she
physically resembles, whose grave she carefully tends, and
whose fate--desertion by a white man--she shares. Jewel's
tie to Jim feeds the hostility of Cornelius, an abusive
but jealous foster parent to her and, as Jim's host and
supposed mentor in the trade of Patusan, something of an
archetypal bad father to himself as well. Supplanted by
Jim as Stein's agent, regarding himself as an "old servant"
(LJ, 310) turned out for a boy, Cornelius also resents his
sexual deposition: "He . . . comes here devil knows from
where . . . devil knows why--to trample on me till I die";
"We shall see! . . . Steal from me? Steal from me
everything! Everything!" (LJ, 328, 329). Cornelius's
treachery in guiding Brown to the ambush of Dain Waris
achieves his persistent aim, Jim's death (LJ, 368, 378,
388, 397), but he himself is killed by Jim's Malay
retainer, Tamb' Itam. The murder is foreshadowed by Jim's
verbal assault on him as "the hateful embodiment of all the
annoyances and difficulties he had found in his path"--a
"swindler, liar, sorry rascal." Jim's invective is halted
only by the silence of the "indistinct figure . . . that
seemed to hang collapsed, doubled over the rail in a weird
immobility. . . . 'Exactly as if the chap had died while I
had been making all that noise'" (LJ, 293).

Cornelius, Jewel's stepfather, doubles for Stein, who,
"greyhaired, paternal," bending with "compassionate and
chivalrous deference" (LJ, 350), becomes her last guardian.
But he has been her covert protector for years; it was he
who paid Cornelius to marry a Dutch-Malay woman abandoned
by a white paramour.[40] Royal Roussel makes a reasonable
guess that this unnamed betrayer, the actual father of
Jewel, is Stein. Marlow surmises that before Jim's
disgrace, Patusan "had been used as a grave for some sin,
transgression, or misfortune" (LJ, 219); and although he
refuses to countenance the possibility of wrongdoing by
Stein, the philanthropist himself alludes to failures in
his past. Admittedly he has not always been able to follow
his advice to Jim, to pursue the dream "ewig--usque ad

finem": ". . . do you know how many opportunities I let
escape; how many dreams I had lost that had come in my
way?" (LJ, 215, 217).[41]

In a competition for Jewel, Stein may substitute for
an earlier father and sexual rival, Jim's Essex parson.
Toward the latter, however, an extra parricidal motive
might emerge. There are two ways for the son to kill the
father, externally as a competitor and internally as part
of himself. After the Patna Jim, though he shuns overt
self-destruction as "not the way" (LJ, 132) out of his
disgrace, seemingly pursues what Edwin Shneidman has called
a "subintentioned death," one in which the victim plays
"subtle, covert, latent, partial, and unconscious roles
. . . in effecting or, more often, in hastening his own
demise."[42] Jim's leitmotif comes to be the assumption of
risk. In the boat from the Patna, for example, he courts
death: "The sun crept all the way from east to west over my
bare head, but that day I could not come to any harm. . . .
The sun could not make me mad. . . . Neither could it kill
me. . . . That rested with me" (LJ, 126). In Patusan he
fearlessly leaps over the Rajah's stockade, dwells in the
house of Cornelius, drinks the Rajah's possibly poisoned
coffee, shoots one would-be assassin and frees three
others, stakes his life on the success of the attack on
Sherif Ali and wins, and then, in the same gamble on
the peaceful withdrawal of Brown's force, loses. Jim's
exploits seem to gratify more than the wish to firm his
courage, though that motive might be expected; his tie to
his father appears to require self-destruction. A quest
for death would be compatible with the urge to kill an
overwhelming parent, introjected in early childhood as his
conscience. Freud placed the origin of conscience, or
the superego, in identifications with the parents, but
particularly the father, in the process by which the
child's Oedipus complex is resolved. The outcome of
sexual conflict is the formation within the ego of a
"precipitate," which assumes a position of dominance;
retaining the character of the father, it "confronts the
other contents of the ego as [a] super-ego."[43] The
existence of a condemnatory introjected parent in Jim could
be inferred from his psychic division. Although after the
Patna he admits only shame, in the sense of condemnation by
others, he endures guilt--self-condemnation--as well.
Marlow says that in justifying himself for the desertion of
the ship, "He was not speaking to me, he was only speaking
before me, in a dispute with an invisible personality, an
antagonistic and inseparable partner of his existence--
another possessor of his soul" (LJ, 93). Two recent

critics, H. M. Daleski and Giles Mitchell, have
treated this inward foe as a Jungian shadow, roughly
comparable to the Freudian id, which has blocked the
realization of Jim's ego ideal of heroic masculinity.[44]
But since the passage follows an elaborate bit of self-
exculpation, the adversary would appear to resemble
the Freudian superego: ". . . one part of the ego sets
itself over against the other, judges it critically, and,
as it were, takes it as its object."[45]

The character of the superego that would be formed by
an internalization of the Essex parson is sufficiently
clear. Jim's "treasured" last letter from home delineates
the standard of conduct expected by a rigid old cleric,
living untested in one of England's "abodes of piety and
peace," "breathing equably the air of undisturbed rectitude" (LJ, 5, 341, 342):

> One can almost see him, grey-haired and serene
> in the inviolable shelter of his book-lined,
> faded, and comfortable study, where for forty
> years he had conscientiously gone over and over
> again the round of his little thoughts about faith
> and virtue, about the conduct of life and the only
> proper manner of dying. . . . He hopes his "dear
> James" will never forget that "who once gives way
> to temptation, in the very instant hazards his
> total depravity and everlasting ruin. Therefore
> resolve fixedly never, through any possible
> motives, to do anything which you believe to be
> wrong." (LJ, 341-42)

By this Calvinist standard no redemption for Jim's
desertion of the Patna appears to be possible. The only
remedy, as foreseen by Stein, is death: "One thing alone
can us from being ourselves cure!" (LJ, 212). Conrad
offers a paradox: Jim dies partly to kill that within
himself which requires self-destruction. Its power in a
crisis has been demonstrated through the insight of Brown.
When not appealing to the id, this satanic manipulator
assumes the mantle of the superego, displaying, as Jeffrey
Berman has said, an "uncanny ability to exploit [Jim's]
guilt" over the leap from the Patna.[46] In this second
role Brown's master stroke is the contrast he insinuates
between his own past and what he divines to be Jim's:

> I came here for food. . . . And what did you
> come for? . . . I would let you shoot me, and
> welcome. . . . I am sick of my infernal luck.
> But it would be too easy. There are my men

in the same boat--and, by God, I am not the
sort to jump out of trouble and leave them in
a d--d lurch. (LJ, 382-83)

In Conrad's anticipation of modern suicidology, a
complex of motives pointing to death overrides Jim's
commitments to Patusan and to Jewel, whom he had promised
never to leave. Conrad has fully developed the wish to
kill and to be killed--along with the wish to die, in a man
who can say, "I have no life" (LJ, 409). In comparison,
other deaths of son figures in the novel have the look of
summary executions, revealing less about the characters'
psychology than about Conrad's own. The abrupt suicide of
Captain Brierly, for example, is announced at the close of
Marlow's tribute to a success story.

He had never in his life made a mistake, never
had . . . a check in his steady rise, and he
seemed to be one of those lucky fellows who
know nothing of indecision, much less of
self-mistrust. At thirty-two he had one of the
best commands going in the Eastern trade--and,
what's more, he thought a lot of what he had.
. . . As I looked at him flanking on one side
the unassuming pale-faced magistrate who
presided at the inquiry, his self-satisfaction
presented to me and to the world a surface as
hard as granite. He committed suicide very
soon after. (LJ, 57-58)

It is possible to wring adequate motives from a scanty
text. Marlow believes that Brierly somehow identified
himself with Jim, whose dereliction on the Patna he was
required to judge; in the process he was "probably holding
silent inquiry into his own case. The verdict must have
been of unmitigated guilt" (LJ, 58). Brierly, then, in
Albert Guerard's words, "recognized in Jim an unsuspected
potential self; he had looked into himself for the first
time"[47] and glimpsed a possible failure. Another critic,
Charles Clark, asserts that the failure is actual, not
potential; Brierly has reason to fear some revelation
of cowardice or other shortcoming by an old Malay who
testifies at the Patna inquiry. The witness "suddenly,
with shaky excitement" pours out "a lot of queer-sounding
names" (LJ, 99) of forgotten men and ships. The target
is clear; he "wanted that white Tuan to know--he turned
towards Brierly, who didn't raise his head--that he had
acquired a knowledge of many things by serving white men on

the sea for a great number of years" (LJ, 98-99).[48]   Thus
Brierly might have had a wish to die, to escape shame. It
also appears that he may not have been on excellent terms
with his father, who sends not a word in reply to the news
of his death: "Neither Thank you, nor Go to the devil!--
nothing! Perhaps they did not want to know" (LJ, 64).
Another suicidal motive imputable to him is a wish to be
killed, to terminate Oedipal guilt. A captain who may
have erred in gaining too early or too proudly the father's
privilege of command, he kills himself with the request
that the ship be given to an older man--his gray-haired
mate Jones, who has described him as "promoted over too
many heads, not counting my own" (LJ, 59). Amazed at the
efforts of the thirty-two-year-old Brierly on his behalf,
Jones tells Marlow that the late captain "wrote like a
father would to a favourite son . . . and I was five-
and-twenty years his senior. . . . I couldn't believe
my eyes. . . . You would think, sir, he had jumped
overboard only to give an unlucky man a last show to get
on" (LJ, 62). In this, Jones may have said more than he
knows.[49] But Conrad has sketched the character of
Brierly in so few strokes that any explanation of his death
must remain tenuous.

The same might be said of Gentleman Brown, the
baronet's son engaged in a sanguinary struggle with the
world for the respect he feels his due. Marlow treats him
as a kind of idealist, whose attack on Dain Waris's force
"was not a vulgar and treacherous massacre" but "a lesson,
a retribution"--an act of "revenge upon the world which,
after twenty years of contemptuous and reckless bullying,
refused him the tribute of a common robber's success" (LJ,
403, 404). As a "latter-day buccaneer," Brown, "the show
ruffian on the Australian coast," is distinguished by "a
blind belief in the righteousness of his will against all
mankind, something of that feeling which could induce the
leader of a horde of wandering cut-throats to call himself
proudly the Scourge of God" (LJ, 352, 370). In general,
Brown's Attilalike posture seems not to have incited
authorial retribution. But a decline in his fortunes is
signaled by a sexual escapade, his elopement with the dying
wife of a missionary. The charm of a moribund woman may
have been the chance she afforded for a gesture of Oedipal
defiance. The husband,

> poor man . . . had been heard to express the
> intention of winning "Captain Brown to a
> better way of life." . . . "Bag Gentleman Brown
> for Glory"--as a leery-eyed loafer expressed
> it once--"just to let them see up above what

a Western Pacific trading skipper looks like."
(<u>LJ</u>, 384)

Brown not only fails to convert but steals the man of God's
wife, and we are told that Brown's "luck left him . . .
very soon after" (<u>LJ</u>, 353). His ship goes on the rocks; he
buys a rotten old schooner and is caught running guns; he
steals a better schooner and it sinks; and finally he
develops asthma, which turns out to be fatal. Freud has
said that the destiny of people who appear dogged by a
malignant fate "is for the most part arranged by themselves
and determined by early infantile influences."[50] Asthma
he declared to be in many cases psychosomatic, and traceable to a single "exciting cause--to the patient's having
overheard sexual intercourse taking place between
adults."[51] These sweeping assertions are consistent
with the history of Conrad's fictional asthmatic. Brown's
breathlessness would symbolically confer on him a paternal
role forbidden a child; it would repeat in symbolic form,
both gratifying and punitive, the sexual replacement of the
father he has just achieved. Conrad, the son of two
persons who eventually died of tuberculosis, might well
have linked breathlessness with parental intercourse. He
may also have considered possible results of sexual guilt
to be self-destructive behavior and psychosomatic illness.
But if such were his beliefs, he did not embody them very
credibly in Brown, whose death, like Brierly's, seems
hastily contrived to meet an authorial need.

A third doomed character is the comic hero of an
anecdote, perhaps a disguised authorial fantasy of sexual
usurpation; Conrad in <u>A Personal Record</u> describes any
novelist as "a figure behind the veil" who in creating
"imaginary things, happenings, and people" is "only writing
about himself" (<u>PR</u>, xv). Conrad's persona Bob Stanton,
showing the steady courage that Jim lacked on the <u>Patna</u>,
attempts to rescue a lady's maid from a sinking ship, but
the panicky woman

> wouldn't leave the ship--held to the rail like
> grim death. The wrestling-match could be seen
> plainly from the boats; but poor Bob was the
> shortest chief mate in the merchant service,
> and the woman stood five feet ten in her shoes
> and was as strong as a horse. . . . One of the
> hands told me . . . "It was for all the world,
> sir, like a naughty youngster fighting with
> his mother." (<u>LJ</u>, 150)

According to Freud, the fantasy of rescuing the mother has
the Oedipal significance of repaying her for the gift of
life by giving her something of equal value--a child. "The
son shows his gratitude by wishing to have by his mother a
son who is like himself: in other words, in the rescue-
phantasy he is completely identifying himself with his
father."[52] In drowning for his gallantry, Stanton-
Conrad seems to pay the penalty for an imagined replacement
of the father. The mother fends off his advances, but, in
what might be called the son's revenge, loses her life
also, in consequence of having preferred the wrong man.

A fourth Oedipal victim, Dain Waris, is a generally
dutiful youth guilty of one sign of presumption: in a
gesture reminiscent of Shakespeare's Prince Hal, he tries
on his own finger the ring that symbolizes Stein's
authority in Patusan; Waris's death in an ambush follows
almost immediately. The phallic act of donning the ring, a
convenient symbol of Patusan's feminized jungle, links
sexual and political aggrandizement; as the next Rajah of
Patusan, he would probably have acquired a wife, or more
wives. But Conrad, though tolerant of the dynastic goals
of two Malays, Dain Maroola and Lakamba, in prior novels,
does not permit Dain Waris to succeed Tunku Allang. The
reason for disallowing an ambition supported by the youth's
own father may be that this third aspirant, as a semi-
European and a potential rival of white rulers, comes
too near his creator. "Of Dain Waris, his own people said
with pride that he knew how to fight like a white man.
. . . he had that sort of courage--the courage in the open
. . . but he had also a European mind," which for Marlow
if not Conrad entails "an unobscured vision, a tenacity
of purpose, a touch of altruism" (LJ, 261-62). Close
proximity to an author, if he suffers from guilt, carries
the risk of guilt by association. Waris contrasts with an
un-European Malay, Jim's servant Tamb' Itam, who marries
and fathers a child and yet survives, apparently outside
the need for Oedipal compromise.

Of those sons who are required to compromise, none in
Lord Jim reaches a solution satisfactory to the author, or
at least none survives--not even Brierly, who adhered to
Marlow's formula of celibacy plus professional achievement.
In the number of dead, Lord Jim is a despairing work; not
surprisingly, it also contains one of Conrad's darkest
perspectives on the father. Besides Doramin, Jim's
elephantine executioner, there are three other paternal
grotesques, reflecting an apparent need to master fear by
comedy. The pajama-clad Patna captain, for example,

becomes in flight a "vast carcass" forcing its way into a tiny gharry, troubling "one's sense of probability with a droll and fearsome[53] effect, like one of those grotesque and distinct visions that scare and fascinate one in a fever" (LJ, 46, 47). "Like a captive balloon" he disappears "into 'ewigkeit'" (LJ, 47). The captain's traits of physical distortion and dehumanization also characterize Cornelius, a "sinister pantaloon" marked even in the blazing sunshine by an effect of "secret slinking," evoking "everything that is unsavoury. His slow laborious walk resembled the creeping of a repulsive beetle" (LJ, 285, 307). In a fourth instance of the grotesque, the distortion is mental. The chief engineer of the Patna, in advanced D. T.'s in a hospital, fends off pink toads by the million. "'The ship was full of them, you know, and we had to clear out on the strict Q. T.,' he whispered with extreme rapidity. 'All pink. All pink--as big as mastiffs, with an eye on the top of the head and claws all round their ugly mouths. Ough! Ough!'" (LJ, 53).[54]

But the most incisive paternal images in Lord Jim are perhaps those of Stein and Marlow, in whom menace is covert. By splitting the father figure, Conrad can imply hidden potentialities while skirting the stress of ambivalent response to a single complex figure like Lingard. Overt betrayals of Jim by the German captain, Cornelius, and Doramin--who had, after all, no obligation to take the life offered him--may reveal a shadow side of Marlow and Stein; though largely benevolent, they remain questionable. Their possible blend of motives, in offering opportunity laced with danger, is epitomized in the anecdote of the "decent middle-aged father," an Abraham who offers "his bit of sacrifice to the sea," his "little willing victim" (LJ, 44-45) of a son, before he himself goes safely ashore.

In Marlow, transformed from a son in Heart of Darkness into a father in Lord Jim, Conrad reveals paternal psychology from the inside. Marlow clearly regards Jim--in looks, "as promising a boy as the sun ever shone on" (LJ, 40)--as a son. "He was a youngster of the sort you like to see about you; of the sort you like to imagine yourself to have been; of the sort whose appearance claims the fellowship of these illusions you had thought gone out, extinct, cold"; ". . . besides the fellowship of the craft there is felt the strength of a wider feeling--the feeling that binds a man to a child" (LJ, 128, 129). Yet when Stein's advice to follow the dream raises in Marlow the prophetic vision of a grave for Jim[55]--

The whisper of his conviction seemed to open

> before me a vast and uncertain expanse, as of a
> crepuscular horizon on a plain at dawn--or was
> it, perchance, at the coming of the night?
> One had not the courage to decide; but it was
> a charming and deceptive light, throwing the
> impalpable poesy of its dimness over pit-
> falls--over graves. (LJ, 215)

--the listener, to rid himself of an awkward "very young
brother" (LJ, 223), acquiesces in this scheme, and Jim is
sent by both men to his death. They act in full knowledge
of the state of Patusan, in which "utter insecurity for
life and property" is "the normal condition"; on arrival
Jim is saved from immediate murder only by "the unex-
pectedness of his coming" (LJ, 228, 251). One might
argue that his romantic nature, and his suicidal bent,
would be gratified by nothing less than life on a razor's
edge, and that his foster parents seek only to accommodate
him. But more compelling paternal motives might be found
in Stein's need to redeem his past failures in Patusan, or
Marlow's dread of Jim as a secret sharer--as Albert Guerard
has said, "another or potential self . . . the criminally
weak self that may still exist."[56] Marlow, "a member of
an obscure body of men held together by a community of
inglorious toil and by fidelity to a certain standard of
conduct" (LJ, 50), cannot help asking:

> Was it for my own sake that I wished to find
> some shadow of an excuse for that young fellow
> . . . whose appearance alone added . . . a
> hint of a destructive fate ready for us all
> whose youth--in its day--had resembled his
> youth? I fear that such was the secret
> motive of my prying. (LJ, 51)

> He appealed to all sides at once--to the side
> turned perpetually to the light of day, and
> to that side of us which, like the other
> hemisphere of the moon, exists stealthily in
> perpetual darkness, with only a fearful ashy
> light falling at times on the edge. He
> swayed me. I own to it. . . . he was one of
> us. (LJ, 93)

> If he had not enlisted my sympathies he had
> done better for himself--he had gone to the
> very fount and origin of that sentiment, he
> had reached the secret sensibility of my
> egoism. (LJ, 152)

Like Brierly, who tried to bribe Jim to flee the court of
inquiry, Marlow evidently fears the presence of a double
who has raised a "doubt of the sovereign power enthroned in
a fixed standard of conduct" (LJ, 50). Even worse, Jim has
led Marlow to question the value of the standard: "There is
never time to say our last word--the last word of our love,
of our desire, faith, remorse, submission, revolt. The
heaven and the earth must not be shaken" (LJ, 225). Unable
to fathom the significance of Jim's conduct on the Patna,
Marlow wavers in imagination between dutiful seaman and
rebel.

Of the threat Jim poses to his work, which includes
the training of maritime officers in the traditional code,
he seems aware. He does not, however, acknowledge its
possible effect on his treatment of the offender. A
narrator of doubtful reliability, he dismisses Jim's role
of man-god in Patusan as merely

> the part into which Stein and I had tumbled
> him unwittingly, with no other notion than to
> get him out of the way; out of his own way,
> be it understood. That was our main purpose,
> though, I own, I might have had another
> motive which had influenced me a little. I
> was about to go home for a time; and it may
> be I desired, more than I was aware of
> myself, to dispose of him--to dispose of
> him, you understand--before I left. (LJ,
> 221)

The semiconscious motive to which Marlow confesses is
a praiseworthy sense of responsibility for a younger
compatriot; going home "must be like going to render an
account," to confront "the spirit that dwells within the
land . . . a mute friend, judge, and inspirer," to which
one must return "with clean hands" (LJ, 221-22). Marlow's
account of himself is open to the same objection he has
has raised to Jim's self-estimate: ". . . no man ever
understands quite his own artful dodges to escape from the
grim shadow of self-knowledge" (LJ, 80).

When Marlow quotes what Brierly has said of Jim, "Let
him creep twenty feet underground and stay there" (LJ, 66),
he is surely asking Stein, whose trading network must
include dull spots as well as perilous ones, to provide a
death. Only when Jim is on his way into danger is Marlow
"freed from that dull resentment which had existed side by
side with interest in his fate"; only then can they address

each other as "dear boy" and "old man" (LJ, 240-41).
Despite an abundance of help rendered to "a nice child"
(LJ, 198), Marlow (like Stein in need of a troubleshooter)
appears to be in part a Laius, as that self-regarding
character has been defined by John Munder Ross. Yet Jim
has engaged in neither the sexual nor the professional
rivalry with Marlow that Freudian Oedipal theory would have
assumed. Conrad in his fourth novel suggests that these
forms of supersession do not exhaust the possible prov-
ocations from youth; it can offend simply by shaking an
elder in his social role--a yoke that, as Jacques Lacan
reminds us, would require in life the suppression of some
portion of the role-player's reality. Conrad has made of
Marlow's sense of identity a Lacanian "construct in the
imaginary."[57]

At the same time, in offering a protagonist no
workable compromise with the father, Lord Jim leaves
unresolved the Oedipal problem raised by Conrad's first two
novels. The attempt to strike a life-sustaining balance,
by which the son could be allowed women in return for the
renunciation of other desiderata, ends in failure. The
only compromise that appears to have satisfied Conrad, even
temporarily, is the one reached for Marlow in Heart of
Darkness: the abandonment of sexual competition with the
father in exchange for survival and professional success.
Significantly, Marlow is a sailor, and he has before him an
ex-seaman, the harlequin, as a model of asceticism. The
persistence of the sea in the minds of two exiles from its
simplicities reflects Conrad's radical hope that man could
attain safety and a state of grace "at any spot a thousand
miles from the nearest land" (NN, 31)--or, it might be
said, from the nearest woman. In Conrad's sea fiction
around the turn of the century he pushed a near belief as
far as its credibility would allow, and somewhat beyond.

4

The Immunity of the
Son at Sea

The brevity of the Conradian son's life span on land, where women abound, contrasts with his almost miraculous survival at sea, in a world of men. In The Nigger of the "Narcissus" (1897), "Youth" (1898), "Typhoon" (1902), and The End of the Tether (1902), his longevity appears to be conditioned on an abstinence from sexual rivalry with the father. In nonsexual competition, however, the son enjoys a wide latitude; in all four works he challenges the father's authority, and in one, "Youth," he assumes command of a ship. Authorial leniency toward filial self-assertion is logical, for all the captains of those stories, despite an undoubted strength, reveal serious defects as commanders. Their portraits reflect both Conrad's official support of paternity and his covert rebellion against it.[1]

Consistency in the application of Conrad's Oedipal compromise contrasts with a fluctuation in artistic quality. A wavering point of view in The Nigger[2] and the excessive length and sentimentality of The End of the Tether show an author less firmly in control than in the two middle works, "Youth" and "Typhoon" (the latter completed by May 1901). But whatever the difficulties of composition, Conrad adhered to his formula; only a residual discontent with a solution that amounts to substitute death for the son may be reflected in the symbolic castration, followed by annihilation, of the conspicuously patriarchal Captain Whalley of The End of the Tether: a splendidly white-bearded "pilgrim" (ET, 181) goes blind and kills himself.

In The Nigger of the "Narcissus," Conrad's refractory sons include the narrator, a member of the crew. This spokesman asserts its "latent egoism of tenderness to suffering" and its "demoralising" anxiety to keep a dying black sailor alive; "through him we were becoming highly humanised, tender, complex, excessively decadent" (NN, 138, 139). The crew's solicitude for James Wait, to the detriment of the ship's discipline, is grounded in each man's sense of his own mortality. Self-interest, in Conrad's view, erodes the solidarity necessary to keep Captain Allistoun's "small planet" (NN, 29) afloat. Wait represents temptation: "I thought I had seen the devil," says the cook of the man who will cast an "infernal spell" over the ship (NN, 19, 37). A second temptation, also inimical to discipline and group survival, appears in the shifty-eyed Donkin, an agitator for seamen's rights. It is the threat inherent in Donkin that produces an Oedipal confrontation with Captain Allistoun. But the two temptations are linked by Allistoun's confinement of Wait to quarters, which leaves the other men to work the ship shorthanded and supplies the pretext for Donkin's attempted murder of the captain.

The only crew member who resists all enticement from duty is the sixty-year-old patriarch Singleton, as "old as Father Time himself" (NN, 24). This "sage" represents a forgotten generation of "real" sailors, "voiceless men--but men enough to scorn in their hearts the sentimental voices that bewailed the hardness of their fate" (NN, 14, 25, 126). These selfless stalwarts are contrasted with modern seamen, who have learned to whine. ". . . the others were strong and mute; they were effaced, bowed and enduring, like stone caryatides that hold up in the night the lighted halls of a resplendent and glorious edifice" (NN, 25). The structure is evidently the British Empire,[3] which, at least in the narrator's official view, would be subverted by Donkin's appeal to working-class discontent, or Wait's to human frailty.

The narrator is perhaps more sensitive to the appeal of Donkin, a mutinous son whom he excoriates in such detail as to seem bewitched. In his introduction of two newcomers to the Narcissus, the description of Wait is brief: "He held his head up in the glare of the lamp--a head vigorously modelled into deep shadows and shining lights--a head powerful and misshapen with a tormented and flattened face--a face pathetic and brutal: the tragic, the mysterious, the repulsive mask of a nigger's soul" (NN, 18). A contrasting set piece for the "votary of change" (NN, 14) becomes an extended caricature:

> His neck was long and thin; his eyelids were red; rare hairs hung about his jaws; his shoulders were

peaked and drooped like the broken wings of a bird;
all his left side was caked with mud which showed
that he had lately slept in a wet ditch. He
had saved his inefficient carcass from violent
destruction by running away from an American ship
where, in a moment of forgetful folly, he had dared
to engage himself; and he had knocked about for a
fortnight ashore in the native quarter, cadging
for drinks, starving, sleeping on rubbish-heaps,
wandering in sunshine: a startling visitor from a
world of nightmares. (<u>NN</u>, 10)

At first glance, according to the narrator:

They all knew him! . . . The man who can't do
most things and won't do the rest. The pet of
philanthropists and self-seeking landlubbers.
The sympathetic and deserving creature that knows
all about his rights, but knows nothing of courage,
of endurance . . . of the unspoken loyalty that
knits together a ship's company. The independent
offspring of the ignoble freedom of the slums full
of disdain and hate for the austere servitude of
the sea. (<u>NN</u>, 10-11)

Although the central event of the novel is the death
of Wait, the prime mover is Donkin as he works a vein of
discontent obvious from the start of the voyage. The Irish
sailor Belfast asserts the need for the crew's solidarity
against the officers and boasts of having thrown tar on
a "lovely" specimen of authority in his white clothes:
"Drowned, blind with tar, he was!" (<u>NN</u>, 8). The way now
lies open for Donkin's brag, "The bloody Yankees been
tryin' to jump my guts out 'cos I stood up for my rights
like a good 'un," and his show of resistance to an early
muster on the <u>Narcissus</u>: "If that's the way of this ship,
we'll 'ave to change all that" (<u>NN</u>, 11-12, 14). But
response to his "altruistic indignation" (<u>NN</u>, 112) is
limited by the personal popularity of the officers and by
the men's inveterate fidelity to the standards they have
set. Opposed by the largely conformist psychology of
the crew, he isolates himself by an overt defiance of
authority. When the first mate knocks out one of his
teeth, the narrator comments approvingly, ". . . men will
be just" (<u>NN</u>, 40). The crew's self-identification with
authority is so close that it sometimes assumes the mate's
disciplinary role. When the ship rolls on her side and
Donkin protests Allistoun's refusal to cut the masts, not a

murmur comes from men who believe this _pis aller_ their only
chance for survival; one sailor even clouts the dissenter
into silence.

Donkin's nearest approach to leadership comes after
the ship has been righted and the unity of officers and men
can no longer be felt as a condition of survival.

> We remembered our danger, our toil--and conveniently
> forgot our horrible scare. We . . . listened to the
> fascinating Donkin. . . . we could not but listen
> . . . to that consummate artist. He told us we were
> good men--a "bloomin' condemned lot of good men."
> . . . Didn't we lead a "dorg's loife for two poun'
> ten a month?" (NN, 100)

> His picturesque and filthy loquacity flowed like a
> troubled stream from a poisoned source. . . . We
> abominated the creature and could not deny the
> luminous truth of his contentions. . . . we had
> saved the ship and the skipper would get the
> credit. (NN, 101-2)

The crew's resentment mounts when Allistoun accuses Wait of
malingering and confines him to quarters: "There's nothing
the matter with you, but you choose to lie-up to please
yourself--and now you shall lie-up to please me" (NN, 120).
The order seems to violate both Wait's right to work, if he
has the urge, and the crew's right to his support. Yet
Allistoun, knowing that Wait is dying, has acted on an
impulse of pity; if the invalid tries to work, he will be
unable to hide his condition from himself. Perhaps only
Allistoun's advancing years could have rendered so hard a
man susceptible to the appeal of Wait's mortality. An
embarrassed captain tells his two mates, "more impressed
than if they had seen a stone image shed a miraculous tear
of compassion," "When I saw him standing there, three parts
dead and . . . no grit to face what's coming to us all--the
notion came to me all at once, before I could think" (NN,
127). The unhappy result of charity has been a near
mutiny, although for most of the crew rebellion goes no
further than a vague determination not to be "put upon"
(NN, 122). Donkin's attempt to murder the captain with a
belaying pin is quickly repudiated: "The hurtling flight of
some heavy object was heard; it passed between the heads of
the two mates. . . . a deafening hubbub arose. Above it
Archie was heard energetically:--'If you do oot ageen I
wull tell!'" (NN, 123). In the words of an unnamed and
representative sailor, "We ain't that kind" (NN, 123). The

continued loyalty of most of his crew assures Allistoun's
victory in a public confrontation with the votary of
mutiny. Astute in psychology as well as seamanship,
the captain outfaces the man who tried to kill him and
then—having returned the weapon to be stowed in its proper
place on the ship—coolly turns his back on Donkin as the
perpetrator of "nonsense" (NN, 137).

The menace of Donkin re-emerges only at the end of the
voyage, after the Narcissus has docked in London. Although
the crew rejects his offer of a drink, as it rejected his
bid for mutiny, he and his gospel of change are fated to
thrive on land. Given a bad discharge by Allistoun, he can
afford to throw it back: "'. . . keep it. I'm goin' ter
'ave a job ashore.' . . . All looked at him. He had better
clothes, had an easy air, appeared more at home than any of
us. . . . 'Yuss. I'ave friends well off. That's more'n
you got. But I am a man'" (NN, 169-70). At the pay table
he denounces the crew in words that point to an unresolved
issue in the novel. The narrator cannot determine whether
manhood signifies the unthinking fidelity of a Singleton or
the self-assertion of a Donkin. The agitator's argument is
both persuasive and unanswered.

> "What 'ave I done to yer? Did I bully yer? Did
> I 'urt yer? Did I? . . . You won't drink? . . .
> Then may ye die of thirst, every mother's son of
> yer! Not one of yer 'as the sperrit of a bug.
> Ye're the scum of the world. Work and starve!"
>   He went out, and slammed the door with such
> violence that [an] old Board of Trade bird nearly
> fell off his perch. (NN, 170)

The scene seems to echo the crashing exit of Ibsen's Nora
in a contemporary literary escape from paternalism.

Conrad's attitude to a rebel is, however, more complex
than Ibsen's broadly sympathetic one. Captain Allistoun
sits "smiling thoughtfully at the cleared pay-table" (NN,
170); a shaken narrator endeavors to dismiss Donkin as the
phenomenon of an unquiet land:

> I never saw them again. . . . Singleton has no
> doubt taken with him the long record of his
> faithful work into the peaceful depths of an
> hospitable sea. And Donkin, who never did a
> decent day's work in his life, no doubt earns
> his living by discoursing . . . upon the right
> of labour to live. So be it! Let the earth and
> the sea each have its own. (NN, 172)

This dichotomy, entirely to the faithful seaman's credit, marks a retreat from a prior contrast, in which a blind-drunk Singleton, unable to write his name at the pay table, was distinguished from a Donkin "grave" and "full of business" (NN, 169). The first sailor has impressed the clerk as "a disgusting old brute," the other as "an intelligent man" (NN, 169). Donkin, a "consummate artist" in rhetoric, may represent a rebel self of his creator, who quarreled with several captains, who once confirmed Donkin's judgment of life at sea--"ce métier de chien" (PR, 122)--and who as early as 1885, ten years before he published Almayer's Folly, declared himself "sick and tired of sailing about for little money and less considera-tion."[4] The voice of disaffection on the Narcissus also appears to express a covert rebel self of the narrator. This observer undercuts his deification of Allistoun--"He, the ruler of that minute world, seldom descended from the Olympian heights of his poop. . . . at his feet . . . common mortals led their busy and insig-nificant lives"--by noticing a "crawling line" of sailors in a gale, pinned up against the shrouds "in attitudes of crucifixion" (NN, 31, 56). The narrator's heroes turn out to be his shipmates, last seen drifting away past the Mint in the "sunshine of heaven . . . like a gift of grace" (NN, 172). From his farewell salute to a partly mutinous crew--"Good-bye, brothers! You were a good crowd" (NN, 173)--the ringleader is not excluded.

The narrator's parting question for his mates--"Haven't we, together and upon the immortal sea, wrung out a meaning from our sinful lives?" (NN, 173)--may assert a common guilt in parricidal urges, conflicting with an opposite set of impulses. A high degree of submission in Conrad's "big children" (NN, 6) of the sea suggests Freud's theory that paternal standards, internalized to form the child's superego, become a means of control by subsequent father figures. "As a child grows up, the role of father is carried on by teachers and others in authority; their injunctions and prohibitions remain powerful in the [superego] and continue, in the form of conscience, to exercise the moral censorship."[5] The crew's motive for rejecting mutiny--"We ain't that kind"--is compatible with an introjection of paternal and paternalistic authority as the basis of self-identification. In the hierarchy of maritime discipline such authority would be particularly strong. But control of mental life by the superego is never complete; besides, even in an adult psyche the superego may never have attained its full maturity. Anna Freud has postulated a preliminary but sometimes durable

stage of superego development, characterized by a defense
she terms "identification with the aggressor"--the
authority from whom the child expects punishment. By this
mechanism a passive role is changed into an active one.
"By impersonating the aggressor, assuming his attributes or
imitating his aggression, the child transforms himself from
the person threatened into the person who makes the
threat." A second defense, closely allied with the first,
is the projection of guilt. The parents' standards have
been introjected, but ". . . the offense is externalized";
thus the ego, though it has learned what is regarded as
blameworthy, defends itself against self-criticism. The
precursor of true morality, which includes the acceptance
of one's own fault, is "vehement indignation at someone
else's wrongdoing."[6] In harmony with Anna Freud's
observations, a majority of crew members on the Narcissus
would appear to have projected parricidal guilt onto
Donkin, and to have imitated the aggressor in meting out
corporal punishment to a scapegoat; Donkin suffers for
others' sins as well as his own. The first mate, Baker,
sets a precedent by knocking out one of his teeth; later a
crew member hits him on the mouth for demanding the masts
be cut. In addition, the narrator casually mentions that
after the storm ". . . we refrained from kicking him,
tweaking his nose, or from accidentally knocking him about,
which last, after we had weathered the Cape, had been
rather a popular amusement" (NN, 102); nevertheless, for
the attempt on the captain Donkin is soundly kicked by
Archie. "And a good job, too!" (NN, 131), says Belfast,
the man who once boasted of tarring an officer.
    The crew's attitude to parricide is thus opposite to
Dostoevsky's in The Brothers Karamazov, as interpreted by
Sigmund Freud: because Dmitri stands ready to commit
parricide, he spares his brothers the necessity; therefore
Father Zossima bows down at his feet. For Dostoevsky a
criminal is "almost a Redeemer, who has taken on himself
the guilt which must else have been borne by others."[7]
On the Narcissus, by contrast, the self-divided sailors
blink their affinity with Donkin. Having heard Belfast's
boasts, and Wait's claim to be malingering,[8] he complains
to Wait with some justice: "I've been treated worser'n a
dorg by your blooming back-lickers. They 'as set me on,
only to turn aginst me" (NN, 152).
    The phenomenon of identification with the aggressor
requires that the parent or other authority figure set an
aggressive example to be followed. Anna Freud did not
probe the motivation of the attacker; but The Nigger of the
"Narcissus," like Conrad's other works, might be examined

for the presence of a Laius as well as Oedipus.
Admittedly, the harm done by Conradian fathers is not
always traceable to a conflict of generations. The
anecdote of the "Plimsoll man" (NN, 107), for example,
merely encapsulates the view that paternity, for one reason
or another, is not to be trusted. Conrad's professed
humanitarian is named for Samuel Plimsoll, an advocate of
the Unseaworthy Ships Bill (1875), which made the white
painted load line, or Plimsoll mark, mandatory on British
ships. In Knowles's account on the Narcissus, Plimsoll's
agent, a "fatherly old gentleman with a white beard" (NN,
107), persuaded a crew in Cardiff to refuse duty on the
ground the vessel was overloaded; by the time a court had
ruled she was not, the kindly patriarch apparently unable
to see beyond the length of his umbrella had disappeared,
and the crew was punished with six weeks' hard labor.

The Plimsoll man represents one paternally sanctioned
approach to salvation, the way of philanthropy and leg-
islation, which unaccountably fails in the novel. Two
other paternal panaceas, the maritime code and religion,
also fail, partially or totally, for reasons that are
clearly assignable to the hubris of an older generation.
For instance, Captain Allistoun, who can seem "with his
eyes to hold the ship up in a superhuman concentration of
effort" (NN, 65), is a flawed Olympian. The narrator's
tribute to his omniscience is not fully warranted: "He was
one of those commanders who speak little, seem to hear
nothing, look at no one--and know everything, hear every
whisper, see every fleeting shadow of their ship's life"
(NN, 125). In fact, his misjudgment of his crew's temper
sparks an aborted mutiny. His motive is compassionate, but
pity, according to Conrad, disguises a "latent egoism of
tenderness to suffering" (NN, 138); Allistoun's concern has
been for his own mortality rather than Wait's.

But a greater danger than mutiny results from the
captain's desire to gain a kind of immortality by setting
a speed record. "He had commanded the Narcissus since she
was built. He loved his ship, and drove her unmercifully;
for his secret ambition was to make her accomplish some day
a brilliantly quick passage which would be mentioned in
nautical papers" (NN, 30-31). The narrator notes that well
into the storm "Captain Allistoun, looking more hard
and thin-lipped than ever, hung on to full topsails and
foresail, and would not notice that the ship, asked to do
too much, appeared to lose heart altogether for the first
time since we knew her" (NN, 52). Not all of this canvas
has been furled when the Narcissus capsizes, the forecastle
doors fly open, and the men watch their "chests, pillows,

blankets, clothing, come out floating upon the sea" (NN,
58). In reference to a needless loss the motif of
crucifixion recurs: ". . . Archie's big coat passed with
outspread arms, resembling a drowned seaman floating with
his head under water" (NN, 58). The maritime code of duty
has offered no protection against a captain's narcissism.
Allistoun's ambiguous credo, ". . . I am here to drive this
ship and keep every man-jack aboard of her up to the mark"
(NN, 133), falls within the code if "drive" means "to impel
forward"; if, as seems probable, it means "to overtask"
both ship and crew, he would appear to have exceeded his
authority.

Allistoun's thirst for immortality is caricatured in
the cook's "pride of possessed eternity" (NN, 115). John
Palmer has correctly identified Podmore as "a tool of
Conrad's theological skepticism,"[9] a man who prays for
the destruction of the ship ("a quick deliverance"--NN, 80)
so that his own soul, held always in readiness to meet its
Maker, may be the only one exempt from hell-fire. Later
the same apostle, relenting enough to try to save Wait's
soul as well, "prayerfully" strips himself of "the last
vestige of his humanity," by pronouncing the terrified
patient "as good as dead already" (NN, 116, 117). "He
lies," gasps Wait; ". . . he is a devil--a white devil"
(NN, 119). What seems Podmore's sole act of real beneficence, the production of hot coffee for the men on
the overturned ship, only serves to extend his "supreme
conceit" to the belief he has performed a miracle; a
"special mercy" has sustained his "walking over the sea to
make coffee for perishing sinners" (NN, 83, 116).

A third father figure, Singleton, "profound and
unconscious" (NN, 130), lacks the self-awareness necessary
to produce a Laius; yet in the ethic he promulgates, and
the example he sets for younger men, he, too, has a
destructive potential. In an era of growing concern for
maritime safety, Singleton, "untouched by human emotions,"
remains indifferent to the rights of seamen: "Ships are all
right. It is the men in them!" (NN, 24, 41). His discovery of his own mortality, in a collapse after thirty
hours at the wheel, does not affect his "chilling air of
resignation" (NN, 130). Like Podmore, this primitive, with
his cannibal tatoos, doubles for Allistoun--not in egotism
but in the barbarism of "hard unconcern" (NN, 130) for
life.

Conrad's denigration of the father often works against
his seeming intention, to present the Narcissus, hier-
archically governed, as a paradigm of the well-ordered
society, in which man's struggle against nature requires

control by an adamantine patriarch from the top. At the
end of the novel England becomes a boat, "the great
flagship of the race" (<u>NN</u>, 163). The ship, or ship of
state, must be guarded against the condition of anarchy
imaged by a <u>Narcissus</u> deserted by her helmsman: she
"trembled from trucks to keel; the sails kept on rattling
like a discharge of musketry. . . . It was as if an
invisible hand had given the ship an angry shake to recall
the men that peopled her decks to the sense of reality,
vigilance, and duty" (<u>NN</u>, 124).

In what may be Conrad's reaction to the foundation in
1887 of the National Amalgamated Sailors' and Firemen's
Union, he has tried to show a demanding captain and code as
part of a benevolent order of the universe. Discontent on
a ship is "a silly exasperation against something unjust
and irremediable that would not be denied"; an "eternal
pity" ordains that toil be "hard and unceasing," lest men
have strength left to ponder "the complicated and acrid
savour of existence" (<u>NN</u>, 90, 103). At least officially,
Conrad offers a defense of paternalism to compare with
Disraeli's <u>Sybil</u> (1845), Eliot's <u>Felix Holt</u> (1866), or the
warnings of Bounderby in Dickens's <u>Hard Times</u> (1854). Like
Eliot's workingmen, Conrad's sailors suffer from "intellectual shortcomings" (<u>NN</u>, 102). Like Bounderby, who
conceived a working class demanding to be "fed on turtle
soup and venison, with a gold spoon,"[10] the narrator of
<u>The Nigger</u> gibes at Utopia: "Our little world," "inspired
by Donkin's hopeful doctrines . . . dreamed enthu-
siastically of the time when every lonely ship would
travel over a serene sea, manned by a wealthy and well-fed
crew of satisfied skippers" (<u>NN</u>, 103). Like Dickens's
cunning agitator Slackbridge, "an ill-made, high-shouldered
man,"[11] the scarecrow Donkin may be motivated by an
egotism stemming from physical deformity. He lacks
altruism or any true sense of solidarity with the class he
champions; his vindictive envy even precipitates the death
of a shipmate. To a man of Donkin's "passionate sense of
his own importance," the "black idol" (<u>NN</u>, 105, 152) Wait
has been rendered intolerable by the homage he receives
from other seamen: "Who's yer to be . . . waited on 'and
an' foot like a bloomin' ymperor. Yer nobody" (<u>NN</u>, 151).
Wait expires on his tormentor's assurance that he will soon
go overboard, and Donkin, at the nadir of Conrad's portrayal of a malcontent, steals the dead man's money.

Yet this betrayal of the ideal of working-class unity
is paralleled by Allistoun's betrayal, in self-interest, of
the ideal of the ship's solidarity. And not only the
depiction of the father but the system of rewards and

punishments works against The Nigger as a defense of
paternalism. The incidence of casualties on the Narcissus
reflects nonconformity to Conrad's private Oedipal compromise, not disobedience to Allistoun's orders. The
paternal sexual prerogative turns out to be decisive.
The only death on the voyage is Wait's, long delayed but
finally occurring soon after he has boasted of a conquest
ashore: "There is a girl. . . . She chucked a third
engineer of a Rennie boat--for me. . . . she would
chuck--any toff--for a coloured gentleman" (NN, 149).
Wait, a Europeanized Negro who speaks the most polished
English on the ship, resembles the Malay Dain Waris of Lord
Jim in nearness to Conrad, and may have been punished
accordingly for sexual indulgence. A parallel victim is
Creighton, the white second mate of the Narcissus. In a
violent storm and capsizing, the only casualty--among more
than a score of men cold, hungry, drenched, moving with
"the negligence of exhausted strength" (NN, 92)--is this
officer, whose leg injury leaves him with a limp. That
Conrad intended a symbolic castration is implied by his
insertion of the lame and lonely sailor Knowles, a butt for
the crew's jokes, as Creighton's comic analog.

> "Jack, you're a terror with the gals."--"He takes
> three of 'em in tow to once, like one of 'em
> Watkinses two-funnel tugs waddling away with
> three schooners behind."--"Jack, you're a lame
> scamp."--"Jack, tell us about that one with a
> blue eye and a black eye. Do." . . . Knowles
> turned about bewildered. (NN, 108-9)

Conrad's excuse for the emasculation of Creighton may have
been supplied at the beginning of the voyage, when the mate
dreamed of a girl "in a light dress, smiling under a
sunshade," who "seemed to be stepping out of the tender
sky" (NN, 22).
      Wait, Creighton, and Knowles are the only young or
younger men sexually linked with women in the novel--unless
one might mention the observers of "two bareheaded women,"
emblematic of "the sordid earth," at the docking of the
Narcissus (NN, 164, 165). "One of the women screamed at
the silent ship--'Hallo, Jack!' without looking at any
one in particular, and all hands looked at her from the
forecastle head" (NN, 164). Conrad leaves it at that. The
three men of the Narcissus who have wives waiting for them
are all marked by some paternal attribute: a godlike
captain, a missionary cook, a boatswain "bearded like a
gigantic Spaniard" and speaking in a "rumbling bass" (NN,
17).

Authorial rigor toward sexual offenses contrasts with leniency to a mutineer and would-be murderer; the gelded Donkin lives to prosper on land. However, his rivalry with Allistoun for power over a ship—in nautical parlance, a female—is couched in sexual terms. The captain rivets his gaze on the Narcissus in a storm "as a loving man watches the unselfish toil of a delicate woman upon the slender thread of whose existence is hung the whole meaning and joy of the world" (NN, 50). A former harpooneer, a man equipped with a gaze "piercing like a dart" (NN, 90), he evidently represents phallic power; when the ship goes over and Donkin refuses to help right her, his captain threatens to brain him with another phallic implement, a belaying pin. Later, Donkin, claiming the same power for himself, throws a pin at the captain but misses. Allistoun returns it publicly, then forces him to put it back where he found it. In the ceremony of replacement, the symbolism of the belaying pin is, if anything, overstressed: Allistoun whipping it from his pocket makes a movement

> so unexpected and sudden that the crowd stepped
> back. . . . He held it up. "This is my affair.
> . . . you all know it; it has got to go where
> it came from." . . . They looked away from the
> piece of iron, they appeared shy, they were
> embarrassed and shocked as though it had been
> something horrid, scandalous, or indelicate,
> that in common decency should not have been
> flourished like this in broad daylight. (NN, 135)

Donkin is, in effect, required to reconstitute the union of father and mother; he rushes at the forerigging and rams "the pin into its hole violently" (NN, 136). But although one ship-woman has been relinquished to a captain-father, Donkin's parting shot, "I'll be even with yer yet" (NN, 136-37), suggests the power he expects to wield, through agitation, over the whole British merchant navy.

What may save him from a fate worse than temporary defeat at the hands of Conrad is his patent lack of interest in actual women. Talk of them leaves him "scandalised," "severe," "disgusted"; on one occasion he is seen feeling "all over his sterile chin for the few rare hairs" to be found there; fellow crew members consider him "a long-headed chap" but "no kind of man" (NN, 101, 106-7, 109, 149). A distinction between manhood in sexuality and manhood in rebellion is perhaps essential to his survival in the Conradian world.

The same rule for the sexual prerogative governs

"Youth," whose married man is a Captain Beard, master of
the ill-fated barque Judea; his name has both paternal and
sexual connotations. At the outset Marlow, in his first
appearance in Conrad's fiction, seems to be involving himself, twenty-two years earlier, in a triangle of captain-
father, son, and wife-mother. Mrs. Beard

> came from Colchester to see the old man. She
> lived on board. . . . Mrs. Beard was an old
> woman, with a face all wrinkled and ruddy like
> a winter apple, and the figure of a young girl.
> She caught sight of me once, sewing on a button,
> and insisted on having my shirts to repair. (Y, 7)

The socks follow, and all the rest of Marlow's outfit; but
Mrs. Beard is soon dispatched by the captain back to
Colchester, and her parting admonition to Marlow makes
clear her preference: "You are a good young man. If you
see John--Captain Beard--without his muffler at night,
just remind him from me to keep his throat well wrapped
up. . . . I noticed how attentive you are to John--to
Captain--" (Y, 9-10).
   The contest with the father--if Beard can be said to
fight--comes on the issue of command. The rise of a green
second mate to the captaincy of the Judea is initially
improbable; Marlow feels himself "a small boy between two
grandfathers"--those "thorough good seamen," the captain
with "fluffy hair . . . like a chin-strap of cotton-wool
sprinkled with coal-dust" (Y, 4, 5) and the first mate
Mahon, who sports a long, snow-white beard. But Beard is
broken by a series of mishaps to his first command, which
he has gained only at the age of sixty; his ship bound for
Bangkok suffers storms, leaks, a collision, a fire in her
cargo of coal, and finally an explosion of coal dust. At
this point Beard, following the example of his paternally
named steward Abraham, goes mad. Marlow scrambling out of
the hold with his hair blown off is eagerly questioned by
his captain: "Where's the cabin-table?" Next Beard wants
to trim the yards. "I don't know if there's anybody
alive," Mahon protests. "Surely," he says, gently,
inflexibly, "there will be enough left to square the
foreyard" (Y, 24). At first "immense in the singleness of
his idea" (Y, 25) that the undecked smoldering shell of the
Judea can still reach Bangkok, he yields somewhat when the
ship spouts flame: he transfers his obsession to salvage.
"One would have thought [he] wanted to take as much as he
could of his first command with him. . . . We said, 'Ay,
ay, sir,' deferentially, and on the quiet let the things

slip overboard. The heavy medicine-chest went that way
. . . green coffee, tins of paint" (Y, 30-31). When an
evacuation to the boats can be postponed no longer, Marlow
by firelight finds his captain asleep and the first mate
feasting with the crew on the ship's stores; the aged Mahon
"with an uncorked bottle" resembles "one of those reckless sea-robbers of old making merry amidst violence and
disaster" (Y, 33). Marlow, who for hours has kept the
boats from smashing into the burning Judea, now saves crew,
first mate, and captain from going down with the ship. He
wakes Beard to give an order: "Time to leave her, sir" (Y,
33). The captain lingers "disconsolately . . . to commune
alone for a while with his first command. Then I went up
again and brought him away at last. It was time. The
ironwork on the poop was hot to the touch" (Y, 34).

De facto captain of the Judea in her last moments,
Marlow soon receives his first de jure command, as the head
of three men in a lifeboat. He promptly compounds his
prior usurpation of authority from a senior captain:

> I was ordered to keep close to the long-boat,
> that in case of bad weather we might be taken
> into her.
>   And do you know what I thought? . . . I
> wanted to have my first command all to myself.
> . . . I would make land by myself. I would
> beat the other boats. Youth! All youth! The
> silly, charming, beautiful youth. (Y, 34)

In Marlow's attitude to aging, "Youth" foreshadows
Lord Jim, in which the same narrator in middle age will
find a younger man's talk of a "clean slate" (LJ, 185) a
reminder of his own "frailty and finitude."[12] "I was
no longer young enough to behold at every turn the
magnificence that besets our insignificant footsteps" (LJ,
185). The short story itself contrasts Marlow narrating at
forty-two with Marlow achieving his first command at
twenty.

> . . . I remember my youth and the feeling that
> will never come back any more--the feeling that
> I could last for ever, outlast the sea, the
> earth, and all men; the deceitful feeling that
> lures us on to joys, to perils, to love, to vain
> effort--to death; the triumphant conviction of
> strength, the heat of life in the handful of
> dust, the glow in the heart that with every year
> grows dim, grows cold, grows small, and expires
> --and expires, too soon, too soon--before life

itself. ($\underline{Y}$, 36-37)

Marlow's hazardous plan for his cockleshell succeeds
("I steered many days. . . . I did not know how good a man
I was till then"--$\underline{Y}$, 36). But his first glimpse of the
East, a feminized landscape like Conrad's Malaysian or
African jungle, hints at a price to be paid for rebellion.
It is not enough that Beard seemed mad, or that he may
have destroyed his own ship by refusing to put into port
when the fire was first detected: "The coast of West
Australia is near, but I mean to proceed to our desti-
nation. . . . No more putting back anywhere, if we all
get roasted" ($\underline{Y}$, 19). Whatever the state of the captain
Marlow has supplanted, he still must make amends for his
Oedipal audacity.

> The mysterious East faced me, perfumed like a
> flower, silent like death, dark like a grave.
> ($\underline{Y}$, 38)

> I have known its fascination since; I have seen
> the mysterious shores, the still water, the lands
> of brown nations, where a stealthy Nemesis lies
> in wait, pursues, overtakes so many of the
> conquering race, who are proud of their wisdom,
> of their knowledge, of their strength. ($\underline{Y}$, 41-42)

Open to both a colonial and a sexual interpretation, these
passages anticipate the Marlow who will renounce Kurtz's
Intended for permanent bachelorhood in Heart of Darkness.
The single-mindedness of Captain Beard in pointing the
burning Judea toward Bangkok is matched by the tenacity of
Captain MacWhirr of "Typhoon," who steams the Nan-Shan
straight through a hurricane. A novice in foul weather,
he rejects the evidence of his falling barometer and the
advice of a navigation manual that storms should be
circumvented. As he explains to his first mate Jukes:

> A gale is a gale . . . and a full-powered
> steam-ship has got to face it. There's just
> so much dirty weather knocking about the world,
> and the proper thing is to go through it with
> none of what old Captain Wilson of the Melita
> calls "storm strategy." ($\underline{T}$, 34)

> Facing it--always facing it--that's the way
> to get through. You are a young sailor. Face
> it. That's enough for any man. ($\underline{T}$, 89)

To escape a 300-mile detour and a large coal bill, he all
but wrecks the ship; in the words of William Bonney, she
"survives the typhoon through no fault of his own."[13]

The fixity of both Beard and MacWhirr falls within
Henri Bergson's definition of the comic as "something
mechanical encrusted on the living"; expecting the
flexibility or suppleness associated with life, we
encounter instead rigidity or mechanism. According to
Bergson, "All that is serious in life comes from our
freedom"; whatever is determined for us--whatever reduces
us to "humble marionettes/The wires of which are pulled by
Fate"--is comic.[14] Freud has assimilated Bergson's
view to his own formula, that the comic depends on an
expenditure of energy "on expectation which has become
superfluous"; the energy not needed can then be "discharged
by laughter." All Bergson's examples of rigidity, he
found, "go back to a comparison between the expenditure on
expectation and the expenditure actually required for an
understanding of something that has remained the same; and
the larger amount needed for expectation would be based on
observation of the multiplicity and plasticity of living
things."[15] What remains the same in MacWhirr is,
according to Charles Schuster, his unflinchingly literal
mind, which produces a "lockstep logic." On storm strategy
the reasoning of the man whose name evokes automatism
proceeds impeccably to a wrong conclusion.

> . . . suppose I went swinging off my course
> and came in two days late, and they asked me:
> "Where have you been all that time, Captain?"
> What could I say to that? "Went around to
> dodge the bad weather," I would say. "It
> must've been dam' bad," they would say. "Don't
> know," I would have to say; "I've dodged clear
> of it." See that, Jukes? (T, 34)[16]

Of the same density are his remarks on the Nan-Shan's
Siamese flag, about which Jukes as a patriotic or jin-
goistic Englishman has complained, "Queer flag for a man
to sail under, sir." But the captain consults the colors
of all nations in his International Signal Codebook and
issues a rebuke: "There's nothing amiss with that flag.
. . . Length twice the breadth and the elephant exactly in
the middle. I thought the people ashore would know how to
make the local flag. Stands to reason" (T, 10).

To his imaginative first mate, MacWhirr at the start
of the voyage is a purely comic figure. But the crisis he
creates will reveal the strength inherent in a dearth of

imagination--"the enemy of men, the father of all terrors"
(LJ, 11), which will bedevil Jukes on the Nan-Shan as it
did Jim on the Patna. In the storm Jukes, forgetting his
intellectual superiority, finds himself "uncritically glad
to have his captain at hand. It relieved him as though
that man had, by simply coming on deck, taken most of the
gale's weight upon his shoulders" (T, 39). When the entire
China Sea seems to have concentrated on the task of washing
Jukes overboard, he keeps on "repeating mentally, with the
utmost precipitation, the words: 'My God! My God!'" (T,
42). This deity, or his human counterpart in Conrad's
secular universe, soon materializes; Jukes is "caught in
the firm clasp of a pair of stout arms. He returned the
embrace closely round a thick solid body. He had found his
captain," that "stranger to the visions of hope or fear"
(T, 42, 48). For Jukes, MacWhirr's "frail and indomitable"
voice, enduring through wind and water, shoving aside the
bellowing hurricane, has an "effect of quietness like the
serene glow of a halo" (T, 44, 46). Possibly only the
illusion of theophany could explain the mate's compliance
with an order to go below and pacify two hundred coolies
fighting over the spilled dollars from their broken sea
chests. At first he resists: ". . . directly, his heart,
corrupted by the storm that breeds a craving for peace,
rebelled against the tyranny of training and command" (T,
53). Yet he goes, and as he reports back to the bridge
over the engine-room speaking tube, his words, in the
youth's excited fancy, mount "as if into a silence of an
enlightened comprehension dwelling alone up there with a
storm" (T, 72).

The creation of a man-god as a defense against the
power of nature recalls Freud's derivation of religious
needs from "the infant's helplessness and the longing for
the father aroused by it." In this depreciatory view,
the common man's notion of a caring Providence, and his
inability to imagine this power except as "an enormously
exalted father," are "patently infantile . . . foreign to
reality . . . humiliating."[17] And indeed, Jukes on the
Nan-Shan has a sense of personal degradation; dependence on
his captain has "weakened his faith in himself" (T, 42).
His reverence for MacWhirr is also a defiance of reality,
for this deity, like the Christian one as seen by Conrad,
has bungled. To R. B. Cunninghame Graham Conrad had
written in 1897:

> . . . I shall be inexorable like destiny and
> shall look upon your sufferings with the idiotic
> serenity of a benevolent Creator (I don't
> know that the ben: Crea: is serene;--but if

he is (as they say) then he <u>must</u> be idiotic.)
looking at the precious mess he has made of
his only job.[18]

The "divine folly" (<u>OI</u>, 273) Conrad attributed to the
man-god Lingard might more properly have been ascribed to
MacWhirr. Lingard, rational in his fashion, sought power
through the exercise of an "infernal charity" (<u>OI</u>, 161);
MacWhirr in steaming through a typhoon has no prospect of
advantage, not even the possible credit of having saved the
ship. The <u>Nan-Shan</u> survives by luck and--if any single
human agency can be called decisive--the skill of her chief
engineer.[19] "'Awful sea,' said the Captain's voice from
above. 'Don't let me drive her under,' barked Solomon Rout
up the pipe. 'Dark and rain. Can't see what's coming,'
uttered the voice. 'Must--keep--her--moving--enough to
steer--and chance it.' . . . 'I am doing as much as I
dare'" (<u>T</u>, 67). Only once, when MacWhirr halts the ship
for a huge wave that he alone can see, does he have a
stronger claim to omniscience than the man in the engine
room. But Jukes is not permanently enamored. When the
storm has passed and he no longer needs to be protected
from nature, he ceases to deify MacWhirr, and may even
react against the role of devotee. In his coda to a
botched voyage, the humiliation of having created, even
momentarily, a god may account for his refusal to laud
MacWhirr's fairness in dividing the spilled dollars equally
among the coolies. Reducing his captain to a lucky
incompetent who has blundered on a solution, the mate
concludes, "I think that he got out of it very well for
such a stupid man" (<u>T</u>, 102).[20]

The Donkinlike second mate, small, shabby, beardless,
one of those sailors who "care for no ship afloat," leaves
the broken, salt-caked <u>Nan-Shan</u> at Fu-Chau with the
pertinent comment, "There's a fellow there that ain't fit
to have the command of a scow" (<u>T</u>, 28, 92). On the
testimony of MacWhirr, a man not given to exaggeration, the
second mate lost his nerve completely in the storm: "Gone
crazy. . . . Rushed at me. . . . Had to knock him down"
(<u>T</u>, 68). This rebel, whose impulses toward the father are
uniformly parricidal, is a simplified variant of the first
mate. One attacks MacWhirr physically, the other verbally,
in ridicule; Jukes alone evinces a possible homosexual
attachment, as in his long, consoling embrace of the
captain, "cheek to cheek," in the tumult of a storm "like
an unbridled display of passion," or by an initial contact
in which "they tumbled over and over, tightening their hug.
. . . Jukes came out of it rather horrified, as though he

had escaped some unparalleled outrage directed at his
feelings" (T, 42, 45, 47). A dread of homosexuality, as
well as of infantile dependency, may figure in his final
rejection of the captain. But whatever the differences
between the two mates, both survive by Conrad's usual
compromise, in which a wide scope in rebellion is allowed
when sexual rivalry with the father has been abjured.
The beardless second mate matches Jukes, unmarried and
unengaged, in celibacy. The only three married men of
"Typhoon," corresponding to the three of The Nigger, are,
once again, all heavily paternal: MacWhirr, "Father" Rout,
and a boatswain fifty years old, hirsute, "resembling an
elderly ape" (T, 49).

MacWhirr, who embodies in some degree all three of
Lingard's paternal traits--though not in the balance in
which Lingard displayed comedy, menace, and protection--may
have been, from the standpoint of ambivalent response, a
dangerous creation for Conrad. It was perhaps in the
interest of psychic safety that his next model of the
father was the monumental Captain Whalley, a hero almost
preternaturally free of comedy. But although the character
of Harry Whalley may represent an escape from complexity,
he is significant for the number and variety of Oedipal
rivalries in which Conrad has involved him. One of these
is a rebellion against the God Whalley takes to be pun-
ishing him with blindness for "a little pride" (ET, 324)
in wanting to live forever. Whalley conceives his interest
in longevity to be the need to continue supporting a married daughter Ivy, whom he named to connote dependency
on himself. But since he has visited Ivy only once in
her years of wedlock, he might be thought to have been
motivated less by love than by the desire for power, and by
pride in the strength that made him her resource. "With
age he had put on flesh a little, had increased his girth
like an old tree presenting no symptoms of decay; and even
the opulent, lustrous ripple of white hairs upon his chest
seemed an attribute of unquenchable vitality and vigour"
(ET, 187). Whalley's concept of a proud God, apt to root
out any hint of pride in a mortal, might have come from an
imago of the father. The captain's august parent had been
a Colonel Whalley, of "distinguished connections"; Harry
"could remember as a boy how frequently waiters at the
inns, country tradesmen and small people of that sort, used
to 'My lord' the old warrior on the strength of his
appearance" (ET, 181). A text repeatedly linked with the
son is the Lord's Prayer, which he recites every morning in
a "loud earnest voice" (ET, 171). Both the proud God and
the desire to propitiate him suggest Freud's contention

"that God is a father-substitute; or, more correctly, that he is an exalted father; or, yet again, that he is a copy of a father as he is seen and experienced in child-hood."[21]

Besides the filial conflict with a deity who was to Conrad--as to Freud--illusory,[22] The End of the Tether probes three other Oedipal rivalries, in all of which Captain Whalley enacts the role of the father. In a triangle like that of Lingard, Aïssa, and Willems, he has sponsored both members of a younger couple. Ivy, the image of his dead wife, "had twined herself tightly round his heart, and he intended her to cling close to her father as to a tower of strength; forgetting while she was little, that in the nature of things she would probably elect to cling to someone else" (ET, 174). When she married, Whalley deemed her choice a "poor stick," destined to fail, and urged her continued reliance on her father: "Mind you write to me openly" (ET, 174, 175). A subsequent collapse of his own fortunes, in the crash of the prestigious Travancore and Deccan Banking Company, effects a castration of the young husband whose dependency he has encouraged along with Ivy's; as though he "had only waited for this catastrophe, the unlucky man, away there in Melbourne, gave up his unprofitable game, and sat down--in an invalid's bath-chair at that, too. 'He will never walk again,' wrote the wife" (ET, 175-76). In a variation on Conrad's usual theme of death to sexually active European sons, this youth lives, but only by turning celibate.

Having in a sense vanquished the husband, Whalley at nearly seventy endeavors to go on as Ivy's prop by commanding the old steamer Sofala. On this vessel Sterne, the ambitious young mate, who has perceived the growing affliction that Whalley tries to conceal, plots to replace him as captain; and Massy, the engineer-owner, can stomach no authority but his own. A "beggar on horseback" (ET, 206) who bought the Sofala with a second prize in the Manila lottery, he perpetuates an old feud with authority. Once too mutinous to keep a berth as an engineer, he has been, until the advent of the impoverished Whalley, too carping to retain the captain required by law and the insurance company. Unable for a time to operate his ship, he has invented a conspiracy of all the captains in Singapore to "bring him to his knees" (ET, 206) because he is an engineer, an upstart among shipowners.

In the classic symptoms of persecutory paranoia as described by Freud, the enmity which the sufferer sees in others is "the reflection of his own hostile impulses against them," the projection outwards of what he does not

wish to recognize in himself.[23] For Freud, in a
hypothesis now generally repudiated by psychoanalysts,
the genesis of paranoia lay in the need to ward off a
"homosexual wishful phantasy"; the principal forms of male
paranoia could "all be represented as contradictions of the
single proposition: '_I_ (a man) _love him_ (a man).'" One
such contradiction is achieved through delusions of
persecution, which "loudly assert: 'I do not _love_ him--I
hate him'"; the reason, taken from an unconscious
projection of hostility, is that ". . . HE PERSECUTES
ME."[24] A Conradian parallel to this view, that paranoia
originates in homosexuality, might be found in the fact
that Massy's enmity comes to center on Whalley, who has a
powerful physical attraction for him. The bass-voiced
patriarch with his phallic emblem, a walking stick, makes
an almost supernatural first impression on the owner of the
Sofala:

> He seemed to have fallen on board from the
> sky. . . . Massy had been struck dumb by
> astonishment in the presence of that imposing
> old man with a beard like a silver plate,
> towering in the dusk rendered lurid by the
> expiring flames of sunset.
> . . . It was a dream. He would presently
> wake up and find the man vanished like a shape
> of mist. The gravity, the dignity, the firm
> and courteous tone of that athletic old stranger
> impressed Massy. He was almost afraid. (_ET_, 270)

But Whalley's appeal is promptly countered by a suspicion
of the 500 pounds he has offered for a partnership in the
Sofala: "What did it mean? . . . what could there be
behind? . . . What is his motive?" (_ET_, 270). Later it
appears that Massy "had never hated any one so much as that
old man who turned up one evening to save him from an utter
disaster" (_ET_, 269) by providing him with a captain.
    However, the theory that paranoia has its origin in
homosexuality has been disputed by (among others) the
post-Freudian analyst Jule Nydes, who considered its actual
root to be Oedipal conflict.[25] Nydes treated the per-
version characteristic of the illness as a regression
from, and a defense against, parricidal impulses toward the
father. The paranoid, who wishes to replace the parent of
the same sex, dreads "retaliation from the introjected
parental superego, which in turn is projected onto
surrogates in the world of contemporary adults." A
regression to homosexuality serves "to appease the father

figure and to insure safety."[26] Massy's long history of
conflict with authority figures would tend to follow
Nydes's view rather than Freud's. Further evidence for the
existence of an intense Oedipal conflict might be obtained
from Massy's compulsive gambling: "The Manila lottery
has been eating him up" (ET, 207). Freud himself, in
"Dostoevsky and Parricide," treated the novelist's mania
for play as a form of self-punishment by which Oedipal
guilt was assuaged by ruin: "He never rested until he had
lost everything." Freud added that Dostoevsky's obsession
with the gaming table was a substitute for autoerotic
satisfaction: "The 'vice' of masturbation is replaced by
the addiction to gambling; and the emphasis laid upon the
passionate activity of the hands betrays this derivation";
moreover, the link between efforts to suppress masturbation
and fear of the Oedipal father is "too well known to need
more than a mention."[27] The latter point seems relevant
to the information that Massy's father was a drunken
boilermaker, probably fearsome, and that the son's maniacal
search for a winning lottery number involves frenetic
activity of the hands in pencilling "a great pile of flimsy
sheets" kept "under lock and key like a treasure" (ET, 265,
266).

Massy's case is complicated by his single impressive
win, from which his obsession with the lottery dates.
Nydes has indicated that to the paranoid or masochist, a
victim of Oedipal conflict, any success he gains may appear
as a dangerous encroachment on the father's authority:
"Success equals incest with the parent of the opposite sex.
Success means murder of the parent of the same sex."[28]
The purchase of a ship may be an untenable success for
Massy, and one which must be undone by an equivalent
failure. According to Whalley's informant Captain Eliott,
when the engineer got a ship of his own, he went

> off his balance all at once: came bouncing
> into the Marine Office . . . switching a
> little cane in his hand, and told each one
> of the clerks separately that "Nobody could
> put him out now. It was his turn. There
> was no one over him on earth, and there never
> would be either." He swaggered and strutted
> between the desks, talking at the top of his
> voice, and trembling like a leaf all the while.
> (ET, 205)

Apart from the phallic cane, a striking detail is Massy's
tremor, which suggests the dread of retaliation noted by

Nydes. Massy may court ruin partly to forestall punishment
by another. He becomes a complex example of Conradian
Oedipal compromise: his survival may have been assured by
celibacy, but a further penalty seems likely to be exacted
from him.

A grain of truth in Massy's belief that Whalley
persecutes him is the imposing old captain's ruse, at the
start of their agreement, in letting himself be taken for
a wealthier man than his 500-pound investment in their
partnership would have indicated.[29] When the Sofala's
worn-out boilers need replacement and Massy has no money
left from the lottery, Whalley declines to put up additional funds; he also means to withdraw his original
investment, to give to Ivy. "You blind devil! It's you
that drove me to it" (ET, 331), cries Massy when he runs
his ship on a reef for the insurance.

In the wreck Whalley, who has weighted his pockets
with the iron Massy used to deflect the ship's compass,
chooses to go down with his last command. His blindness,
insufficiently countered by reliance on the compass and the
eyes of a Malay serang, has made the Sofala unseaworthy.
The wish to die, in a "presumptuous Titan" physically and
morally at the end of his tether, is paramount; in a last
letter to Ivy he has written: "God seems to have forgotten
me. I want to see you--and yet death would be a greater
favour" (ET, 305, 338). In William Moynihan's reading of
The Golden Bough, the name Sofala comes from a region in
Africa in which kings revered as gods were expected to kill
themselves for any bodily defect. Whalley, a king in his
"physical splendor, his captaincy, and his fatherhood,"
kills himself for the defect of failing sight, which
signifies the end of his power.[30] His arrival at total
blindness coincides with the Sofala's terrific double crash
against the reef: "The light had finished ebbing out of the
world" (ET, 333).

In the castration and killing of Whalley, Conrad has
carried out the acts fantasied by Belfast against a ship's
officer in The Nigger of the "Narcissus": "Drowned, blind
with tar, he was!" (NN, 8). By creating and destroying a
character of whom he stands in some awe, Conrad demonstrates the ambivalence of a primitive or a child
toward the father. For Freud, the ruler of a primitive
people is both revered and hated[31]; when his subjects
perceive any sign that his power to do them good is
limited, their underlying hostility, now unchecked by any
considerations of prudence, demands his death; hence the
custom of Sofala. But in The End of the Tether it is not
Ivy and her husband, Whalley's beneficiaries, who require a

death; it is Conrad. The prototype of his attitude is
discernible in one of Freud's comments on the parent-child
relationship: "A son's picture of his father is habitually
clothed with excessive powers . . . and it is found that
distrust of the father is intimately linked with admiration
for him."[32]

The mate Sterne's belief "that no skipper in the world
would keep his command for a day if only the owners could
be 'made to know'" (ET, 239) corresponds to Conrad's
portrayal not only of Whalley but of Captains Allistoun,
Beard, and MacWhirr as well; each puts his ship and all
aboard in danger. Ideal paternity--that is, benevolence
without an alloy of menace--is ascribed in four works of
sea fiction only to figures rarely seen, like Solomon Rout
of "Typhoon" and an anonymous passenger on the Sofala:

> When the mate made an abrupt start, a little
> brown, half-naked boy, with large black eyes,
> and the string of a written charm round his neck,
> became panic-struck at once. He dropped the
> banana he had been munching, and ran to the
> knee of a grave dark Arab in flowing robes,
> sitting like a Biblical figure. . . . The
> father, unmoved, put out his hand to pat the
> little shaven poll protectingly. (ET, 259)

The ideal father is so briefly glimpsed as to raise a doubt
that Conrad believed in the possibility of his existence.

In relation to Oedipal conflict, the narrator's
assertion in The Nigger of the "Narcissus," "The true peace
of God begins at any spot a thousand miles from the nearest
land" (NN, 31), does not signify that the war of generations has ceased but rather that the formula for the
son's survival has been found in a world without women.
Even the murderous Donkin, the usurping Marlow, the
criminal Massy, and the "instinctively disloyal" (ET, 239)
Sterne--who never joins a ship without the intention of
supplanting his commander--can be tolerated. Conrad's
confidence in his Oedipal solution was sufficiently strong
after The End of the Tether that he abandoned the
simplified world of the sea and attempted in three
political novels to apply the formula of celibacy-
and-rebellion to men on land.

5

The Failure
of a Compromise

For Kafka's protagonist K. the father's power must be
challenged at the center, by the son's unremitting effort to
penetrate the Castle; similarly, Conrad, not content with
the struggle of father and son on ships, at the periphery
of human affairs, transferred the Oedipal contest of his
fiction to the seats of power. In what are usually termed
his political novels, Nostromo (1904), The Secret Agent
(1907), and Under Western Eyes (1911), the son's rebellion
is successively mounted in a South American country colo-
nized by foreign investors, in Victorian England, and in
czarist Russia. However, as in The Castle, in which the
power to be wrested from the father is political, economic,
and sexual, political and personal considerations in these
three novels mingle, in what Frederick Karl has called
Conrad's "magic mountain," his vision of the breakdown of
Western civilization.[1]

A continuity of the "political" novels with earlier
Conradian fiction, which most readers have taken to be
essentially personal and psychological, is supplied by the
embodiment of the state in a series of fathers who prove, in
varying degrees, impotent, comic, or menacing; its failure
is their failure. Moreover, Conrad has recourse, at least
in Nostromo and The Secret Agent, to the same Oedipal
compromise as in prior works. In each of these two novels
he gives to one son figure a latitude in nonsexual competition that is paid for, as before, by sexual abstinence.
Unlike Nostromo and Decoud in the first, or Stevie and the
doomed Ossipon in the second, Charles Gould and the Professor survive their rebellions. So do the narrator and
Leggatt in "The Secret Sharer," the short story Conrad
interrupted Under Western Eyes to write. But in the

Russian novel itself the assassin Haldin, though he appears
to have met the requirement of sexual self-denial, does not
survive; nor does the hero Razumov, who is scarcely less
abstinent. Conrad's Oedipal compromise appears to have
foundered on a fictional reenactment of Freud's primal human
crime, the actual murder of the father.

The more limited rebellions of Nostromo and The Secret
Agent do not imply that the fathers have achieved a better
justice, either personal or social. In Nostromo the Latin
American country of Costaguana, having gained its independence from Spain, exists in perpetual turmoil; a military band in Sulaco, its western capital, "plays sometimes
in the evenings between the revolutions" (N, 11). By a
fracturing of chronology the novel approaches what Joseph
Frank has called "spatial form,"[2] in which events appear
simultaneous, and all revolutions are one. Strictly
speaking, however, a circular movement is visible in the
relation of Sulaco, or the Occidental province, to the rest
of the country: from the federation advocated by the elder
statesman Don José Avellanos to the unity imposed by his
ferocious persecutor Guzman Bento, to the separation
achieved by the journalist Martin Decoud, to a future
unification plotted by Cardinal-Archbishop Corbelàn. This
cycle is superimposed on a much longer historical movement,
beginning with the Spanish conquest, in which successive
waves of foreigners exploit the country and the misery of
the common people is perennial. "The heavy stonework of
bridges and churches left by the conquerors proclaimed the
disregard of human labour, the tribute-labour of vanished
nations" (N, 89). In the novel's present, the power of king
and church is gone, but "at the sight of some heavy ruinous
pile overtopping from a knoll the low mud walls of a village," a guide for foreign visitors will remark: "Poor
Costaguana! Before, it was everything for the Padres,
nothing for the people; and now it is everything for these
great politicos in Sta. Marta, for negroes and thieves" (N,
89). The thieving politicians, however, are lackeys of the
American-owned San Tomé silver mine, the "Imperium in
Imperio" which Conrad indicates as the oppressor of the
future: "There is no peace and no rest in the development of
material interests" (N, 135, 511). The power of the mine
is evidently to be broken by organized labor and its ally
Cardinal-Archbishop Corbelàn, the impending "savior" of the
country under the slogan "wealth for the people" (N, 511).
But a "fanatical" (N, 194) priest also advocates the
restoration of confiscated property to the church. His
anticipated triumph seemingly represents a return to the
original European oppressor in Costaguana, the padre.

In the quicksand of political futility Conrad focuses
on the struggles of three young men: Nostromo, the Genoese
factotum of the blancos, or white oligarchs of Sulaco;
Charles Gould, the English administrator of the San Tomé
mine; and Martin Decoud, a native son turned Frenchified
dilettante. The first of these is labeled by Conrad a "man
of the People," the embodiment of their "courage . . .
fidelity . . . honour," which are made available to the
foreign masters of Sulaco "whenever there is something
picturesque to be done" (N, xiii, 224, 515). An orphan who
has left behind in Italy only an abusive uncle, Nostromo
acknowledges what Daniel Schwarz calls "the patrimony of
materialism"[3] when he promises to take care of Sir John,
the traveling English chief of Sulaco's railway, "as if [he]
were his father" (N, 43). Among the materialists a second
surrogate parent is the Oceanic Steamship Navigation Company's Captain "Fussy Joe" Mitchell, for whom Nostromo is
a dutiful foreman of the lightermen, or Capataz de Cargadores. A simple Conradian sailor out of his depth on
land, Mitchell boasts of having "discovered" and "made" (N,
473) Nostromo,[4] and proudly lends him for any dangerous
bit of work. Eventually the factotum, like Rossini's
Figaro, notices the use that others are making of him.
". . . Nostromo here and Nostromo there--where is Nostromo?
Nostromo can do this and that--work all day and ride all
night" (N, 417). His most famous exploits relate to the
central event of the novel, the rising of General Montero,
the War Minister, and his brother Pedrito against the reform
government of Don Vincente Ribiera, the "hope of honest
men," the advocate of "good faith, order, honesty, peace,"
but also the protector of foreign interests (N, 117). At
the head of his cargadores Nostromo rescues the deposed
president-dictator from a mob. In another legendary feat of
the same revolution his 400-mile, six-day dash to Cayta to
summon the blancos' General Barrios to the defense of Sulaco
saves the mine and the newly formed Occidental Republic.

A byword for incorruptibility, he is nevertheless
ultimately corrupted, by an ill-conceived mission to cheat
the approaching Monterist forces of a shipment of San Tomé
silver. The lighter carrying the silver collides in the
darkness of Sulaco's Golfo Placido with an enemy transport,
and the cargo has to be landed outside the harbor, on the
island called the Great Isabel. When Nostromo, having crept
back into Sulaco, learns that his "fool's business" (N, 430)
with the treasure is--like his return alive--considered by
the blancos of no importance, he deems himself betrayed.
According to the English doctor, Monygham, the first
European he meets, the treasure should have been saved to

bribe the Monterist Colonel Sotillo, or simply handed over
to him. But for Nostromo, a man of consummate vanity, to be
unimportant is to be destroyed; the "very essence, value,
reality" of his life has "consisted in its reflection from
the admiring eyes of men" (N, 525). Any interest in his
exploit "would have restored to him his personality--the
only thing lost in that desperate affair" (N, 434). But
Monygham, ignoring him, fixes on a scheme to prevent Sotillo
from joining forces with the other Monterists; the colonel
must be distracted by a treasure hunt in the waters of the
harbor, and meanwhile Nostromo must ride to Cayta to fetch
Barrios. "Terrible in the pursuit of his idea," Monygham
cares only for the protection of the wife of Charles Gould;
to all others, including himself, the doctor is, as Nostromo
perceives, "a dangerous man" (N, 434, 438). The factotum
begins to empathize with Hirsch, the luckless merchant whom
Monygham allowed to be tortured by Sotillo for information
about the silver, and finally shot. Concluding "that
everything is permitted to the rich"--that is, to his
paternal exploiters--Nostromo in "revenge" decides to keep
their silver (N, 435, 541). He devises a prudent and
gradual disposal in foreign ports: "I must grow rich very
slowly" (N, 503).

Deserting the complacent Captain Mitchell, who has
used him to enhance a prodigious self-importance, Nostromo
is left with his first and most influential father in
Costaguana--Giorgio Viola, the man for whom he jumped ship.
The young sailor replaced Viola's dead boy, endeavoring to
be for the old man "all his son would have been" (N, 468).
But Viola's expectations run high. A heroic votary of
nationalism and popular democracy, and one who had fought
with Garibaldi, he resembles Apollo Korzeniowski in patriotism and disappointment. When the cause of a united
Italy passed from the idealistic Garibaldi to the cynical
politician Cavour, Viola, unable to live under Cavour's
king, emigrated to South America. The impossibility of the
white-haired republican's ideals is symbolized by his
habitual gaze upward at the snowy dome of Higuerota, "whose
cool purity seemed to hold itself aloof from a hot earth"
(N, 26). Even for Viola, a zealot turned innkeeper and
paterfamilias, daily life has become a distraction from the
cause of liberty. "He had been one of the immortal and
invincible band of liberators who had made the mercenaries
of tyranny fly like chaff before a hurricane. . . . But that
was before he was married and had children" (N, 25).

Viola's old-fashioned liberalism has little relevance
to what would today be called a Third World country,
commandeered by foreigners; but his ideology has had an

impact on Nostromo. For Robert Hodges, Viola has passed on
to his protégé two dominant attitudes: an "austere contempt
for all personal advantage" (N, 31), and a distrust of the
upper classes. The first view, which Hodges sees as based
on "the cult of the hero, Viola's worship of Garibaldi,"[5]
may account for Nostromo's record of flamboyant and poorly
rewarded service to the oligarchs; Viola, says Dr. Monygham,
has "encouraged much of the Capataz's confounded nonsense"
(N, 320). But Hodges fails to note the contradiction
between Viola's "fanaticism" (N, 21) in castigating the rich
and his desire that Nostromo should risk his life for their
safety, comfort, and profit. The second attitude contrasts
sharply with Viola's rebuke to the blanco journalist Martin
Decoud, who has asked him whom he is really for. Viola's
stern reply, "For the people," meets the rejoinder, "We are
all for the people--in the end." "Yes," growls Viola, "and
meantime they fight for you. Blind. Esclavos!" (N, 168).
Viola's willingness to make a blind slave of Nostromo may
derive partly from a grudge against youth because it is
young. Nostromo, cocksure at twenty-four, taunts Viola,
sunk in age and defeat, for taking aid from Mrs. Gould. She
is undoubtedly a

> "rich benefactress. Hey! old man of the people.
> Thy benefactress. . . ."
>   "I am old," muttered Giorgio Viola. "An
> Englishwoman was allowed to give a bed to
> Garibaldi lying wounded in prison. The greatest
> man that ever lived. A man of the people,
> too--a sailor. I may let another keep a roof
> over my head. . . . Life lasts too long
> sometimes." (N, 471)

Conrad implies by juxtaposition that anger can override the
logic of Viola's ideology. In the next paragraph Nostromo
asks whether he should undertake the 400-mile sprint to
Cayta--"Am I to try--and save all the Blancos?"--and Viola
replies, "You shall do it as my son would have" (N, 471).
    Viola's heroic ideal fails Nostromo when the rich
overlook his peril in shifting the San Tomé treasure away
from Sulaco. He then embraces for the first time the old
man's other precept, the distrust of wealth. "Kings,
ministers, aristocrats, the rich in general, kept the people
in poverty and subjection; they kept them as they kept dogs,
to fight and hunt for their service" (N, 415).[6] But
Nostromo acts on this bias differently from his mentor.
Abandoning the role of the Capataz-factotum, he acquires
another public identity as Captain Gian' Battista Fidanza, a

"patron of secret societies, a republican like old Giorgio, and a revolutionist at heart (but in another manner)" (N, 525). That other manner is not so much political--though Viola the nationalist would not have understood the socialist or communist oratory of the secret societies' "pale photographer, small, frail, bloodthirsty" (N, 562)--as it is financial. The old man despises money, but Nostromo, who employs his schooner in disposing of the silver bars, has joined the rich.

Insofar as Nostromo has been shaped by Viola's ideas-- either in the cult of the hero or in the religion of democracy--he has been harmed by them. The result of disillusionment, coupled with a disdain for the rich, has been the protégé's unexpected degradation into a liar and a thief. Conrad has paralleled a relationship of spiritual fatality by making Viola Nostromo's killer in a physical sense. The victim is shot stealing across the Great Isabel, now the property of the old man as lighthouse keeper, to collect from its cache more of the silver for clandestine sale. The hoard which he has "yearned to clasp, embrace, absorb, subjugate in unquestioned possession" (N, 529) has become a partial substitute for a sexual object; the Great Isabel, named for a woman, is another of Conrad's feminized landscapes: wedge-shaped, with a ravine in which the treasure lies buried. Silver for Nostromo supersedes ties to actual women. Bent on saving it from the Monterists, he refuses the plea of the dying Teresa, the only woman he can remember having called mother (N, 470), to fetch her a priest. His later attachment, to Giselle Viola, is also subordinated to the treasure; their elopement is precluded by his obsession with the wealth secreted, without the family's knowledge, on the island. Nevertheless, Viola's bullet does end a sexual rivalry between surrogate father and son, and one of long standing. Teresa, a wife younger than her husband, may have been in love with the Capataz (N, 319); so, unquestionably, are both of Viola's daughters. The result is somewhat obscure. After Teresa's death, Nostromo tells Giselle that "your dead mother" is a barrier between them; the girl, seemingly aware of this obstacle, replies, "Poor mother! She has always . . . She is a saint in heaven now, and I cannot give you up to her" (N, 539).

Nostromo himself senses at times that he is "fated" (N, 524) to marry within the Viola family. On his own testimony, none of his "magnificent and carelessly public . . . amours" around Sulaco has meant much; he tells Decoud, ". . . as to those girls that boast of having opened their doors to my knock, you know I wouldn't look at any one of them twice except for what the people would say" (N, 129,

297). In a public scene with a gypsy "spitfire," she can wring from him only the dubious assurance, "I love thee as much as ever. . . . but thou must not ask me to swear it on the Madonna that stands in thy room" (N, 128, 129). For Joseph Dobrinsky the encounter suggests an unawakened sexuality in the robust Capataz.[7] Yet when this hero directs a girl to cut off his silver buttons in a mock castration, the laughter of an admiring crowd connotes no lack of virility. His indifference to the Morenita may only indicate the focusing of his sexuality, in dread and fascination, on a love that will bring him into open rivalry with Viola.

In courting Giselle, the younger daughter, Nostromo escapes an incestuous tie, since Linda, the elder girl, resembles Teresa, the dead mother. He also dodges the relationship he assumes to exist between Viola and Linda: the father "would be glad to keep the eldest, who had his wife's voice" (N, 530). But when the suitor comes to ask Viola for Giselle, the request proves unutterable. Seized by "a sudden dread," the "fearless and incorruptible Nostromo" cannot pronounce a name: "For my wife! . . . It is time you--" (N, 531). Sudden fear may evince an irruption from the unconscious--an intuition that the widower Viola intends to keep Giselle as a wife substitute, in what Mrs. Gould has termed the "prison" (N, 514) of the island. On grounds never made clear, Viola has uniformly rejected Giselle's suitors, including at least one railway engineer and the Sulaco native Ramirez--an "honest, lovelorn swain" (N, 516), yet detested by Viola. Indeed, the old man's behavior would be consistent with a motive neither specified nor forbidden by the text: an unwillingness to part with either daughter. He offers Nostromo only the one whom Nostromo will never marry. Though long paired by the elder Violas with the dark, fierce Linda, this suitor has made his choice of the blond Giselle--Sulaco's town beauty-- sufficiently plain to be noticed by Linda, and perhaps by her father as well.

Viola, without inquiring which of his daughters is wanted, calls Linda to be betrothed; Nostromo, afraid of being forbidden the island, fails to state his preference. The omission costs him his life, in circumstances far from pellucid. According to the father, the man he shot without warning in the dark was Ramirez, the thwarted lover now thought to be plotting the abduction of Giselle. "Old Viola," in the words of Dr. Monygham, "does not allow any trifling with his honour. He has grown uneasy and suspicious since his wife died" (N, 516). But the seeming mistake in identity may represent a murderous intent,

conscious or unconscious. Viola's age and reputation for
senility leave his acumen, like the elder Bacadou's in "The
Idiots," in doubt. But either before or after the shot he
has recognised the intruder on the island; Ramirez, he says,
"cried out in son Gian' Battista's voice" (N, 563). The
suggestion of a deliberate sacrifice is strengthened by
Conrad's doubling of Nostromo and Ramirez. Both want
Giselle; both have been Capataz de Cargadores, Ramirez
having served as Nostromo's protégé and successor.

Viola's own death, just after Nostromo's, may result
from a remorse that neither Freud nor Conrad would have
found incompatible with fear and hatred of an Oedipal
rival--one who could not be defeated by any other means.
The novel's final page appears to confirm Nostromo's sexual
superiority. On the news of his death, Linda appears erect
on the lighthouse, "with her arms raised above her head as
though she were going to throw herself over. 'It is I who
loved you. . . . I! Only I! . . . I shall never forget
thee. . . . Never! Gian' Battista!'" (N, 566). As a
substitute for Viola, the elderly Dr. Monygham,

> pulling round in the police-galley, heard
> the name pass over his head. It was another
> of Nostromo's triumphs, the greatest, the most
> enviable, the most sinister of all. In that
> true cry of undying passion . . . the genius
> of the magnificent Capataz de Cargadores
> dominated the dark gulf containing his
> conquests of treasure and love. (N, 566)

That Linda has executed the leap her pose implied would
account for the description of her love as Nostromo's "most
sinister" triumph. Of Viola's three women, this one, whom
her fiancé rejected, and who at the time of her suicide
believes the Garibaldino to be still living, provides the
most dramatic evidence of the son's victory over the father.
Her final act is foreshadowed in the betrothal scene. In
the presence of Viola, now left "solitary," his "best-loved
daughter" tells a younger man: "I was yours ever since I
can remember. I had only to think of you for the earth to
become empty to my eyes. . . . The world belongs to you, and
you let me live in it" (N, 532).

Oedipal rivalry in the novel's other son-victim,
Martin Decoud, is less clear-cut. In the skeptical young
Costaguanero called from Paris by the exigencies of the
Monterist revolution, Conrad initially sketches an "idle
boulevardier" (N, 152), an uncommitted habitué of newspaper
offices, an aspiring but dabbling poet. This ornament, who

apparently would fight for nothing, is the subject of
heavy moralizing by the narrator. A life of "dreary
superficiality . . . covered by the glitter of universal
blague" has induced in him "a mere barren indifferentism
posing as intellectual superiority" (N, 152).   To French
friends he describes the atmosphere of his country as opéra
bouffe in which spilt blood is real. "Of course, government
in general, any government anywhere, is a thing of exquisite
comicality to a discerning mind; but really we Spanish-
Americans do overstep the bounds. No man of ordinary
intelligence can take part in the intrigues of une farce
macabre" (N, 152). According to the narrator, Decoud
has "pushed the habit of universal raillery to a point where
it blinded him to the genuine impulses of his own nature";
he has "no faith in anything except the truth of his own
sensations"; he imagines himself drinking aesthetic pleasure
from a spectacle in which every belief, "as soon as it
became effective, turned into that form of dementia the gods
send upon those they wish to destroy" (N, 153, 200, 229).

However, this "exotic dandy" (N, 229), unlike Conrad,
proves incapable of forsaking a distracted homeland. Don
José Avellanos--like Viola, a patriot probably modeled on
Apollo Korzeniowski--appeals to his godson in Paris to
collect a thousand rifles for Ribiera's defense against the
insurgent Monteros. Decoud's sister has "never seen Martin
take so much trouble about anything in his whole life" (N,
154). "It amuses me" (N, 154), he says, and announces his
intention of accompanying the rifles to Sulaco--apparently
to visit Antonia, Avellanos's severely patriotic daughter.
Eight years before, as a schoolgirl, she had attacked
Decoud's "pose of disabused wisdom," and made him falter in
his affectation of "amused superiority" (N, 155). Once in
Costaguana, the defeated wit, employing a different tack,
becomes in a burst of energy the savior of his country--at
least until the next revolution. Accepting the role
assigned him by Avellanos, he founds and edits a newspaper,
the Porvenir, to counter the Monterist press. And when the
rebel army proves victorious, he alone of the notables of
Sulaco vigorously opposes the city's surrender. Spurred by
what he claims to be his love for Antonia, he makes "an
impassioned appeal to their courage and manliness" (N, 236)
in proposing a separatist state. At its inception he risks
his life, perhaps already forfeited by his journalistic
attacks on the Monteros, to help Nostromo get the silver
away from Sulaco; only an uninterrupted flow of treasure
will guarantee the support of the American financier Holroyd
for the nascent Occidental Republic.

In Decoud's own effort to reconcile skepticism with

commitment, he proclaims himself a lover but not a patriot; whatever he does is for Antonia: ". . . I, the man with a passion, but without a mission, I go . . . to play my part in the farce to the end" (N, 246). Yet as he drifts with the silver on the dark waters of the Golfo Placido, even his love begins to seem a pose: ". . . his passionate devotion to Antonia into which he had worked himself up out of the depths of his scepticism had lost all appearance of reality" (N, 267). His suicide after only ten days alone on the Great Isabel supports the narrator's concept of a hollow man. Decoud dies from "solitude and want of faith in himself and others" (N, 496).

> After three days of waiting for the sight of
> some human face, Decoud caught himself
> entertaining a doubt of his own individuality.
> It had merged into the world of cloud and
> water, of natural forces and forms of nature.
> In our activity alone do we find the sustain-
> ing illusion of an independent existence as
> against the whole scheme of things of which
> we form a helpless part. Decoud lost all
> belief in the reality of his action past and
> to come. (N, 497)

He shoots himself, falls into the gulf, and is "swallowed up in the immense indifference of things" (N, 501).

For Harry Marten, the two Decouds, the skeptical onlooker and the seemingly committed participant, can be reconciled by an assumption of supreme egotism; the need to strike a pose, to be noticed, to be judged important, rather than actual commitment, governs Decoud. His patriotism, his love, even his sense of identity depend on the presence of an audience; he is Conrad's "emblem for the man without faith in an external ideal--any ideal."[8] Marten's val-uable analysis might have been sharpened by a consideration of the kind of activity that sucks the realistic Decoud into Costaguana. The identity to be assumed is that of a successful Oedipal challenger, the supplanter of Avellanos sexually, with Antonia, and politically, as leader of the blancos of Sulaco.

The ordinary father-son rivalry has evidently been displaced from Decoud's biological parent--an elderly shadow in Paris, ruled by an unmarried daughter-wife, the "handsome, slightly arbitrary and resolute angel" (N, 223) who is Martin's sibling, correspondent, and confidante. Martin leaves this woman behind. But in the unmar-ried Antonia, he and Avellanos contend for a second

daughter-wife, one who has replaced her mother as the old
man's preserver after his ordeal at the hands of Guzman
Bento. As a widower, Avellanos "depended very much upon the
devotion of his beloved Antonia. He accepted it in the
benighted way of men, who, though made in God's image, are
like stone idols without sense before the smoke of certain
burnt offerings" (N, 140). Conrad's emphasis on Antonia's
beauty, particularly on her "full figure" and "full red
lips" (N, 149), hints an erotic motive in the father's
possessiveness. But the daughter is also conveniently
learned, a combined nurse and secretary to her obtuse
parent.

The sacrifice of Antonia is made partly on behalf of
an unworkable "theory of political purity" (N, 182), which
includes the payment of debt to foreign investors; Avellanos
cements their hold on Costaguana. As Decoud bitterly
observes, the country "is like a treasure-house, and all
these people are breaking into it, whilst we are cutting
each other's throats. . . . We are a wonderful people, but
it has always been our fate to be . . . exploited!" (N,
174). The younger man's "indictment" (N, 171) is disregarded by Avellanos as though he had not heard. A
leader moribund before Decoud's challenge, the garrulous
"Nestor-inspirer" of the blancos, and chief prop of the
ineffectual Ribiera, can only hope that his devotion to his
country will be "enshrined" in a history "for the reverent
worship of posterity" (N, 142, 144). Both his life and his
soul seem "overtaxed by so many years of undiscouraged
belief in regeneration" (N, 149). The end nears when the
sheets of his historical treatise, Fifty Years of Misrule,
are fired out as gun wadding, to be "blown in the wind,
trampled in the mud" (N, 235). In the Monterist crisis of
Sulaco Decoud by his demand for secession and resistance
insures that an already frail Avellanos will not survive.
As the new leader of the blancos writes to his sister:

> I bent my ear to his withered lips, and made
> out his whisper, something like, "In God's name,
> then, Martin, my son!" I don't know exactly.
> There was the name of God in it, I am certain.
> It seems to me I have caught his last breath.
> . . .
> He lives yet, it is true. I have seen him
> since; but it was only a senile body. . . . I
> know that Don José has really died there, in
> the Casa Gould, with that whisper urging me to
> attempt what no doubt his soul, wrapped up in
> the sanctity of diplomatic treaties and solemn
> declarations, must have abhorred. (N, 236)

When Antonia asks Decoud, emerging from the debate over
Sulaco's future, "Have they killed my father in there?" he
asserts a dubious mandate: "Your father himself . . . has
told me to go on." "He has?" cries Antonia. "Then, indeed,
I fear he will never speak again" (N, 238, 239). Dispas-
sionately viewing her tears for the apostle of political
rectitude, Antonia's fiancé concludes: ". . . whether I
escaped or stayed to die, there was for us no coming
together, no future" (N, 239). Even if both survive the
revolution, apparently, no marriage will ensue. Forced
to choose between her father and Decoud, Antonia has
rejected the challenger.

Sexually unsuccessful, politically ascendant, Decoud
has engaged in an Oedipal struggle in which the fruits of
victory closely resemble those of defeat, and in which
the rewards, if any, must lie in the fact of competition.
Rivalry yields an activity in which he can "find the
sustaining illusion of an independent existence as against
the whole scheme of things of which we form a helpless
part." Decoud the political leader, like Bolivar the
Liberator, believes America to be "ungovernable" (N, 186).
Decoud the lover is irritated by Antonia's gravity, against
which he has "often felt his familiar habit of ironic
thought fall shattered" (N, 191). Her talk only sometimes
rouses in him "a sudden unwilling thrill of interest. Some
women hovered, as it were, on the threshold of genius,
he reflected. They did not want to know, or think, or
understand. Passion stood for all that" (N, 183).
Antonia's passions, however, are directed more to politics
than to persons, for she appears indifferent to his
survival. He remembers her at sixteen as "very terrible
. . . a sort of Charlotte Corday in a schoolgirl's dress; a
ferocious patriot" who "would have stuck a knife into Guzman
Bento" or "sent me to stab him without compunction" (N,
180). Eight years later, in Sulaco, he tells her: ". . .
you do keep me here writing deadly nonsense. Deadly to me!
It has already killed my self-respect. . . . It's a sort of
intellectual death; but there is the other one in the background for a journalist of my ability" (N, 180). Decoud,
without hope of pardon by the rebel general he has called
"a gran' bestia three times a week" (N, 180), has in mind
a convent handy for executions. "I shall go to the wall,"
he announces "with a sort of jocular desperation" (N, 181).
Antonia does not argue the point, but neither does she
consider fleeing with him to safety.

The suicide of Decoud, a disappointed man, is readily
explainable in terms of Karl Menninger's threefold scheme:

the wish to kill, the wish to be killed, and the wish to
die; the improbability is not in the motivation but in
Conrad's having given it to many more young men than older
ones. Most evident in Decoud is the wish to die, when the
loss of his audience has removed the illusion that either
Antonia or the separatist state is worth fighting for.
Jeffrey Berman has called attention to the affinity of his
descent into the Stygian waters with the theory of a death
instinct that Freud advanced in Beyond the Pleasure Principle in 1920, sixteen years after the publication of
Nostromo:

> Speculating on the existence of an instinctual
> force of unknown origins, Freud maintained
> that this instinctual drive inheres within all
> life, impelling it "to restore an earlier state
> of things which the living entity has been
> obliged to abandon under the pressure of
> external disturbing forces." . . . Arguing
> that the "death instinct," as he called it,
> is more primitive and more elementary than
> the pleasure-principle which is displaced by
> it, Freud maintained that it implies neither
> the quest for pleasure nor pain but the urge
> to be released from both sensations. . . .
> Since the sheer process of living demands
> an exhausting and finally exhaustive exertion
> of energy to maintain one's identity apart
> from an indifferent or hostile environment,
> the individual longs for a return to
> inanimate matter, "to the quiescence of the
> inorganic world." "If we are to take it as
> a truth that knows no exception that
> everything living dies for internal reasons
> . . . becomes inorganic once again--then
> we shall be compelled to say that 'the aim
> of all life is death.'"[9]

The strong pull of the gulf on the imagination of Decoud, a
man with scant interest in life to offset its fascination,
is felt as soon as he and Nostromo have floated away in the
lighter from the noise and danger of revolutionary Sulaco.

> . . . the enormous stillness, without light or
> sound, seemed to affect Decoud's senses like
> a powerful drug. . . . it would have resembled
> death had it not been for the survival of his
> thoughts. In this foretaste of eternal peace
> they floated vivid and light, like unearthly

clear dreams of earthly things that may haunt
the souls freed by death from the misty
atmosphere of regrets and hopes. (N, 262)[10]

When he kills himself and falls into the gulf, he ends a
movement begun in the dark, still house of Giorgio Viola,
where Teresa is dying. The return to what Conrad, as well
as Freud, saw as the "immense indifference of things" is
foreshadowed as Decoud ends a letter to his sister. "With
the writing of the last line there came upon Decoud a moment
of sudden and complete oblivion. He swayed over the table
as if struck by a bullet" (N, 249).

As in Berman's reading, critical discussion of Decoud's
urge to suicide has been, so far as I am aware, restricted
to the single issue of the wish to die. But the other two
motives in Menninger's scheme might be easily derived from
Oedipal relationships in which Avellanos is both the father
of Antonia and the friend and godfather of Decoud. When Don
José lies dying, the most likely remaining target of the
son's homicidal impulse is the beautiful Antonia, whom he
accuses of keeping him in Costaguana at his peril, and who
embodies her father's ideals. Decoud's charge that she
would gladly kill him may be a projection of his own
antipathy to her. An opposite wish in him, the longing to
be killed, may appear in his "fatal touch of contempt for
himself" (N, 300). Parricidal urges have probably led
to guilt even though Avellanos, gripped by a fanatical
patriotism and desire for personal immortality, did not
hesitate to assign his godson a militant role which might
lead to his death. Like Nostromo, Decoud has allowed
himself to be used. His last utterance, "It is done" (N,
501), recalls Kayerts's Christlike posture at the close of
"An Outpost of Progress"; redeeming no one and perhaps fully
comprehending nothing, both men die as sacrifices to the
father.[11]

That the basis for Conrad's condemnation of "son
Decoud" (N, 200) is sexuality is confirmed by the fate of
Antonia, which reasserts the principle that women properly
belong to the father; she never marries but lives with her
uncle Corbelàn and breathes his unionist politics as she did
the federalism of Avellanos. Had Decoud been active in the
political sphere alone, he would probably have been allowed
to survive as a successful contender with his elders. The
son's right of asexual revolt is confirmed in Nostromo by
the survival of Charles Gould, the administrator of the
San Tomé mine. As the new "King of Sulaco"--"the other
Carlos"--he replaces the ousted King Charles IV of Spain (N,
48, 93). He also, as the third generation of an English

family in Costaguana, supplants his murdered uncle Henry
Gould, former president of the country's western province.
More directly Charles supersedes his father, by operating at
a profit the silver concession that ruined the elder Gould.
As a kind of forced loan to the Costaguanan government it
was bestowed on an unwilling proprietor and his descendants
in perpetuity. The grantee, one of the country's wealthiest
merchants, was required to pay at once five years' royalties
on the estimated output of a ruined property; other exac-
tions followed. Ignorant of mining, unable to throw off
this fatal gift, he ended by writing Charles, at school in
England, of almost nothing else.

> He implored his son never to return to Costaguana,
> never to claim any part of his inheritance there,
> because it was tainted by the infamous Concession;
> never to touch it, never to approach it, to forget
> that America existed, and pursue a mercantile
> career in Europe. And each letter ended with
> bitter self-reproaches for having stayed too
> long in that cavern of thieves, intriguers,
> and brigands. (N, 57)

Robert Hodges aptly describes the father's counsel as
"objectively sound," but so emotionally given as to
constitute, in effect, "an appeal for loyalty"; the passion
with which the elder Gould advises his son to abandon the
mine "makes that advice a call for revenge."[12] Hodges
fails to cite a passage which suggests an unconscious intent
to involve Charles: "To be told repeatedly that one's future
is blighted because of the possession of a silver mine . . .
is calculated to excite a certain amount of wonder and
attention" (N, 57).
    The father's double attitude to Charles--protective in
warning him away from the mine, dangerous in making it
irresistible to him--is matched by Charles's ambivalence to
his parent. In Freud's account of the son's mixed attitude
to the father:

> In addition to the hate which seeks to get rid
> of the father as a rival, a measure of tender-
> ness for him is . . . habitually present. The
> two attitudes of mind combine to produce iden-
> tification with the father; the boy wants to
> be in his father's place because he admires
> him and wants to be like him, and also because
> he wants to put him out of the way.[13]

Charles's reading of the desperate letters is sympathetic to
a lonely widower, of whom he can say, "Ever since I was ten
years old he used to talk to me as if I had been grown up"
(N, 73). Yet Charles is also coolly reflective, in an
embryonic resolve to prosper where his inept parent has
failed. He studies mining engineering, and on the death of
his father he returns at once to Costaguana to take up
his forbidden inheritance. His opinion of the father's
financial debacle reflects that parricidal impulse which
Edwin Shneidman has designated "blame"[14]: "I think
sometimes that poor father takes a wrong view of that San
Tomé business"; "They corrupted him thoroughly, the poor old
boy. . . . But now I shall know how to grapple with this"
(N, 60, 63). Yet the persistence of the negative Oedipal
impulse appears in his need to make disobedience--at least
to the father's stated wish--seem obedience. As Robert
Hodges has said, Nostromo is "a major study of rational-
ization and self-deception."[15] The death of Charles's
beleaguered parent, an event "closely affecting his own
identity," fills him with a desire for action, that

> friend of flattering illusions. Only in the
> conduct of our action can we find the sense
> of mastery over the Fates. For his action,
> the mine was obviously the only field. It was
> imperative sometimes to know how to disobey
> the solemn wishes of the dead. He resolved
> firmly to make his disobedience as thorough (by
> way of atonement) as it well could be. The
> mine had been the cause of an absurd moral
> disaster; its working must be made a serious
> and moral success. He owed it to the dead
> man's memory. (N, 66)

Material success, Charles reasons, will be moral success,
the fulfillment of a duty to redeem the failure of the dead.
But material success is also to be a moral success in the
deliverance of a continent. Clothing his will to power "in
the fair robes of an idea" (N, 239), Charles proclaims:

> What is wanted here is law, good faith, order,
> security. . . . I pin my faith to material
> interests. Only let the material interests
> once get a firm footing, and they are bound to
> impose the conditions on which alone they can
> continue to exist. That's how your money-
> making is justified here in the face of
> lawlessness and disorder. It is justified
> because the security which it demands must

be shared with an oppressed people. A
better justice will come afterwards. That's
your ray of hope. . . . And who knows whether
in that sense even the San Tomé mine may not
become that little rift in the darkness which
poor father despaired of ever seeing? (N, 84)

Occasional lapses into the second person--"your money-
making," "your ray of hope"--suggest, however, that
Gould has not yet fully convinced himself. For added
support he invokes his uncle Henry, the former president of
the Occidental Province, who supposedly "was no politician.
He simply stood up for social order out of pure love for
rational liberty and from his hate of oppression. . . . He
went to work in his own way because it seemed right, just as
I feel I must lay hold of that mine" (N, 64).

An infusion of American capital removes, according to
Charles, the real ground of his father's ban on mining: the
fear that the son would waste his life in a vain search for
financing. "That was the true sense of his prohibition,
which we have deliberately set aside" (N, 73). Disobedience may also be extenuated by Charles's acquisition of a
substitute father, the financier Holroyd, from whom his
"sentimental" (N, 238) faith in materialism may stem. The
affairs of Sulaco are remote-controlled from San Francisco
by this millionaire hobbyist, who preaches, with "the
temperament of a Puritan and an insatiable imagination of
conquest" (N, 76), the gospel of manifest destiny:

Time itself has got to wait on the greatest
country in the whole of God's Universe. We
shall be giving the word for everything:
industry, trade, law, journalism, art,
politics, and religion. . . . We shall
run the world's business whether the world
likes it or not. The world can't help
it--and neither can we. (N, 77)

Holroyd, whose name suggests "Holy rod"[16] or "Holy rood,"
justifies economic imperialism by the export of "the purer
forms of Christianity" (N, 80) to Catholic Costaguana. By
endowing churches, to allow God a share of profits from
the mine, the financier has reduced his deity to a kind of
partner in "the religion of silver and iron" (N, 71). The
novel's more puissant immortal is the fifty-eight-year-old
Holroyd himself, the head of a consortium. As the European
chief engineer of Sulaco's railroad explains to a skeptical
Dr. Monygham: "To be a millionaire, and such a millionaire

as Holroyd, is like being eternally young. The audacity of
youth reckons upon what it fancies an unlimited time at its
disposal; but a millionaire has unlimited means in his
hand--which is better" (N, 317). He would not, however, use
them for the rescue of Charles Gould, should the younger man
stand in any dire need of assistance: "We will go with you
as long as the thing runs straight. But we won't be drawn
into any large trouble"; ". . . we shall know how to drop
you in time" (N, 79, 82).

Charles's ability to find these terms "agreeable" (N,
82) may signify an appetite for risk, as retribution for
parricidal urges. Although he can speculate on whether
Holroyd's talk is "the voice of destiny" or "clap-trap" (N,
83), and although he has a phallic leitmotif, the equestrian
spur, he shows a vein of submission. Apart from rational-
izing disobedience, his chief concession to the father
is the sexual renunciation that typically insures the
survival of Conradian youth. In the "subtle conjugal
infidelity" (N, 365) by which he neglects his wife for the
mine, a guilty son forfeits the right to a son of his own.
The novel shows him in the act of choosing between sexual
and asexual replacement of the father. After the elder
Gould has died, in ignorance of his son's intent both to
marry and to operate the mine, Charles simultaneously
contemplates two forms of Oedipal usurpation. Before asking
his fiancée's consent to the mining venture, he stares
fixedly at "a heavy marble vase ornamented with sculptured
masks and garlands of flowers, and cracked from top to
bottom" (N, 61). The flawed female symbol of the vase
foreshadows a childless marriage[17]--a necessity if incest
is to be averted. Emilia's maternal attitude to Gould--her
"poor boy" (N, 62)--accords with his sense that she replaces
his dead mother. In describing to his bride her future home
in Sulaco he says: "I lived there once, as a small boy, with
my dear mother, for a whole year, while poor father was away
in the United States on business. You shall be the new
mistress of the Casa Gould" (N, 64). But when Emilia
assumes this position, neglect ensues. Gould's subsequent
avoidance of his wife leaves her, appropriately, to the
company of an older man, Dr. Monygham.

In Nostromo, as in prior Conradian works, the dominant
paternal trait emerges as menace. Of three son figures in
the South American novel, Gould alone survives; but for
him, as for Nostromo and Decoud, life is impaired by the
spiritual legacy of a father, actual or substitute, who has
died in defeat. At the personal level Avellanos, "a genuine
old Roman--vir Romanus--eloquent and inflexible" (N, 169),
sacrifices Decoud to a futile dream; Viola warps Nostromo;

the elder Gould, except for a managerial capability he
did not foresee in Charles, would have ruined his son by
embroiling him in the mine. At the social level the older
men are unable to secure a linear and progressive movement in the affairs of Costaguana. One cause of its
circularity--in which, as Royal Roussel has said, ". . .
revolution is inevitably transformed into an autocracy,
which in turn gives rise to revolution"[18]--is a trait
shared by most of the novel's father figures. Like Captain
Beard in "Youth," or MacWhirr in "Typhoon," they have become
dangerous through enslavement to a fixed idea. Guzman
Bento, for example, has

> ruled the country with the somber imbecility of
> political fanaticism. The power of Supreme
> Government had become in his dull mind an object
> of strange worship, as if it were some sort of
> cruel deity. It was incarnated in himself, and
> his adversaries, the Federalists, were the supreme
> sinners . . . as heretics would be to a convinced
> Inquisitor. (N, 137)

He shares the absolutist mentality of his torturer, Father
Beron. Another sinister cleric, Corbelàn, that "strenuous
priest with one idea" (N, 200), foments a revolution with
the aid of his protégé, Hernandez the former bandit, a
military genius whom he has created Minister of War. Even
Dr. Monygham becomes dangerous in the "fanaticism of his
devotion" (N, 453) to Mrs. Gould; and two honorable old
soldiers, Don Pépé and Father Romàn, would, in service to
their ideal of fidelity, blow up the mine for Charles Gould
if need be.
    In this plan of destruction the novel shows a son in
the process of aging into the rigidity, or autocracy, of
the fathers. As the youthful heir to the mine Charles is
"prepared to stoop for his weapons" (N, 85)--to follow his
father in the bribery and intrigue necessary to do business
in Costaguana--yet he has regrets. "For a moment he felt as
if the silver mine, which had killed his father, had decoyed
him further than he meant to go" (N, 85). Later, however,
he will conceive of the mine as "symbolic of abstract
justice" (N, 402), sanctioning whatever he wants to do.
"The mine had got hold of Charles Gould with a grip as
deadly as ever it had laid upon his father" (N, 400). In an
"almost mystic view . . . of his right" (N, 402) he resolves
to destroy it rather than let the Monterists have it. As he
assures Pedrito, he "would never let the mine pass out of

his hands for the profit of a Government who had robbed him of it. The Gould Concession could not be resumed. His father had not desired it. The son would never surrender it. He would never surrender it alive" (N, 402). He has told Hirsch: ". . . I have enough dynamite stored up at the mountain to send it down crashing into the valley . . . to send half Sulaco into the air if I liked" (N, 204). "A man haunted by a fixed idea," says the narrator, "is insane" (N, 379).

An assumption of progressive insanity in Charles Gould may serve to bridge a gap in the novel. Conrad fails to explain why the mine, which Captain Mitchell terms "a great power . . . for good and evil" (N, 486), should change radically from the first category to the second. Initially, despite its paramilitary organization and its impersonal numbered villages, the stable Gould concession appears beneficial; it overrides the politicians of Costaguana, who are uniformly wicked or inept. The mine has signified to the common people "honour . . . prosperity . . . peace," "well-being, security, and justice" (N, 397). Charles's optimistic faith that material interests could create a better society appears to be justified by the late, prosperous Sulaco of which Mitchell is cicerone. A believer, like Gould, in the possibility of a linear movement, he can speak of the "great future" of the sepa- ratist cause, which has saved the San Tomé mine "intact for civilization" (N, 483). But for Mrs. Gould in the novel's coda:

> There was something inherent in the necessities
> of successful action which carried with it the
> moral degradation of the idea. She saw the San
> Tomé mountain hanging over the Campo, over the
> whole land, feared, hated, wealthy; more soulless
> than any tyrant, more pitiless and autocratic than
> the worst Government; ready to crush innumerable
> lives in the expansion of its greatness. (N, 521)

And for Dr. Monygham, ". . . the time approaches when all that the Gould Concession stands for shall weigh as heavily upon the people as the barbarism, cruelty, and misrule of a few years back" (N, 511). These comments evidently refer to an objective change in the mine, not to that alteration in the popular view of it which has produced the revolutionary activity of Nostromo and the secret societies, and which might be termed a revolution of rising expectations (". . . the men have grown different"--N, 511). Gould is destined to become another tyrant, and thus to extend circularity in

Costaguana. But unless one accepts Conrad's psychology of
crystallization, this inevitability may be difficult to
grant. Nostromo presents evidence of colonialism but, as
Michael Wilding has noted, no sign of current exploitation
to compare with the famous grove-of-death passages in Heart
of Darkness.[19]

Despite his fear of rigidity, however, Conrad's
attitude to the fixed idea is not wholly negative; Nostromo
often couples it with heroic stature. Don Pépé and Father
Romàn have been intrepid campaigners and Viola a disinterested warrior for liberty. "His austere, old-world
Republicanism had a severe, soldier-like standard of
faithfulness and duty, as if the world were a battlefield
where men had to fight for the sake of universal love and
brotherhood, instead of a more or less large share of booty"
(N, 313). Corbelàn, whose scar testifies to his "apostolic
zeal," has "come out of the wilds to advocate the sacred
rights of the Church with the same fanatical fearlessness
with which he had gone preaching to bloodthirsty savages,
devoid of human compassion or worship of any kind" (N, 194).
Avellanos as a prisoner has existed only "to prove how much
hunger, pain, degradation, and cruel torture a human body
can stand without parting with the last spark of life" (N,
137-38); and yet he has praised his tormentor Guzman Bento
as a patriot.

Conrad's ambivalence toward the idealists of Nostromo
suggests his attitude to his father--as Najder has said, one
of "admiration and contemptuous pity."[20] The combination
may not have been tenable; authorial anxiety can perhaps be
glimpsed in the transition from Nostromo to Conrad's next
novel, The Secret Agent, which is subtitled A Simple Tale.
A description on the whole misleading is apt in one respect:
the portrayal of the father has been simplified. As in the
shift from the complex Captain MacWhirr of "Typhoon" to the
two-dimensional Captain Whalley of The End of the Tether,
Conrad has abandoned an uneasy mix of paternal traits. In
the London of The Secret Agent, that "cruel devourer of the
world's light," with "darkness enough to bury five millions
of lives" (SA, xii), no father figure at either the social
or the personal level excites admiration. In particular,
the revolutionaries are categorized by a "dislike of all
kinds of recognized labour" (SA, 53). Man does not revolt
against the advantages and opportunities of a given society,
but

> against the price which must be paid for the same
> in the coin of accepted morality, self-restraint,
> and toil. The majority of revolutionists are the
> enemies of discipline and fatigue mostly. There

> are natures, too, to whose sense of justice the
> price exacted looms up . . . enormous . . .
> humiliating . . . intolerable. Those are the
> fanatics. The remaining portion of social rebels
> is accounted for by vanity, the mother of all noble
> and vile illusions, the companion of poets,
> reformers, charlatans, prophets, and incendiaries.
> (SA, 53)

The gibe might be taken as evidence of authoritarianism in
the narrator (or Conrad), except that the legal guardians of
society turn out to be lumped with their opponents: "The
terrorist and the policeman both come from the same basket.
Revolution, legality--counter moves in the same game; forms
of idleness at bottom identical" (SA, 69).

In Conrad's fictional version of the attempted bombing
of the Greenwich Observatory by anarchists in 1894, the
self-seeking hero Verloc is simultaneously vice-president
of a revolutionary society, an agent provocateur for the
Russian Embassy, and a police informer; in private life he
is bourgeois, respectably married, domesticated. "Burly in
a fat-pig style," he has devoted himself to indolence with
"a sort of inert fanaticism" (SA, 12, 13). Nevertheless,
as he makes his way to an appointment at the Embassy, his
self-image entails the protection of London's "opulence and
luxury": ". . . the whole social order favourable to their
hygienic idleness had to be protected against the shallow
enviousness of unhygienic labour" (SA, 12). But the Embassy
takes a less favorable view of his usefulness. A man well
past forty suddenly finds himself "menaced in what is
dearest to him--his repose and his security" (SA, 52); he
must produce a dynamite outrage within a month or be fired
from the secret service. According to First Secretary
Vladimir, "The proper business of an 'agent provocateur'
is to provoke" (SA, 25). The deliberations of a Milan
conference for the suppression of political crime must be
prodded. "England lags" in repression; "this country is
absurd with its sentimental regard for individual liberty"
(SA, 29). Since the "sacrosanct fetish" of the day is
science, and since "madness alone is truly terrifying,"
Vladimir proposes to destroy the inoffensive first meridian
(SA, 33). On this mission Verloc employs his wife's half-
witted younger brother Stevie to carry the explosive;
the youth stumbles and blows himself up instead of the
observatory. In sacrificing to his own welfare the object
of Winnie Verloc's maternal passion, Verloc has ended her
"supreme illusion," that he and Stevie "might be father and
son" (SA, 187). The possibility of a Laius had not occurred

to the woman who married Verloc, seven years previously, to
gain for Stevie a protector.

Verloc is the novel's paradigm of self-indulgent
fatherhood, in or out of the Establishment. On the revolutionary side the "ticket-of-leave apostle" Michaelis,
"round like a distended balloon" from fifteen years of
imprisonment, is kept by a wealthy and infatuated old lady
(SA, 48, 50). Sequestered in her country cottage, he can
"moon about the shady lanes for days together in a delicious
and humanitarian idleness" (SA, 53). Or, in small rooms
that duplicate his cell, he can pen in "guileless vanity"
(SA, 120) an endless autobiography, for a fashionable pub-
lisher who has offered ₤500. To a Utopian Marxist whose
ideas are "inaccessible to reasoning," capitalism will
automatically destroy itself by its internal contradictions,
and then the world will turn into "an immense and nice
hospital, with gardens and flowers, in which the strong are
to devote themselves to the nursing of the weak" (SA, 107,
303). Michaelis's attitude of benign dependency contrasts
with the fiery preaching of another kept man, Karl Yundt,
for whom a capitalist economy feeds on the people and law is
"the pretty branding instrument invented by the overfed to
protect themselves against the hungry. . . . Can't you smell
and hear . . . the thick hide of the people burn and siz-
zle?" (SA, 47-48). But Yundt, the inciter of others,
has "never in his life raised personally as much as his
little finger against the social edifice" (SA, 48).

In a society symbolized by Stevie's drawings of circles
in "cosmic chaos" (SA, 45), the anarchic instinct for self-
preservation is equally strong among the guardians. At
the top is the weak-eyed Great Personage Sir Ethelred, an
unready Home Secretary who wishes to be spared the details,
and hence the reality, of any question. His comfortable
notion of social reform, admired only by his young secretary
Toodles, is the nationalization of British fisheries.
The quotidian struggle of the haves and have nots is the
business of Chief Inspector Heat, "familiar to the great
public as . . . one of its zealous and hard-working pro-
tectors" (SA, 101). He nonetheless resembles "a certain
old fat and wealthy native chief," purportedly a colonial
friend to the English but "principally his own good friend,
and nobody else's. Not precisely a traitor, but still a man
of many dangerous reservations in his fidelity, caused by a
due regard for his own advantage, comfort, and safety" (SA,
118). The Inspector's reputation has been built largely on
Verloc, a source concealed from his department: ". . . I
would deal with the devil himself" (SA, 132). To shield his
informant in the investigation of the bombing, he intends to

frame Michaelis, against whom evidence can easily be
fabricated. The successful effort of Heat's immediate
superior, the Assistant Commissioner, to clear a man whose
innocence no one doubts are not--despite the label of "an
energetic Don Quixote" (SA, 115)--prompted by idealism.
The great lady who is the apostle's benefactress has also
befriended the Assistant Commissioner; he cannot risk losing
her by the sacrifice of her adored revolutionist and salon
ornament.

The target of three rebels, Stevie, Ossipon, and the
Professor, would appear to be Sir Ethelred's society at
large. Revolt in The Secret Agent looks, on the surface,
purely political, without any personal relationship between
the son and the hated father. Yet since Conrad will require
for the son's survival the same Oedipal compromise in the
social milieu as in the personal one, he in effect treats
political unrest as what Freud said it was: an extension of
a personal conflict in childhood. In the adult's attitude
toward the authority of the state, ". . . the father-
relation is the decisive factor."[21] One fictional
biography in The Secret Agent affirms the relationship.
Stevie as a child was defended against the father by
the somewhat older Winnie--the boy's sister and, as the
supplanter of an "impotent" (SA, 242) parent, his acting
mother as well. After the death of the boy Winnie
considered "much more mine than mother's" (SA, 275):

> . . . she had the vision of the blows
> intercepted (often with her own head), of
> a door held desperately shut against a man's
> rage . . . of a poker flung. . . . And all
> these scenes of violence came and went
> accompanied by the unrefined noise of . . .
> a man wounded in his paternal pride,
> declaring himself obviously accursed since
> one of his kids was a "slobbering idjut and
> the other a wicked she-devil." (SA, 242)

Winnie's "deviltry" may have consisted of her choice of the
brother over the father, and an erotic demonstration of this
preference. Stevie's adult desire to make a cabman and his
horse happy by taking them to bed with him derives from his
own consolation by Winnie, years before, by the same method:
"To be taken into a bed of compassion was the supreme
remedy" (SA, 168).

A child's history of beatings may explain what Conrad
calls Stevie's "morbid dread of pain" (SA, 169). The novel
appears to bear out Freud's concept of repressed affect:

"When there is a _mésalliance_ . . . between an affect and its
ideational content," so that the affect appears disproportionate, it "belongs to some other content, which is
unknown (_unconscious_)."[22]   The repressed content refers
to Stevie's relationship to his father, in which, as for
Freud's Rat Man, physical abuse has produced in the victim
an uncontrollable fury. Freud's patient became a coward
"out of fear of the violence of his own rage. His whole
life long . . . he was terribly afraid of blows, and used to
creep away and hide, filled with terror and indignation,
when one of his brothers or sisters was beaten."[23]   In a
similar "return of the repressed,"[24] Stevie's commisera-
tion with the underdog always ends in the desire for
revenge. "The tenderness of his universal charity had two
phases as indissolubly joined and connected as the reverse
and obverse sides of a medal. The anguish of immoderate
compassion was succeeded by the pain of an innocent but
pitiless rage" (_SA_, 169).[25]   Once an office boy for a
milk company, he was fired for lighting fireworks on the
staircase; ". . . two other office-boys in the building had
worked upon his feelings by tales of injustice" (_SA_, 9).
After he reads in an anarchist tract of a German officer who
nearly tore the ear off a recruit, his sister complains: "I
had to take the carving knife from the boy. . . . He can't
stand the notion of any cruelty. He would have stuck that
officer like a pig if he had seen him then" (_SA_, 60). When
a night cabman beats his "steed of apocalyptic misery" in
order to support a wife, four children, and a habit of
drink, Stevie concludes that "somebody . . . ought to be
punished for it--punished with great severity"; he "knew
what it was to be beaten. He knew it from experience" (_SA_,
167, 171, 172). His willingness to carry Verloc's dynamite
seems a reaction partly to this episode, and partly to
Yundt's rhetoric of branding and cannibalism, which
according to Winnie drove the literalistic hearer "out of
his mind" (_SA_, 59).

The novel contains hints that his social revolt derives
not only from a conflict with his actual father but also
from one with Verloc, for whom he supposedly feels only
"reverence and awe"; the boy "would go through fire for
you," Winnie assures her husband--and Stevie does (_SA_, 182,
184). In Freud's theory to explain the ambivalence of the
Rat Man toward his father, an intense conscious love is the
condition of a repressed hatred for the same person. Far
from extinguishing the hatred, the love only drives it into
the unconscious; there, "safe from the danger of being
destroyed by the operations of consciousness," it can
flourish unchecked. "In such circumstances the conscious

love attains as a rule, by way of reaction, an especially
high degree of intensity, so as to be strong enough for
the perpetual task of keeping its opponent under repression."[26]   Such a division of affect would be a natural
response in Stevie to the intrusion of Verloc, a good provider but also a rival for Winnie.   Repressed hatred may
govern a scene of Verloc's return from the Continent.
Stevie carries off the traveler's bag "with triumphant
devotion" (SA, 182); but the bag is a female symbol and the
devotion may be to Winnie instead of Verloc.   Symbolically
deprived of his wife, the father is then stripped of
manhood, as a sexual prop repeatedly linked with him
disappears: "Before his extended arm could put down the hat
Stevie pounced upon it, and bore it off" (SA, 184).[27]

Verloc's attitude to his wife's brother is one of
superficial toleration and covert hostility.   By the bombing
an older man removes a younger rival, and a troublesome
wedding gift--one more to provide for--in a predictable
mishap; Stevie stumbles over a tree root, as does the police
constable who comes to investigate.   Ostensibly Verloc has
employed his brother-in-law because nothing worse than the
asylum can befall an incompetent if he is caught with
dynamite.   But an additional motive is suggested when Winnie
informs her husband, "You . . . seem to have grown quite
fond of him of late" (SA, 189).   "Mr. Verloc, tying up the
cardboard box into a parcel for the post, broke the string
by an injudicious jerk, and muttered several swear words
confidentially to himself" (SA, 189).   Oedipal rivalry
surfaces when he presses his claim on a grieving wife after
the death of the son-brother: "Do be reasonable. . . . What
would it have been if you had lost me?" (SA, 234).[28]

In Winnie's anguished vision of events in Greenwich
Park, ". . . after a rainlike fall of mangled limbs the
decapitated head of Stevie lingered suspended alone, and
fading out slowly like the last star of a pyrotechnic
display" (SA, 260).   This death, a symbolic castration, is
avenged by Stevie--through Winnie, his sister and double--by
the phallic act of stabbing Verloc with the carving knife.

> As if the homeless soul of Stevie had flown for
> shelter straight to the breast of his sister,
> guardian, and protector, the resemblance of her
> face with that of her brother grew at every
> step, even to the droop of the lower lip, even
> to the slight divergence of the eyes. (SA, 262)

As might be expected, the murder is triggered by Verloc's
sexual summons to his wife: "'Come here,' he said in a

peculiar tone . . . intimately known to Mrs. Verloc as the note of wooing" (SA, 262). Winnie now chooses the son over the father.

A sexual triangle figures in the death of another son character, even though he waits to approach Winnie until she has been widowed. This second sacrifice to an author's possible Oedipal conflict is the anarchist Comrade Ossipon, ex-medical student, author of a pornographic pamphlet, and dependent on many women instead of the one who suffices for a Yundt or a Michaelis. Erroneously believing Verloc to have been the man blown up in Greenwich Park, Ossipon means to inherit Winnie, together with Verloc's dingy shop (his "ostensible business"--SA, 3) and whatever the triple agent had in the bank. But this successor, on finding that Verloc was killed by Winnie instead of a bomb, becomes "terrified scientifically" (SA, 290) of a woman he classifies as a degenerate. Ossipon's rejection of social authority contrasts with his abject submission to the gospel of a spiritual father, Lombroso, the theorist of criminal types. The teeth having fixed Winnie to her lover's satisfaction as a "murdering" (SA, 297) type, potentially dangerous to himself, he pockets her money and abandons her. However, he proves unable to enjoy his windfall. Conrad explains that his knowledge of the reason for Winnie's subsequent suicide from a cross-Channel boat is intolerable to a man alone; for the rest of humanity, as a newspaper puts it, "An impenetrable mystery seems destined to hang for ever over this act of madness or despair" (SA, 307). Conrad would have us believe that Ossipon, burdened with the knowledge he cannot share,

> could face no woman. . . . He could neither think, work, sleep, nor eat. But he was beginning to drink with pleasure. . . . His revolutionary career, sustained by the sentiment and trustfulness of many women, was menaced by an impenetrable mystery. (SA, 310)

> Already he bowed his broad shoulders, his head of ambrosial locks, as if ready to receive the leather yoke of the sandwich board. (SA, 311)

Ossipon's profound reaction to the death of one woman seems unlikely in a seducer of his experience. In the abrupt transformation of a Don Juan into a monk, with overtones of an early grave, the operative psychology seems to be less Ossipon's response to moral isolation than his and Conrad's to Oedipal guilt. The blond Ossipon, a double for the blond Stevie, is a sexual replacement for the father

Verloc; the fact that Verloc is dead before supersession occurs has been, for Conrad, no excuse. Ossipon himself reflects that "Verloc had been a good fellow, and certainly a very decent husband as far as one could see" (SA, 274). The victor's discomfort as the rival of an older man would imply that more than Lombroso, or even preoedipal terrors, lies behind his fear of Winnie as lethal: "He saw the woman twined round him like a snake. . . . She was not deadly. She was death itself" (SA, 291).

In The Secret Agent, as in Nostromo, the surviving son figure is the least active sexually; as before, the extent of his asexual revolt seems immaterial to Conrad. The privileged rebel of The Secret Agent is the bomb-carrying Professor, whose "device is: No God! No master" (SA, 306). The "Perfect Anarchist" (SA, 302) claims superiority to the London police by virtue of his willingness to blow himself up; he cannot be taken alive. As the police know, he walks always with his left hand closed on an india-rubber ball, which, if pressed, will actuate the detonator of an explosive to destroy everyone within a radius of twenty feet. Even the famous Inspector Heat dares not test the Professor's mettle. Life has such a hold on Heat that the sight of this adversary induces nausea; Heat is "human" (SA, 94). Joseph Fradin has suggested that the Professor's hand on the ball in his pocket--the "supreme guarantee of his sinister freedom" (SA, 81), the expression of his will to power--has an onanistic as well as an existential significance[29]; it would appear also that his large padlocked cupboard, the locus of the treasured explosive, is a kind of substitute woman. If so, these modest gratifications suffice. A deficiency in virility, suggested by cheeks "merely smudged by the miserable poverty of a thin dark whisker," frees this chemist to pursue without distraction his "perfect detonator," to the goal of destroying "what is" (SA, 62, 69, 306). Like Shaw's Undershaft, he accommodates as merchant of death all comers. The result, by the logic of Conrad's Übermensch, must be the elimination of the weak, to the end that he shall rule. "'The source of all evil! They are our sinister masters. . . . They have power. They are the multitude. . . . Exterminate, exterminate! That is the only way of progress. . . .' 'And what remains?' asked Ossipon in a stifled voice. 'I remain--if I am strong enough'" (SA, 303-4). Like Nostromo, who adapted Viola's hatred of the rich to justify theft, the Professor has altered a heritage of paternal ideology; he has warped Christian righteousness into a righteousness of ambition, and then of destruction. Like Conrad, he derives from a father whose status in no way confers status on the son.

Of humble origin, and with an appearance really
so mean as to stand in the way of his considerable
natural abilities, his imagination had been fired
early by the tales of men rising from the depths
of poverty to positions of authority and affluence.
The extreme, almost ascetic purity of his thought,
combined with an astounding ignorance of worldly
conditions, had set before him a goal of power and
prestige to be attained without the medium of arts,
graces, tact, wealth--by sheer weight of merit
alone. On that view he considered himself
entitled to undisputed success. His father, a
delicate dark enthusiast with a sloping fore-
head, had been an itinerant and rousing preacher
of some obscure but rigid Christian sect--a man
supremely confident in the privileges of his
righteousness. In the son, individualist by
temperament, once the science of colleges had
replaced thoroughly the faith of conventicles,
this moral attitude translated itself into a
frenzied puritanism of ambition. He nursed it
as something secularly holy. To see it thwarted
opened his eyes to the true nature of the world,
whose morality was artificial, corrupt, and
blasphemous. The way of even the most justi-
fiable revolutions is prepared by personal
impulses disguised into creeds. (SA, 80-81)

The meanness of this motivation does not prevent Conrad
from leaving the Professor as the novel's unsolved problem,
"frail, insignificant, shabby, miserable--and terrible in
the simplicity of his idea calling madness and despair to
the regeneration of the world. Nobody looked at him. He
passed on unsuspected and deadly, like a pest in the street
full of men" (SA, 311). The author has obvious affinities
with a character who declares: "All passion is lost now.
The world is mediocre, limp, without force" (SA, 309). The
Professor, like his creator, desires to move its "immense
multitude," "thoughtless like a natural force," and yet
"what if nothing could move them? Such moments come to all
men whose ambition aims at a direct grasp upon humanity--to
artists, politicians, thinkers, reformers, or saints" (SA,
81, 82). In likening the artist to an anarchist, Conrad
advertises his own outlaw self--as he did in lumping the
vanity of "poets" with that of "reformers, charlatans,
prophets, and incendiaries" (SA, 53).
    The nihilistic Professor is probably the supreme

example of his principle of compromise, by which an Oedipal struggle for power could be expiated by asceticism. From the security of The Secret Agent he moved to Under Western Eyes, in which his carefully wrought agreement, adumbrated in An Outcast of the Islands and developed in Heart of Darkness, collapsed. But before he abandoned his fictional solution, he broke off the writing of his Russian novel to produce "The Secret Sharer"--a brief return to the simplicities of his sea fiction, in which the Oedipal problem had been mastered by the deletion of women and asexual revolt condoned. Leggatt, the uninhibited chief mate of the Sephora, has killed a crew member who resisted an order, the hazardous command to reef a foresail in "a sea gone mad" (SS, 124). Archbold, the Sephora's captain, may have funked the order; Leggatt insists he gave it, and saved the ship. In his account, as James Hamilton has noted, the killing of the unruly seaman was "clearly a displacement of Leggatt's rage at the captain's inability to perform under stress."[30] According to Leggatt, after the main topsail blew away Archbold "whimpered about our last hope. . . . It worked me up into a sort of desperation. I just took it into my own hands and went away from him, boiling, and--" (SS, 124). Of his attack on the sailor the mate says: ". . . I had him by the throat, and went on shaking him like a rat. . . . Then a crash as if the sky had fallen on my head." A ten-minute "smother of foam" fixes his intent: "It's clear that I meant business, because I was holding him by the throat still when they picked us up. He was black in the face" (SS, 102). If the captain instead of Leggatt actually gave the crucial order, Leggatt's rage could be referred to an unsuccessful effort to usurp command. The narrator, however, accepts the outlaw's version of events on the Sephora: "The same strung-up force which had given twenty-four men a chance, at least, for their lives, had, in a sort of recoil, crushed an unworthy mutinous existence" (SS, 124-25). A sympathetic listener hides Leggatt on his own ship and sails perilously near shore to let him escape as "a free man, a proud swimmer striking out for a new destiny" (SS, 143). Two young men collude to evade maritime justice and Conrad approves, for both survive.

The moral of "The Secret Sharer," written in 1909, was compatible with contemporary psychoanalytic theory: the protagonist cannot fully become a captain until he recognizes the existence of a Leggatt in himself. Parricide in the story refers not only to Leggatt's bid for power on the Sephora but to the narrator's lawful assumption of command on his own ship. His contact with a fugitive he persistently labels as his "other self," "double,"

"reflection," "secret sharer," and so on, leads, on his own
testimony, to an increase in fitness to command (SS, 100,
101, 105, 114). The youngest man on board, except for the
second mate, and "untried as yet by a position of the
fullest responsibility," he confesses himself at the
beginning of the tale a "stranger" to his ship and to
himself: ". . . I wondered how far I should turn out
faithful to that ideal conception of one's own personality
every man sets up for himself secretly" (SS, 93, 94). At
the end, after his risky maneuver to bring the ship under
Koh-ring's "towering black mass like the very gateway of
Erebus," he claims "the perfect communion of a seaman with
his first command" (SS, 143). The narrator's road to
professionalism has evidently been his "mysterious communication" (SS, 99) with an instinctual, irrational
self, an id hitherto repressed. He first sees Leggatt from
the ship as a nocturnal "headless corpse" in the "sleeping
water" below--suggesting an intrusion of the unconscious
(SS, 97). The initial symbolism of the unconscious accords
with the concealment of Leggatt in his own stateroom below
decks, with the whispered conversation of two men who wear
identical sleeping suits, and with the narrator's sense of
distraction: "I was constantly watching myself, my secret
self. . . . It was very much like being mad" (SS, 114).
    Eventually the narrator begins to sound like Leggatt,
an unrepentant Cain from whose scorn no elder is safe. Like
Lord Jim, the culprit is a parson's fallen son who can never
go home again; but unlike Jim, he declines submission to the
verdict of the community. ". . . you don't see me coming
back to explain such things to an old fellow in a wig and
twelve respectable tradesmen. . . . What can they know
whether I am guilty or not--or of what I am guilty, either?
That's my affair" (SS, 131-32). Reverting to the Sephora,
he describes Archbold as

> afraid of the men, and also of that old second
> mate of his who had been sailing with him for
> years--a grey-headed old humbug; and his steward,
> too, had been with him devil knows how long--
> seventeen years or more--a dogmatic sort of loafer
> who hated me like poison, just because I was the
> chief mate. . . . Those two old chaps ran the ship.
> Devil only knows what the skipper wasn't afraid of
> (all his nerve went to pieces altogether in that
> hellish spell of bad weather we had)--of what the
> law would do to him--of his wife, perhaps. Oh,
> yes! she's on board. (SS, 107)

Leggatt's contempt is aped by the narrator when Archbold
comes in search of the killer he is required to give up.
The narrator mocks his visitor's adherence to law as an
"obscure tenacity" which "had in it something incomprehensible and a little awful; something . . . mystical"
(SS, 118). Even the senior captain's excellent record
supplies a pretext for ridicule: "Seven-and-thirty virtuous years at sea, of which over twenty of immaculate
command, and the last fifteen in the Sephora, seemed to have
laid him under some pitiless obligation" (SS, 118-19). His
side of events during the storm is suppressed: "It is not
worth while to record that version" (SS, 117). A clue to it
might be the fact that Leggatt the parricide obtained his
post by family influence, not merit (SS, 119). But the
question of nepotism, like that of Leggatt's veracity, is
passed over by a narrator whose communion with a secret self
makes objectivity difficult.[31] It might be supposed that
the tenacious and legalistic Archbold, who resembles the
tenacious and literalistic MacWhirr of "Typhoon," would have
faced a storm with MacWhirr's imperturbability. Neither
captain could fall prey to imagination, that faculty which
is consistently in Conrad's fiction "the enemy of men, the
father of all terrors" (LJ, 11).

A disdain for the legalism of Archbold--"if that was
his name" (SS, 117)--is a disdain for honor, duty, and
the code of the sea.[32] Appropriately, it precedes the
narrator's hair-raising maneuver at Koh-ring, which defies
seamanship but which, if he can be believed--and I think he
can--makes him a seaman. The implication is that henceforth
he will operate within tradition. Read in Oedipal terms,
the story suggests that one must first kill the father,
and know that he does so, in order to become the father.
Freud's economic theory supplies a reason why a connection
should exist between self-knowledge and an increase in the
ability to command. The pressure exerted by the repressed
in the direction of consciousness requires an "unceasing
counter-pressure" to balance it; "thus the maintenance of a
repression involves an uninterrupted expenditure of force,
while its removal results in a saving from an economic point
of view."[33] The moment at which a part of the unconscious
becomes conscious falls as the narrator risks his ship and
the lives of all on board to put Leggatt, that strong
swimmer, nearer shore than he need be. The young captain's
statement, ". . . on my conscience, it had to be thus
close--no less" (SS, 141), registers an acceptance of the
parricidal guilt he shares with Leggatt. Almost immediately
thereafter he turns, for the first time, from introspection
to the problems of his craft: ". . . I forgot the secret

stranger ready to depart, and remembered only that I was a
total stranger to the ship. I did not know her. . . . How
was she to be handled?" (SS, 141). What seems a maturation
would imply that the cost of abrogating repression, in a
process which has brought the narrator "as near insanity
as any man who has not actually gone over the border" (SS,
130), has been warranted.

Professional, but not sexual, success is permitted
under Conrad's Oedipal compromise. In "The Secret Sharer"
the limits of Oedipal self-assertion are indicated by the
behavior of the narrator's hat. If, as in The Secret Agent,
this article represents male sexuality, both he and Leggatt
submit to the deprivation characteristic of Conrad's younger
heroes. The narrator makes his renunciation by bestowing
the hat on Leggatt--his instinctual self but also a separate
person--as they part. The murderer is henceforth to be a
vagabond on the earth; "I saw myself wandering barefooted,
bareheaded, the sun beating on my dark poll" (SS, 138).
Leggatt makes his renunciation by losing the hat in the
water. Now floating, it becomes a "saving mark" (SS, 142)
to tell an inexperienced captain how his ship is responding.
". . . I watched the hat. . . . It was drifting forward,
warning me just in time that the ship had gathered sternway.
'Shift the helm,' I said" (SS, 142). In symbolic terms,
this order, which enables ship, crew, and captain to
survive, is made possible by a sacrifice of sexuality.

But in Under Western Eyes the ascetic sacrifice proves
insufficient; not by coincidence, it would seem, this novel
is also his first work in which an actual murder of the
father occurs. The bomb from the hand of Haldin kills--
along with bystanders--an archetypal paternal figure,
the repressive and "fanatical" (UWE, 7) minister de P--,
representing the little father of all Russians, the czar.
De P--

> served the monarchy by imprisoning, exiling, or
> sending to the gallows men and women, young and
> old, with an equable, unwearied industry. In his
> mystic acceptance of the principle of autocracy
> he was bent on extirpating from the land every
> vestige of anything that resembled freedom in
> public institutions; and in his ruthless perse-
> cution of the rising generation he seemed to aim
> at the destruction of the very hope of liberty
> itself. (UWE, 7-8)

In the preamble to a state paper he has declared "that 'the
thought of liberty has never existed in the Act of the

Creator. . . . It was not Reason but Authority which
expressed the Divine Intention. God was the Autocrat of the
Universe'" (UWE, 8). The killer of de P-- does not survive
the end of the novel, even though he appears to have made
Conrad's typical Oedipal concession of sexual abstinence:
"Men like me leave no posterity" (UWE, 22). Abjuring wife
or mistress, he also fails to exert a claim on the women of
his own family, a mother and sister whom he has persuaded to
leave Russia. In contrast to Decoud's sister and confidante, Natalia Haldin to her brother is only the vehicle
through which his revolutionary ideas can be perpetuated.
"Not a bad little girl my sister. She has the most trust-
ful eyes of any human being that ever walked this earth.
She will marry well, I hope. She may have children--sons
perhaps" (UWE, 22).

As the fates of Aïssa, Doramin, and Leggatt would
demonstrate, a Conradian murderer is not necessarily
punishable; but Haldin is punished with torture and death.
His crime is neither justified by the atrocious character of
the victim nor expiated by the remorse of the killer, who
terms his deed "weary work" (UWE, 16) and expects an early
martyrdom:

> "This is not murder--it is war, war. My spirit shall
> go on warring in some Russian body till all falsehood
> is swept out of the world. . . . a new revelation
> shall come out of Russia. . . . [The Russian soul]
> has a mission, I tell you, or else why should I
> have been moved to do this--reckless--like a butcher
> --in the middle of all these innocent people--
> scattering death--I! I! . . . I wouldn't hurt a
> fly!" . . .
>   Haldin sat down abruptly, and leaning his head
> on his folded arms burst into tears. (UWE, 22)

The son of a docile provincial official, "the soul of
obedience," he, like Charles Gould, has had to invoke an
uncle as sanction for rebellion: "They say I resemble my
mother's eldest brother, an officer. They shot him in '28"
(UWE, 23). In addition Haldin, like de P--, claims divine
guidance, but the younger man's use of the deity is so
introspective as to connote uncertainty. As in Nostromo, a
fixed idea can only gradually crystallize in the mind of its
host. "Did I exult? Did I take pride in my purpose? Did
I try to weigh its worth and consequences? No! I was
resigned. I thought 'God's will be done'" (UWE, 23). In
any case, the recourse to what Conrad could only regard as
an illusion did not, for him, extenuate Haldin's murder of
the father.

Authorial condemnation extends to Haldin's double
Razumov, who is guilty only of covert sympathy with the
parricide he finds concealed in his room. His conscious
response to a known rebel--in appearance, a phallic emblem,
"tall and straight as an arrow" (UWE, 63)--is one of rejection, even before he learns precisely what Haldin has done.
Razumov's terror of this acquaintance on sight may spring
from a latent doubt of his own fidelity to the czar.

> All black against the usual tall stove of white
> tiles gleaming in the dusk, stood a strange figure.
> . . . It loomed lithe and martial. Razumov was
> utterly confounded. It was only when the figure
> advancing two paces asked in an untroubled, grave
> voice if the outer door was closed that he regained
> his power of speech. (UWE, 14)

Only now does the objective reason for fear emerge. The
killer's prompt confession, "It was I who removed de P--
this morning," gives Razumov the sense of his own life in
ruins: "Everybody Haldin had ever known would be in the
greatest danger" (UWE, 16, 20). But even though Haldin in a
room can be only a "visitation" (UWE, 32), the host listens
minute by minute to the story of a murder and wonders why he
has not told this man to go away. The answer lies in his
own unacknowledged urge to parricide. Haldin's ally in the
student whose quiet, laborious existence he has imperilled
is Razumov's submerged rage at the father he has met once,
in an attorney's office, and recognized only by "a light
pressure" of the hand, "like a secret sign. The emotion of
it was terrible" (UWE, 12). This father, in whom personal
and social paternity meet, is the elderly Prince K--, "a
senator, a dignitary, a great personage" (UWE, 40). Through
the attorney as guardian he makes Razumov a modest allow-
ance, but from the heights of domestic splendor he refuses
to recognize an illegitimate son. Warned that any vaunt
of his family tree would be dangerous to his future,
Razumov can only admire from a distance his privileged
half sisters. "Presently they would marry Generals or
Kammerherrs and have girls and boys of their own, who
perhaps would be aware of him as a celebrated old professor,
decorated, possibly a Privy Councillor, one of the glories
of Russia--nothing more!" (UWE, 13). "As lonely in the
world as a man swimming in the deep sea," Conrad's hero has
"his closest parentage . . . defined in the statement that
he was a Russian" (UWE, 10-11).
        In Josiane Paccaud's Lacanian view, Razumov, denied the
Name-of-the-Father, and hence deprived of a place in the

symbolic order--that of language, the family, and society--
is automatically barred from any stable relationship with
his fellows.[34]   Clearly his isolation facilitates his
betrayal of Haldin to the police. Caught between the
"lawlessness of autocracy" and the "lawlessness of revolution" (UWE, 77), seeing no one to intercede for him, he
becomes the prisoner of his peril. The realities of
Russia work against a duplication of the "Secret Sharer"
plot, in which an outlaw could be sheltered in defiance of
legality. In safety Razumov has never professed more than a
vague liberalism, "easily swayed by argument and authority"
(UWE, 5); in jeopardy he readily imagines himself imprisoned
or deported,

> his life broken, ruined, and robbed of all hope.
> He saw himself--at best--leading a miserable exist-
> ence under police supervision, in some small, far-
> away provincial town, without friends to assist his
> necessities. . . .
> He saw his youth pass away from him in misery
> and half starvation--his strength give way, his
> mind become an abject thing. He saw himself creep-
> ing, broken down and shabby, about the streets--
> dying unattended in some filthy hole of a room,
> or on the sordid bed of a Government hospital.
> (UWE, 21)

Dispatched on Haldin's errand, to find the sledge
driver Ziemianitch for an escape, Razumov saves himself for
the nonce by a conversion to autocracy. Conceiving the
vast, snowy expanse of Russia to be "inanimate, cold, inert,
like a sullen and tragic mother hiding her face under a
winding-sheet," or a "monstrous blank page awaiting the
record of an inconceivable history," he sees his country
as enveloped in a "sacred inertia" which must be held
inviolate (UWE, 32-33).

> It was a guarantee of duration, of safety, while
> the travail of maturing destiny went on--a work
> not of revolutions with their passionate levity
> of action and their shifting impulses--but of
> peace. What it needed was not the conflicting
> aspirations of a people, but a will strong and
> one: it wanted not the babble of many voices,
> but a man--strong and one! (UWE, 33)

In a metaphor of penetration, connoting a submissive and
homosexual attitude to the father, Conrad adds: "The grace

entered into Razumov. He believed now in the man who would
come at the appointed time" (UWE, 34). "Everything was not
for the best. . . . But absolute power should be preserved--
the tool ready for the man--for the great autocrat of the
future" (UWE, 35).

Razumov in his ordeal of rebellion and loyalty conforms to Anna Freud's mechanism of identification with the
aggressor. In ascribing his own parricidal impulses to the
"sanguinary fanatic" (UWE, 34) Haldin, he meets her test of
projection. Moreover, if the Russian autocracy--headed by
the little father, the czar--is broadly interpreted as a
punitive parental figure, Razumov meets the test of imita-
tion of the aggressor's methods.[35] If he is found by
the police to have harbored an assassin, he can expect what
no Englishman in his place could envision: being "beaten
with whips as a practical measure . . . of investigation
or of punishment" (UWE, 25). Razumov allays his fear by
assuming the active role, that of the beater. In a reversal of ordinary parent-child relationships, he vents on a
father-substitute, the sixty-year-old Ziemianitch, his
accumulated wrath at Prince K--, toward whom he consciously
feels "no bitterness" (UWE, 11). On finding Haldin's driver
too drunk to be roused for the escape, he thrashes him until
the stick breaks. Razumov reasons like the great autocrat
of the future: "Children" require a master; "ah! the stick,
the stick, the stern hand" (UWE, 31).

Having persuaded himself that the role of "Judas" to
Haldin's Christ is a patriotic duty, Razumov desires to have
his "act of conscience" ratified by another mind (UWE, 38,
115). "No human being," declares the narrator, "could bear
a steady view of moral solitude without going mad" (UWE,
39). Specifically, the approval sought is that of the
father, the Freudian author of conscience and a nominal
protector. At first Razumov gains acceptance. Overcom-
ing an initial vexation, the "mobile, superficial . . .
ex-Guards officer . . . experienced in nothing but the arts
of gallant intrigue and worldly success" (UWE, 42) promises
to see him through an extraordinary peril. Razumov, to be
sure, minimizes any possible annoyance by setting aside
their personal connection: "A young man having no claim upon
anybody in the world has in an hour of trial involving his
deepest political convictions turned to an illustrious
Russian--that's all" (UWE, 42). Yet the Prince shows some
affection; Razumov gasps, feeling "a momentary pressure on
his arm," and hears the assurance, "You have done well"
(UWE, 42).

K-- goes so far as to defend his son, in a subsequent

interview, against General T--, a grotesque authoritarian
intent on establishing Razumov's complicity with Haldin.
"And you say he came in to make you this confidence like
this--for nothing--à propos des bottes," remarks the General
(UWE, 48). For Razumov, T-- is a "goggle-eyed imbecile"
incarnating the suspicion, anger, and ruthlessness of "a
political and social régime on its defence" (UWE, 45, 84).
By the credo of a man "unable to understand a reasonable
adherence to the doctrine of absolutism" (UWE, 84):

> I detest rebels. These subversive minds! These
> intellectual debauchés! My existence has been built
> on fidelity. It's a feeling. To defend it I am
> ready to lay down my life--and even my honour. . . .
> But pray tell me what honour can there be as against
> rebels--against people that deny God Himself. (UWE,
> 51)

> They shall be destroyed. (UWE, 50)

Against T--'s "merciless suspicion" (UWE, 48), however, the
Prince exacts assurances that the future of an honorable
young man will be guaranteed, and that neither the son's
role in the Haldin affair nor the father's will be made
public.

K--'s insertion of himself is significant. In the
carriage from General T--'s, Razumov listens to paternal
speeches in which ". . . natural sentiment struggled with
caution"; encumbered with a "proud and violent" wife, K--
fears any future contact with the son from whom he soon
glides away, leaving Razumov "alone on the edge of the
pavement" (UWE, 52, 53). He subsequently rids himself of
an embarrassment by getting an unsettled traitor into the
Russian secret service abroad. The youth is subjected to
a second interrogation, this one by a seemingly milder
inquisitor--the bearded, "Socratic" (UWE, 90) Councillor
Mikulin. The latter praises the political confession of
faith which the police have found tacked up in Razumov's
room, although the first word of the third line evinces
some dissatisfaction with the status quo, and the rest, in
facile parallels, might demonstrate only the writer's need
to convince himself of his orthodoxy.

> History not Theory.
> Patriotism not Internationalism.
> Evolution not Revolution.
> Direction not Destruction.
> Unity not Disruption. (UWE, 66)

Mikulin, undeceived, blandly assures him: "I understand your liberalism. I have an intellect of that kind myself" (<u>UWE</u>, 294). Razumov's liberalism is, in fact, scarcely an affair of the intellect. In a waking dream he has "beheld his own brain suffering on the rack--a long, pale figure drawn asunder horizontally with terrific force in the darkness of a vault" (<u>UWE</u>, 88), an apt symbol of the unconscious. General T--'s statue of "an adolescent figure, running"-- Spontini's "Flight of Youth" (<u>UWE</u>, 43)--is emblematic of Razumov's desire to bolt from his own parricidal impulses as well as from the autocracy. Yet when he asks permission to retire--"simply to retire"--Mikulin's reply, "Where to?" is prophetic (<u>UWE</u>, 99). A strong thread in his tangle of motives is dependence on paternal "Olympians" (<u>UWE</u>, 306) for approval of his role in Haldin's death. Hence he responds eagerly to the later, unofficial summons of the astute policeman whom Conrad likens to the devil. Like his con- version to autocracy, Razumov's induction into the ranks of police spies is less a matter of political conviction than of psychic need. The "obscure, unrelated" student,

> in the moment of great moral loneliness, was
> allowed to feel that he was an object of interest
> to a small group of people of high position.
> Prince K-- was persuaded to intervene personally,
> and on a certain occasion gave way to a manly
> emotion which, all unexpected as it was, quite
> upset Mr. Razumov. The sudden embrace of that
> man, agitated by his loyalty to a throne and by
> suppressed paternal affection, was a revelation
> to Mr. Razumov of something within his own
> breast. (<u>UWE</u>, 307-8)

Nevertheless, he has felt an "immense disappointment" (<u>UWE</u>, 98) on first learning of K--'s involvement. Although not devoid of paternal solicitude, K--, like Stein and Marlow with Jim, or Mitchell and Viola with Nostromo, or Verloc with Stevie, reaches a pinnacle of self-interest at which the sacrifice of the son becomes imperative. Razumov expresses a displaced contempt for the Prince when he pres- sures a friend, the rebel playboy Kostia, into stealing from Kostia's rich father to finance the journey of a police spy to Switzerland. Alone at dawn, in what the revolution- aries believe to be his escape from Russia, Razumov at the train window tosses Kostia's small brown paper parcel of money into the snow.

Razumov's destruction, begun in Russia, is completed by the Geneva revolutionaries, who in a parody of fatherhood receive an assassin's supposed accomplice as their protégé. His confession to them, at a time when he enjoys absolute safety, is a virtual suicide. He has declared himself "washed clean" (UWE, 357)--by a prior confession to Natalia --of Haldin's death.[36] But a full motivation to self-destruction could still exist in the wish to kill a neglect-ful father; the wish to be killed, to expiate the guilt of parricidal wishes; and the wish to die, to escape a "prison of lies" (UWE, 363) in which he has discovered his own medi-ocrity. He has written Natalia that he will "confess, go out--and perish" (UWE, 361). "He had done with life. . . . Now his scorn extended to himself. 'I had neither the sim-plicity nor the courage nor the self-possession to be a scoundrel, or an exceptionally able man'" (UWE, 362).

The hearers of Razumov's second confession accommodate him in the wish for self-destruction. Although a kindly and intelligent-looking speaker, with a "halo" of silvery hair, urges that "after this piece of sincerity he cannot be dangerous any longer" (UWE, 367), the father's offer of protection proves, as usual in Conrad's fiction, illusory. Sentence is passed and executed on Razumov by Nikita Necator, who was apparently intended to combine two other traits of Conradian paternity, comedy and menace. Misshapen, squeaking in the "falsetto of a circus clown," moving Razumov to "a stare on the verge of horror and laughter" (UWE, 266), the killer of gendarmes exemplifies Conrad's rather unsuccessful use of the grotesque to quell fear of the father. In deafening Razumov and leaving him to be run over by a tram, this specimen indulges an older man's envy of the revolutionary fame (however spurious) of Haldin's putative accomplice. "We have been hearing of nothing but Mr. Razumov for months," complains Nikita, "exasperated like a fashionable tenor by the attention attracted to the performance of an obscure amateur" (UWE, 265, 267).

Given the psychology of the Conradian father, it is hardly surprising that an executioner could be found among Razumov's elders. What is startling is that Conrad should condemn the sexually reticent hero, who has skirted the form of Oedipal rivalry his creator deemed unpardonable. An attempt seems to have been made to save him by means of the usual compromise. Conrad abandoned the plan of the novel he had announced in a letter to Galsworthy: Razumov was to marry Natalia, and the resemblance of the couple's child to the martyred brother was to elicit a confession of betrayal.[37] But in the completed novel, Razumov, though referring obscurely in a diary to a plan to "steal

[Natalia's] soul" (UWE, 359) as a form of revenge on Haldin,
keeps his distance from the girl; and he achieves a complete
break by confessing his betrayal of Haldin, as well as
his (unspecified) design on her.[38] He adds as a kind of
afterthought, "I felt that I must tell you that I had ended
by loving you" (UWE, 361). The tenuousness of their relationship approaches the negations of a passage from the
first American edition: ". . . he did not recognize women as
women. There had been literally no feminine influence on
his life. . . . no woman had ever influenced a dream of
his, taken up a moment of his time, or awakened any of his
dormant feelings."[39] A corroborative passage appears in
the Dent edition of 1923, after Razumov tells Natalia that
he never knew his dead mother: "I've never known any kind of
love" (UWE, 360).

Peter Ivanovitch, one of Razumov's potential rivals
for Natalia had Razumov been more active, is virtually a
caricature of the paternal sexual prerogative. Like Yundt,
Michaelis, and Ossipon in The Secret Agent, he is a revolutionary kept by one or more women, but he alone has
gained fame by trading on his dependency. A "heroic
fugitive" (UWE, 125) liberated by feminine aid from a
czarist prison camp, he has escaped across Siberia and sat
down in Western Europe to pen a best-selling autobiography.
From a protracted self-analysis there rises "like a white
figure from a dark confused sea the conviction of woman's
spiritual superiority--his new faith confessed since in
several volumes" (UWE, 121). Besides preaching "the cult
of the woman" he practices it, "under the rites of special
devotion to the transcendental merits of a certain Madame de
S--, a lady of advanced views, no longer very young" (UWE,
125) but extremely well off. However, a Priapus identified
by such props as a file, a length of chain dangling from the
waist, and a silk top hat does not restrict himself to his
patroness. In the words of Tekla, her dame de compagnie,
he "must direct, inspire, influence. . . . He can't bear
thinking of any one escaping him" (UWE, 237). The escape
would evidently be at least partly from his sexuality,
though this quality is not dependable. In a passage cited
by Helen Rieselbach, Peter's failure to draw Natalia into
his orbit amounts to impotence. Having proclaimed, "I want
you to be a fanatic," he raises "for a moment one thick arm;
the other remained hanging down against his thigh, with the
fragile silk hat at the end" (UWE, 129).[40]

Despite the stress on sexuality, when Razumov comes to
wish a "hairy and obscene brute" dead, the motive is not
sexual rivalry but the danger from Peter's interrogation of
a reticent "Brutus" inclined to "play with the greatness of

the great man" (UWE, 208, 219, 228). Musing impenetrably
behind dark glasses, the leader who believes a political
chasm "has to be filled up" with dead bodies--including that
of his listener--becomes to the younger man "suddenly so
odious that if he had had a knife, he fancied he could have
stabbed him . . . with a horrible triumphant satisfaction"
(UWE, 209, 211).

The moment leaves out of account three women--Natalia,
Mme. de S--, and Tekla--for whom Razumov might have
contended with Peter. Both Mme. de S-- and Tekla are
possible wife-mother figures--like Mrs. Beard in "Youth,"
slim but aged. Mme. de S--, a professed "supernaturalist"
in politics, enjoys talking to a handsome young man--for she
"was not always in a mystical state of mind" (UWE, 219,
222). Razumov may concede an initial attraction when he
describes her as "a witch in Parisian clothes" (UWE, 215).
But he soon rejects her as potentially deadly--skeletal,
grotesque, "like a galvanized corpse out of some Hoffman's
Tale" (UWE, 215); in effect, he treats her as the untouch-
able property of Peter Ivanovitch. He accepts only Peter's
castoff Tekla, whose two years as the secretary of the great
feminist have soured her on genius. Razumov wins her by
politely taking off his hat to a woman starved for the
rudiments of civility. At the end of the novel, crippled
and growing weaker every day, he is faithfully tended by a
"Samaritan" (UWE, 379) with an irresistible vocation. Dying
he gains, as Bernard Meyer has pointed out, the nurturing
mother he never had in infancy.[41] But there is no sign
that his attitude to Tekla alters from the opportunism he
shows on first noting a forlorn woman's attachment to
himself. "It was a great piece of luck for him, he
reflected; because women are seldom venal after the manner
of men, who can be bought for material considerations. She
would be a good ally" (UWE, 235).

His primary orientation appears homoerotic, and
directed to father figures. Conrad's metaphor of grace
entering into him as he conceives his great autocrat of the
future supports Robert Armstrong's conclusion that his
punishment by the revolutionaries has the significance of a
homosexual rape; Nikita's blows on the ears, bursting the
drums, seem to "split his head in two" (UWE, 369).[42] As
Karl Menninger has noted in cases of actual suicide, the
method is often chosen to yield erotic satisfaction.[43]
After Razumov's near suicidal second confession, the choice
is Nikita's; but it provides an equivalent of the knife that
the hero anticipated, perhaps with pleasure.

The confusion in Razumov's sexuality is one possible
index of authorial stress; another is the breakdown of a

compromise permitting celibates to survive; still another,
the confusion in the depiction of the narrator. The insertion of a _soi-disant_ obtuse observer, a pair of Western
eyes, is an effort to gain psychic distance from disturbing
material. The English teacher of languages insists he has
"no comprehension of the Russian character" (UWE, 4). But
this phenomenon as he portrays it includes the same Freudian
or post-Freudian psychology of the unconscious that Conrad's
non-Russians have manifested; what the teacher does not,
or will not, know may be less national than human. He may
suppress his understanding, as when he says of Tekla's
masochistic attachment to Razumov, ". . . I did not want
to meditate very long on the inwardness of this peculiar
episode" (UWE, 375); his statement recalls Conrad's
defensive rejection of Freud: "I don't want to get to the
bottom. . . . I want to look on reality as something rough
and coarse over which I pass my fingers. Nothing more."[44]
But often the teacher does, in spite of himself, get to
the bottom, as in the motivation he supplies for Haldin's
confidence in Razumov. "Amongst a lot of exuberant talkers
. . . a comparatively taciturn personality is naturally
credited with reserve power" (UWE, 6), he writes. And
in addition Haldin is doubtless to be credited with an
awareness that Razumov has parricidal impulses matching
his own; he merely overestimates their relative strength.
Razumov's revolutionary fame, in both Moscow and Geneva,
among both dissidents and policemen, reflects the ability
of others to see what he himself would deny. The narrator
registers a deadlock between authoritarian and rebel selves
when he shows Razumov writing his police report under a
statue of Rousseau. It is also clear that Razumov resists
political (or Oedipal) definition to the end.

> After all, it is [the revolutionaries] and not I
> who have the right on their side!--theirs is the
> strength of invisible powers. So be it. Only
> don't be deceived, Natalia Victorovna, I am not
> converted. Have I then the soul of a slave? No!
> I am independent--and therefore perdition is my
> lot. (UWE, 361-62)

The narrator's insight is further revealed when he
selects as a significant datum Razumov's perception of
Nikita as a double agent, and a double of Haldin's betrayer.
"A squeaky voice screamed, 'Confession or no confession, you
are a police spy!' . . . Razumov looked at the famous slayer
of gendarmes in silent disgust. 'And what are you?' he
said, very low" (UWE, 367). Razumov's charge by

"inspiration" (UWE, 380) is confirmed by Mikulin's later
betrayal, to Peter Ivanovitch at a chance meeting in a
railway carriage, of a killer in two camps. Politically
absurd, the episode is credible in Freudian terms. Despite
his possession of a wife and children, Nikita, symbolically
falsetto-voiced and almost hairless, retains some aspects of
a rebellious son; as an impartial killer he threatens the
revolutionary power structure along with the autocratic one.
All that revolution can effect, says Conrad in the Author's
Note, "is merely a change of names" (UWE, x); there are only
two classes, the rulers and the ruled. Hence the bass-
voiced, paternal Peter Ivanovitch, aspiring to be head of
a theoretically feminist state, and the bearded, paternal
Mikulin, the czar's policeman, have more in common with each
other than either has with Nikita. Insofar as he is a son
figure, a convergence of fathers to destroy him resembles
the paternal collaboration of Marlow and Stein, or Doramin
and Stein, in dispatching Jim, or that of three paternal
figures in summoning Razumov to his fatal entry into the
secret service. An envelope arrives in the handwriting of
the attorney who is Razumov's unofficial guardian; inside is
a second envelope addressed in Prince K--'s hand, and within
that, the message written by Mikulin (UWE, 303).

The writing of Under Western Eyes was interrupted by a
physical and psychic breakdown, lasting for months, in which
the author threatened to destroy the manuscript, jabbered
in Polish, and held, in the words of his wife, delirious
"converse with the characters"[45] of his Russian novel.
Bernard Meyer speculates that Conrad "had developed a
psychosis as a complication of an acute infectious-toxic
process" which precipitated "a latent psychic disorder."[46]
Within the novel, the attempt--however intermittent--to
erect the barrier of an unseeing narrator invites inquiry
into the precise nature of the dangerous material that
Conrad had hoped to distance. From the standpoint of
Oedipal conflict, much of Under Western Eyes is familiar
from earlier work--for example, the contrast of reticent
younger men with exemplars of the paternal sexual prerogative. Besides Peter Ivanovitch, this privileged
older generation includes the libertine Prince K--; the
"lifelong lover" Ziemianitch; General T-- and Nikita as
heads of families; the sybaritic bachelor Mikulin, "an
enlightened patron of the art of female dancing"; and even
the diffident narrator, Natalia's confidant, who confesses
himself deeply attached to her, though "fated" to be a mere
spectator of some inscrutably Russian drama in which she is
a participant (UWE, 283, 305, 339). But if Under Western
Eyes offers little that is new in Oedipal sexual conflict,

it is unique in the autobiographical resonance of its
nonsexual rivalry. The relationship of a Russian novel in
which the hero remarks, "Visionaries work everlasting evil"
(UWE, 95), to Conrad's own tragic childhood, dominated by
the visionary Apollo, in Russia and Poland is inescapable.
Conrad, exile, seaman, and struggling writer, was, like
Haldin and Razumov, blighted by his personal and social
paternity. His view of the Russian autocracy was no more
sanguine than Apollo's, but father and son differed on the
necessity or feasibility of combating it.

> The ferocity and imbecility of an autocratic rule
> rejecting all legality and in fact basing itself
> upon complete moral anarchism provokes the no
> less imbecile and atrocious answer of a purely
> Utopian revolutionism encompassing destruction
> by the first means to hand, in the strange
> conviction that a fundamental change of hearts
> must follow the downfall of any given human
> institutions. (UWE, x)

What this last "political" novel—that "drama of autocracy
. . . not played on the great stage of politics" (UWE, 338)
—may have taught Conrad was the potential crime of his own
revolt against his father's fanaticism. Even when murder
had been displaced from the revolutionary Apollo to the
autocratic de P--, his imagination was haunted by parricide.

6

Quietus

Conrad's emergent psychic disorder in 1910, though perhaps due partly to the tragic events of his past, was not
entirely so. Bernard Meyer cites the current provocation of
an estrangement from his friend and collaborator, Ford Madox
Ford, or Hueffer, over the latter's liaison with Violet
Hunt, a woman eleven years Ford's senior. The affair with a
symbolic mother, who credited herself with having saved Ford
from suicide, left Conrad both scandalized and envious.[1]
It might be said that Ford had realized the Oedipal goal of
numerous Conradian heroes and, by implication, of their
creator. The terms of Conrad's indignation are suggestive:
he denounced Ford as a "spoilt kid."[2] But the senior
author also resented the loss of his protégé's attention and
support. Meyer, who places Conrad's greatest fiction in the
so-called Hueffer decade, 1899-1909, ascribes this achievement partly to the presence of a "secret sharer."[3] Ford,
the neglected son of a prominent music critic, Francis
Hueffer, and an artist mother, daughter of the pre-
Raphaelite painter Ford Madox Brown, had, like Conrad,
been frustrated in childhood attachments. Meyer theorizes
that as a consequence he had, like Conrad, grown up with
"a highly fragile sense of personal worth and personal
identity." Psychic divisions in Ford--which prompted H. G.
Wells's comment, "What he is really or if he is really . . .
nobody knows now and he least of all"[4]--probably rendered
him more sympathetic to those in Conrad. In Meyer's view,
what Marlow says about Jim could equally well have been said
by Ford about a Conrad split between rebel and conforming
selves: "He was not speaking to me, he was only speaking
before me, in a dispute with an invisible personality, an
antagonistic and inseparable partner of his existence--

another possessor of his soul. . . . [He] did not want a
judge. He wanted an ally, a helper, an accomplice."[5]
The Marlow-Jim comparison suggests the dynamic of the Ford-
Conrad friendship--the attempt to achieve an ideal parent-
child tie, to compensate for past deprivation. Significantly, Ford, the younger, sometimes essayed the role of
father to Conrad.[6]

Deprived of a "mirroring companionship" that had
sustained him for ten years, and fearful that "the mad
devils leering at him during his illness" would return,
Conrad, in Meyer's opinion, deserted the faith he had
expressed in the preface to The Nigger of the "Narcissus"
(1897): ". . . the artist descends within himself, and in
that lonely region of stress and strife . . . he finds the
terms of his appeal" (NN, vii-viii). Apparently no longer
psychologically able to withstand the journeys to the
underworld that had produced his great subjective fiction of
the Hueffer years, Conrad opted for an art of the surface;
he re-created himself as "a literary Captain MacWhirr, who
had 'just enough imagination to carry him through each
successive day, and no more.'"[7] Following Thomas Moser
and Albert Guerard, Meyer finds a "radical change" in most
of the fiction after 1910, the "exteriorization of the
source of suffering. . . . when trouble comes to the
protagonist he is no way responsible for it. 'The fault
lies elsewhere, in other people.'"[8] Meyer treats the
expulsion or projection of evil in the late fiction as a
total exoneration of son figures with whom Conrad might
have identified himself.

> . . . the poignant inner mental conflict of
> the early Conrad was replaced by conflict
> with the outer world, and doubting, troubled
> men, like Marlow of "Heart of Darkness," and
> hapless souls like Jim or Decoud, caught in a
> neurotic web of their own creation, gave way
> to simple innocent creatures who, as pawns of
> fate, struggle with indifferent success against
> external influence, external accident, and
> external malevolence.[9]

Since Oedipal sexual conflict continues in Conrad's
fiction after 1910, the view that the source of suffering
has been wholly externalized is a surprising one for a
psychoanalytic critic. It may reflect an uncritical
acceptance of the later Conrad's disavowal of complexity: "I
want to look on reality as something rough and coarse over
which I pass my fingers. Nothing more."[10] Meyer's

concept of filial innocence in the later work is, however,
justified in the sense that the expression of nonsexual
Oedipal rivalry has been sharply reduced. As a look at
Victory (1915), The Shadow-Line (1917), The Rover (1923),
and Suspense (1925) will demonstrate, Conrad refused to
grant post-1910 protagonists the scope in asexual revolt
that he had allowed the Marlow of the Congo, or sea heroes
through "The Secret Sharer," or Charles Gould, or Decoud, or
the Professor--or even, in the first novels, Almayer and
Willems. But since his portrayals of the father after 1910
suggest an unabating authorial impulse to revolt, one might
infer that its expression by the son encountered a more
powerful resistance than in prior fiction; after he had
created Razumov, Conrad may have stifled in his heroes a
kind of impulse of which, in himself, he had stood in sudden fear. His subsequent decline as a writer bears out his
own credo of 1897: the artist must find the "terms of his
appeal" in a descent into "that lonely region of stress and
strife" which constitutes the inner self (NN, viii).

Since he had long deprecated sexual rivalry with the
father, a curb on nonsexual competition signified that the
self-assertion of an ideal protagonist would approach zero.
This cipher is the start of Victory, in which the philosophy
of the hero's father establishes a ban on all activity for
the son. Heyst's life, like Decoud's in Nostromo, is a
study in the feasibility of detachment. The prescription of
the elder Heyst is total disengagement. "Look on--make no
sound," he urges; ". . . cultivate that form of contempt
which is called pity" (V, 174, 175). By the father's doctrine, the universe is devoid of meaning, or of any that
can be apprehended by the human mind: "Man on this earth is
an unforeseen accident which does not stand close investigation" (V, 196). A second precept is that ". . . all
action is bound to be harmful. It is devilish. That is
why this world is evil upon the whole" (V, 54). Nevertheless, the philosopher of inaction, a mentor located in
"the broad, human path of inconsistencies" (V, 176),
never in his own turbulent lifetime has ceased to act.
"'Look on--make no sound,' were the last words of the man
who had spent his life in blowing blasts upon a terrible
trumpet which had filled heaven and earth with ruins, while
mankind went on its way unheeding" (V, 175). His activity
is all the more striking because, having begun life in the
high idealism, or egotism, of romantic hopes, he has suffered more than common disappointment.

> . . . the elder Heyst had begun by coveting all
> the joys . . . those of the fools and those of
> the sages. For more than sixty years he had

> dragged on this painful earth of ours the most
> weary, the most uneasy soul that civilisation
> had ever fashioned to its ends of disillusion
> and regret. One could not refuse him a
> measure of greatness, for he was unhappy in
> a way unknown to mediocre souls. (V, 91)

His persistence in inconsistency may be due to an illusion prominent in Nostromo: "Only in the conduct of our action can we find the sense of mastery over the Fates" (N, 66). If so, it is a consolation he would deny his son, along with the opportunity to supplant him. Heyst, Sr., husband, father, and writer, intends his son to be none of these. His precepts may veil the desire to eliminate a potential competitor. In other contexts, Conrad has written in the same novel: ". . . at the bottom, deep down . . . our unexpressed longings lie"; "for the use of reason is to justify the obscure desires that move our conduct, impulses, passions, prejudices and follies, and also our fears" (V, 75, 83). The father's teaching is at once protective and destructive; to be spared disillusionment, the son is to be denied life.

Axel, his father's pupil in close companionship at the impressionable years between eighteen and twenty-one,[11] emerges from tutelage with "a profound mistrust of life" (V, 91) and a decision to drift as his defense against involvement. The father dies; the son roves to the age of thirty-five, idealizing his life as "a solitary achievement, accomplished not by hermit-like withdrawal with its silence and immobility, but by a system of restless wandering, by the detachment of an impermanent dweller amongst changing scenes." By this method he expects to pass through life "without suffering . . . invulnerable because elusive" (V, 90).

Declaring himself "the most detached of creatures in this earthly captivity" (V, 198-99), he nevertheless fails his father's ideal. The first lapse appears in his emotional tie to the man who had taught him "that he who forms a tie is lost. The germ of corruption has entered into his soul" (V, 199-200). After the funeral of the philosopher he supposes he should hate, as a "destroyer of systems, of hopes, of beliefs" (V, 175), the son finds himself instead mourning, and obliged to rationalize the lapse.

> He became aware of his eyes being wet. It was
> not that the man was his father. For him
> [paternity] was purely a matter of hearsay
> which could not in itself cause this emotion.

> No! It was because he had looked at him so
> long that he missed him so much. (V, 175)

His love for his father, in violation of the father's dogma,
confuses the negative Oedipal attitude with the positive, or
parricidal, one; the same act satisfies both love and hate.

Heyst's second involvement is the rescue of a man who
becomes a substitute father, approaching the original in the
capacity for dominance. Heyst lends the distressed Captain
Morrison the amount of a small fine to save Morrison's brig
from seizure. The recipient promises repayment; but since
his extreme altruism as an island trader leaves him nothing
with which to repay, he insists on annexing Heyst as a
lodger and a partner in his newly formed Tropical Belt Coal
Company. The Samaritan, to stifle the emotions of what
he considers a "harrowing scene" (V, 19) of gratitude,
reluctantly agrees. A hostile impulse toward Morrison
springs from the inevitable conflict of substitute and
actual fathers. As Janet Butler Haugaard has pointed out,
Heyst, Jr., has probably desired the death of the man by
whom his "scornful temperament" was "beguiled into action,"
in violation of Heyst, Sr.'s teaching (V, 65). The son's
resentment of the guilt of apostasy appears in his caustic
comment on a partner obsessed with making "everybody's
fortune" from "black diamonds" (V, 3, 202).

> His mind was like a white-walled, pure chamber,
> furnished with, say, six straw-bottomed chairs,
> and he was always placing and displacing them
> in various combinations. But they were always
> the same chairs. He was extremely easy to live
> with; but then he got hold of this coal idea--
> or, rather, the idea got hold of him. It
> entered into that scantily furnished chamber of
> which I have just spoken, and sat on all the
> chairs. (V, 202)[12]

When Morrison, who has gone back to England to push his
idea, dies of a bad cold in a wet Dorsetshire summer, the
junior partner's sense of guilt suggests the Freudian
principle that the omniscient internal authority of the
superego equates a death wish with an act of murder.[13]

But although a friend suggestively labels the defunct
coal scheme "dead as Julius Caesar" (V, 28), Morrison's
demise is in fact a climatic accident, part of that external
malevolence critics have marked in Conrad's later fiction.
Heyst's guilt is not that of Decoud, another negator drawn
into action by the dreams of an older man. Decoud, by

rejecting Avellanos's political program as chimerical, substituting his own, and superseding his godfather in councils of state, seems actually to have brought about the surrogate father's death; at least in Antonia's opinion, her father has been killed by her lover's separatist creation (N, 238-39). Heyst, on the other hand, though he regards Morrison's coal scheme as a bubble, considers it a game he must, out of loyalty, play energetically; unlike his predecessor, he acts within the limits set by the father.

If Decoud offers one useful point of comparison with Heyst, the Marlow of Heart of Darkness provides another. The son of a writer in Victory's manifest content, a philosopher whose imaginative style reveals some delving in the unconscious--". . . men love their captivity. To the unknown force of negation they prefer the miserably tumbled bed of their servitude" (V, 220)--Heyst might have super- seded this father artistically, as Marlow did Kurtz. Coal, the raw material dug from the earth in Victory, has for Joseph Dobrinsky the same import as fossil ivory in Heart of Darkness: "the buried private ore" on which art depends.[14] Conrad refers in the first sentence of Victory to "a very close chemical relation between coal and diamonds." Both are carbon; the second--organized into a crystalline system, cut, and polished--is analogous to the finished product of the creative process. But Heyst in manifest content is no artist; of a literary parent he can only say, "I am he, all but the genius" (V, 199). His self-abasement, like the harlequin's before Kurtz--"I have no great thoughts" (HD, 132)--registers the force of an overpowering father. In Conrad's earlier and bolder fiction, however, a Marlow could rise up to ridicule the model of filial servitude: "Sometimes I ask myself whether I had ever really seen him--whether it was possible to meet such a phenomenon!" (HD, 140). In Victory, by contrast, the hero is a son who submits, and who never questions the existence of a duty to do so.

Despite the restricted nature of his involvement in life, Heyst's existence becomes structured on a conflict of impulses; no compromise is possible. Secluding himself on the island of Samburan amid the ruins of the coal venture, he reincarnates his parent by importing the philosopher's books, furniture, and portrait from London; ". . . there is a soul in things" (V, 176). In the religious vocabulary that deifies the elder Heyst, these objects become "relics" before which the son is a "remorseful apostate" (V, 177). In the words of Schomberg, a malicious hotelkeeper of Sourabaya, after the death of Morrison he has turned "her- mit from shame" (V, 31). But Heyst lacks the "hermit's

vocation"; on an errand in town while Schomberg's orchestra
murders silence, he feels "sudden pity" for a hopeless girl
musician--like Morrison, "harassed, dejected, lonely" (V,
31, 70, 72).   This second rescue impulse, however, derives
partly from the sexual attraction of Lena or Alma or
Magdalen: "He looked at her anxiously, as no man ever looks
at another man; and he positively forgot where he was" (V,
71).

In the rescue of Lena Heyst not only disobeys his
father's edict of disengagement but, by Freudian theory,
indulges his Oedipal longing for a dead mother.   In a
passage previously cited for the Bob Stanton episode of Lord
Jim, Freud expatiated on the erotic significance of rescuing
a woman.   From the son's point of view, he repays his mother
for the gift of life by giving her another life; he "shows
his gratitude by wishing to have by his mother a son who is
like himself: in other words, in the rescue-phantasy he is
completely identifying himself with his father.   All his
instincts . . . find satisfaction in the single wish to be
his own father."[15]   In general, the fantasy of saving a
woman is said to gratify an Oedipal wish; in particular,
Lena conforms to the kind of mother figure described in
Freud's "A Special Type of Choice of Object Made by Men."
The first condition for this surprising maternal substitute
is the need for a third party injured by the liaison; to
be attractive, the woman must seem to belong to someone
else.[16]   In Victory Lena is claimed by two married and
bearded Germans, Zangiacomo and Schomberg--the first an
"artist"-pimp, perhaps the shadow or id of the once
respectable hotel proprietor.   Lena also meets Freud's
second condition, which is, roughly, "love for a pros-
titute"[17]; the woman's fidelity is problematical.
Schomberg characterizes Lena by a single "infamous" word;
she herself tells Heyst, "I am not what they call a good
girl"; and he reflects, at their first meeting, on the
potential deception in her smile (V, 47, 198).   But jealousy
is essential to Freud's special choice.   The woman must
convince the man that she needs him, "that without him she
would lose all moral control" and sink accordingly.   "He
rescues her, therefore, by not giving her up."[18]   In
Victory the unprotected Lena--whose mother abandoned the
family and whose father lodges in a home for incurables--
expresses a fear of Schomberg's advances: ". . . it isn't
easy to stand up for yourself when you feel there's nothing
and nobody at your back.   There's nothing so lonely in the
world as a girl who has got to look after herself" (V, 85).
"Don't you throw me over now," she warns Heyst.   "I should
have to live, to be sure, because I'd be afraid to kill

myself; but you would have done a thousand times worse than killing a body" (V, 86). Heyst, however, meets the two conditions set by Freud for the lover of such a woman: fidelity and the desire to rescue and redeem.[19] He is Christ (the name rhymes with his surname) to a Magdalen—one of the girl's actual names.

Freud explained the otherwise puzzling features of his special object choice as derivatives of the infant's fixation of love on the mother.[20] The "injured third party" is, of course, the father; the "loose" character of the woman is requisite to the son's realization of a fantasy of possessing the mother.[21] Heyst's opponents in this undertaking are his actual father and two living men (or two aspects of one man) who assert the sexual prerogative of the Conradian parent. A fight between Schomberg and Zangiacomo over the Swede's appropriation of Lena ends in their joint pursuit of the couple: ". . . they seemed quite ready to fall upon . . . Heyst . . . and kill him on the quay" (V, 49). This convergence of paternal figures fails of its purpose, but a later coalition sparked by Schomberg succeeds. He never forgives Heyst for the conquest of Lena, who embodied to a forty-five-year-old man a promise of rejuvenation. To Schomberg, "the girl so . . . basely decoyed away would have inspired him to success in a new start" (V, 96). The sexual grudge is added to a commercial one: Schomberg, the proprietor of a European table d'hote, a self-styled "benefactor" (V, 194) of white men in the tropics, has failed to receive from Heyst the patronage he deemed his due. When three brigands invade his hotel, Schomberg, to gain release and revenge, diverts these "envoys of the outer world" (V, 329) to Samburan with the lie that Heyst is worth plundering.

Schomberg behaves like an avenging avatar of the elder Heyst, whose "living word" (V, 196) the son affronts with Lena. Axel has installed the girl in his Samburan bungalow, the father's very temple, under the father's portrait, which Donald Dike has correctly perceived as an icon.[22] "There must be a lot of the original Adam in me, after all" (V, 173), muses the culprit. Adam's sin of sexual disobedience, for which God condemned him to death, is also Heyst's against a godlike father. To the philosopher, of all forms of action, the sexual was the most reprehensible; it brings "out of the lightless void the shoals of unnumbered generations" (V, 174), new victims of that cheat which is life.

After an unsatisfactory tryst with Lena in the jungle, the wayward son goes back to the bungalow to consult one of his father's books on the deceptions of love. He

read, shrinking into himself, composing his
face as if under the author's eye, with a
vivid consciousness of the portrait . . .
above his head; a wonderful presence in its
heavy frame on the flimsy wall of mats,
looking exiled and at home, out of place
and masterful, in the painted immobility
of profile.
    And Heyst, the son, read: "Of the
stratagems of life the most cruel is the
consolation of love--the most subtle, too;
for the desire is the bed of dreams."
    . . . He abandoned himself to the
half-belief that something of his father
dwelt yet on earth--a ghostly voice,
audible to the ear of his own flesh and
blood. (V, 218-19)

Almost immediately the gambler Jones arrives as a second
avatar of that injured party. A gentleman and a rover,
Jones mirrors his unwilling host. But the intruder who
calls himself "retribution" (V, 379) also doubles for the
hero's father. Each opposes the liaison of Heyst and Lena:
Heyst, Sr., forbade sexuality; the woman-hating Jones is a
homosexual. Each is dead, Heyst, Sr., in actuality, the
ailing Jones as a "skeleton" who is "travelling west" (V,
100, 390). Each has rejected life: Jones is a bored seeker
of "new impressions" for whom "nothing's worth while,
nothing's good enough," and the father has evolved a
philosophy of "universal nothingness" (V, 150, 219, 385).
Each resembles Satan as a rebel against law and society.
The philosopher's claim of "absolute moral and intellectual
liberty" matches Jones's claim of self-dependence "as if the
world were still one great, wild jungle without law" (V, 91,
113).[23] In a paraphrase of Job 1:7, in which the devil
comes "from going to and fro in the earth, and from walking
up and down in it," Jones's Satanic identification becomes
explicit:

Having been ejected, he said, from his proper
social sphere because he had refused to conform
to certain usual conventions, he was a rebel
now, and was coming and going up and down the
earth. . . . I told him that I had heard that
sort of story about somebody else before.
. . . Then he said:
    "As to me, I am no blacker than the
gentleman you are thinking of, and I have
neither more nor less determination." (V,

317-18)

But Jones, like the elder Heyst, is also a god figure. Both the philosopher and the gambler display the god-devil ambivalence that Freud described in "A Seventeenth-Century Demonological Neurosis," and that Conrad attributed to his prototypical father, the Lingard of the early Malaysian novels, the man of "infernal charity" (OI, 161). Jones's arrival at Samburan conforms to Polynesian myths of the advent of "gods" as well as "demons" (V, 228). According to Wilfred Dowden, Jones stating his credentials--"I am he who is" (V, 317)--equates himself with the god of Exodus 3:14, who spoke from the burning bush: "And God said unto Moses, I AM THAT I AM."[24]

This deity promised to smite the ungodly; Lena, appropriately, has awaited "retribution from an angry Heaven" (V, 354) for her sin of living with Heyst, unmarried, of her own free will. Conceiving herself as Eve, she accepts blame for the loss of their paradise (if it could be called that) on Samburan: "Woman is the tempter" (V, 354). Heaven's wrath is plain to her in the sky of their last evening--black clouds broken by "a crimson crack like an open wound" (V, 355). Since Jones was first sighted from the island--"Sail ho!" (V, 190)--her mind has dwelt upon the deluge. Unlike another guilty pair, Willems and Aïssa, Heyst and Lena escape inundation, but their deaths follow a cosmic rebuke: ". . . the thunder growled distantly with angry modulations of its tremendous voice, while the world outside shuddered incessantly around the dead stillness of the room where the framed profile of Heyst's father looked severely into space" (V, 401). The father's position at the eye of this storm makes him appear its controller and voice. As in the apotheosis of Lingard at the climax of An Outcast of the Islands, the moral dictates of religion become conflated with the paternal sexual prerogative. In Victory, in addition, the demand for abstinence reflects the elder Heyst's philosophy of disengagement. But all three prohibitions work to the same end: the son is punished by death for sexuality.

The father-Jones similarity aggravates Heyst's ordinary paralysis, his "complete silence of unused faculties" (V, 390). Even when he has the chance to overpower Jones, to protect himself and Lena, he remains inert, in deference to his father's demand for passivity.

. . . by simply shouldering Mr. Jones, he could have thrown him down and put himself by a couple of leaps, beyond the certain aim of the revolver; but he did not even think of

that. His very will seemed dead of weariness.
He moved automatically, his head low, like a
prisoner captured by the evil power of a
masquerading skeleton out of a grave. ($\underline{V}$, 390)

Heyst is also inhibited by his doubts of Lena, whom he
does not understand and who does not understand him. With
a revolver in his back he finds her "tenderly" ($\underline{V}$, 391)
bending over a groveling worshipper--Jones's "secretary"
Ricardo, a foot fetishist. Whatever her attraction to this
feral admirer, whose attempted rape she has kept secret, she
is conscious only of a desire to save Heyst, by disarming
or castrating Jones's follower; Ricardo she understands
well enough to coax his knife away from him. In a Freudian
interpretation, Heyst's impulse to rescue her in Sourabaya
was symbolic of his wish to give her a child, himself; at
the end of the novel her complementary desire, in seeking to
rescue him from the invaders of Samburan, is to bear him.
The meaning of the rescue fantasy depends on the sex of its
author: in a man it signifies "making a child, i.e. causing
it to be born," in a woman "giving birth oneself to a
child."[25] Conrad's very language implies maternity in
Lena: Heyst's "danger brought a sensation of warmth to
her breast. She felt something stir in there, something
profound, like a new sort of life" ($\underline{V}$, 303). But Heyst,
knowing nothing of her vague plan for his salvation, can
only gape at her apparent infidelity. Candle flames "sear
his very brain with the radiation of infernal heat" ($\underline{V}$,
392). When Jones, intent on shooting his faithless
paramour, commands, "Stoop a little" ($\underline{V}$, 393), a transfixed
Heyst fails to obey. The bullet fired over his shoulder
grazes Ricardo on the floor but fatally wounds Lena.

Although a man's rescue of a woman signifies, in
psychoanalytic terms, an Oedipal wish, and although Lena
meets Freud's specifications for a mother substitute, Heyst
has limited her maternal role by choosing a sexual object of
lower social class. Until he runs off with the daughter of
a music hall performer, he has never been linked with any
woman. The sudden gravitation of a leisured Swedish baron
to a girl reared in poverty, "almost a child of the streets"
($\underline{V}$, 78), suggests Freud's theory in "On the Universal
Tendency to Debasement on the Sphere of Love": a disunion of
love and desire, originating in the need to avoid incest,
characterizes civilized man. To ensure "a completely normal
attitude in love," wrote Freud, two currents of feeling must
unite: "the affectionate and the sensual." But in only "a
very few educated people" are the two strains duly fused in
one object; the man "almost always feels his respect for the

woman acting as a restriction on his sexual activity, and only develops full potency when he is with a debased sexual object."[26] In Freud's analysis, the tender feelings are reserved for the erotic objects of childhood, chiefly the mother, and for later women who resemble them. Toward these "higher" objects, however, any sensual attraction raises the specter of incest.[27]

Heyst might have placed either of two interpretations on Lena's seeming infidelity with Ricardo. She could have become for him the immoral mother of "A Special Type of Choice of Object Made by Men," who acquires her full value to the lover only by rousing his jealousy; or she could be the degraded figure that Jones sees when he whispers to Heyst of the "mud souls" and "mud bodies" of the "vile populace" (V, 392). Heyst's choice from these alternatives appears in his response to Lena's sacrifice and her "victory" in gaining possession of Ricardo's knife (a token triumph, since the invaders have brought an "armoury" of other weapons--V, 402). Lena had expected that after "a great exaltation of love and self-sacrifice, which is woman's sublime faculty," happiness "would burst on her like a torrent, flinging at her feet the man whom she loved" (V, 317, 353). Dying, she complains to Heyst:

> "Oh, my beloved . . . I've saved you! Why don't you take me into your arms and carry me out of this lonely place?"
>   Heyst bent low over her, cursing his fastidious soul, which even at that moment kept the true cry of love from his lips in its infernal mistrust of all life. He dared not touch her. (V, 406)

His final attitude implies the rejection of a dangerous mother imago, one which would unite tenderness and sensuality, in favor of a lower object appealing to sensuality alone--that is, he comes off closer to "On the Universal Tendency to Debasement in the Sphere of Love" than to "A Special Type of Choice of Object." Like D. H. Lawrence's Paul Morel, he retains an inner split.[28] In vain Lena has urged Heyst, "You should try to love me!" (V, 221). Virtually his last words, ". . . woe to the man whose heart has not learned while young to hope, to love--and to put its trust in life" (V, 410), may reflect not so much an experience of love as a statement of his own case, in which this quality is absent or deficient. If, as Menninger has suggested, the method of suicide is erotically significant,[29] Heyst's choice of fire might indicate a yearning for the emotional warmth he has repressed or lacked.

His presumed suicide can be fully explained in terms of
his own psychology. The wish to kill might be directed to
the father, the man "responsible for what my existence
is" (V, 195)--a parent whose standard of disengagement
is cruelly high, and yet incorporated into the son's
conscience, as Apollo's chimera of rebellion had been
incorporated into Conrad's. A sense of guilt is inevitable.
As a sexual rebel the younger Heyst is Adam; in attempting
and failing to realize the father's ideal he was a Christlike victim; finding himself committed to Lena, he "turned
on his back, flung his arms crosswise on the broad, hard
bed" (V, 90) of the tropics. Like Kayerts and Decoud, he
is a son-sufferer, though not a redeemer. In the wish to
be killed, for failure to live up to a paternal ideal, his
submission might resemble Jeffrey Berman's account of Lord
Jim's capitulation to Doramin: "A Kafkaesque yielding to
the oedipal father in which the son has already passed the
judgment of death upon himself even before the authoritarian
father has a chance to execute the sentence."[30] To the
guilt of apostasy might be added the onus of parricidal
wishes and that of his responsibility, real or imaginary,
for the fates of Morrison and Lena. After the death of
Morrison, Heyst admits to a "disgust" at himself; after
Lena's death, Captain Davidson, probably the last to see him
alive, remarks, "I suppose he couldn't stand his thoughts
before her dead body--and fire purifies everything" (V, 330,
410). A further result of the loss of Lena, the last person
in life to interest him, might be his wish to die. The
faith of his father, that life cheats, has been vindicated
--perhaps because he could abide neither detachment nor
involvement. As the narrator remarks, ". . . incompleteness
of any sort leads to trouble" (V, 31).

Of three European sons in Victory, Heyst, Jones, and
Ricardo, none survives the end of the novel. In a hasty
denouement, Conrad dispatches the latter two as a putative
murderer and suicide. In Captain Davidson's reconstruction,
Jones came on the unfaithful Ricardo and "shot him neatly
through the heart" (V, 411). Davidson speculates that Jones
next went down to the wharf to look for his boat and Pedro,
the marauding trio's "brute force" (V, 329), but found
neither. Isolated, marooned, Jones "tumbled into the water
by accident--or perhaps not by accident. . . . Who knows?
. . . I could see him huddled up on the bottom between two
piles, like a heap of bones in a blue silk bag, with only
the head and the feet sticking out" (V, 411).

Conrad's summary justice suggests the operation of a
retributive mechanism beyond artistry. Of the three dead

sons, Heyst and Ricardo were involved with a woman; Jones
and Ricardo were social rebels. The homosexual gentleman
of the latter pair, an "outcast of his vices," lived by
gambling, "mostly fair" (V, 137, 269). His follower
rejected employment for wages as

> worse than slavery. You don't expect a slave
> that's bought for money to be grateful. And if
> you sell your work--what is it but selling your
> own self? You've got so many days to live and
> you sell them one after another. . . . Who can
> pay me enough for my life? (V, 145)

In brief, each of the three combined some form of self-
assertion with membership in Conrad's own race. Victory
reaffirms an authorial double standard, dating from the
creation of Dain Maroola in Almayer's Folly, by which
the nonwhite youth, remote from Conrad, is privileged.
The surviving son of Victory, heir to Heyst's island of
Samburan, is his Chinese servant Wang. Once a rootless man
like Heyst, Wang married an Alfuro woman of the island and
assumed leadership of her village. Under pressure of the
invasion by Jones and company, he steals Heyst's revolver,
deserts him, refuses him and Lena sanctuary in the village,
murders the anthropoid Pedro, and sets him adrift in Jones's
boat--all in "obedience to his instincts" (V, 181), and all
with Conrad's approval or indifference, for no penalty is
ever imposed on this self-seeker from another race. Like
prior works, Victory implies that Conrad carried a burden of
guilt not transferable to sons remote from himself.

The conditions of life for European sons in his late
fiction are further probed in the short novel The Shadow-
Line, which might be compared with "The Secret Sharer," an
earlier account of ordeal and maturation in a first command.
Both narrating captains have made the Conradian renunciation
of women. But in The Shadow-Line an insecure youth seems to
bargain for survival by an explicit promise of celibacy. An
abundance of sexually charged language has made it clear
that his only woman is the ship.

> A ship! My ship! She was mine, more
> absolutely mine for possession and care
> than anything in the world; an object of
> responsibility and devotion. She was there
> waiting for me, spellbound, unable to move,
> to live, to get out into the world (till I
> came), like an enchanted princess. . . .
> A sudden passion of anxious impatience
> rushed through my veins and gave me such a

> sense of the intensity of existence as I have
> never felt before or since. I discovered how
> much of a seaman I was, in heart, in mind, and,
> as it were, physically--a man exclusively of
> sea and ships; the sea the only world that
> counted, and the ships the test of manliness,
> of temperament, of courage and fidelity--and
> of love. (SL, 40)

The suggestion of the chief mate Burns that the captain
may one day be a husband and father is almost indignantly
rebuffed: "As to the wife-and-child (some day) argument it
had no force. It sounded merely bizarre" (SL, 70).

An undeclared love object is probably the ship's cook
Ransome, that "priceless man" and "consummate seaman," with
"soul as firm as the muscles of his body" (SL, 112, 126).
Despite his weak heart, he proves indispensable through a
Bangkok-to-Singapore passage bedeviled with fever and calms.
This "intelligent, serene" sailor possesses a "well-
proportioned figure," a "soft, cultivated voice," a
"pleasant, quiet gaze," and movements full of "grace" (SL,
67, 73, 87, 92, 94). As Robert Hodges has said, "No other
male in all of Conrad's prose is described in such a loving,
almost caressing fashion."[31] In the intimacy of two
strangers who feel an instant and "mysterious communication"
(SS, 99), "The Secret Sharer" has overtones of a similar
tie--compatible with an absence of women at sea, and with
Freud's theory that homosexuality may represent a "retiring
in favour of someone else," e.g., the father to whom women
might be thought to belong.[32]

Inversion becomes more likely if, as Jule Nydes has
asserted, this sexual choice represents a regression from,
and a defense against, parricidal wishes. A regression to
homosexuality serves "to appease the father figure and to
insure safety from retaliation."[33] The need for such a
defense still exists in Conrad's late fiction, although
a notable distinction between "The Secret Sharer" and
The Shadow-Line can be made in terms of audacity. The
narrator of the short story doubles for the aggressive mate
Leggatt, a fugitive killer who tried to wrest command from a
living captain; the narrator of the novel strives only to
achieve the lawful replacement of a dead captain--one who
was, moreover, in his latter days, mad, a would-be "Flying
Dutchman in the China Sea" (SL, 94). To supersede a
betrayer of nautical tradition is permissible, even a duty.
The youth's precursor

> spent most of his time day or night playing
> the violin. . . .

> . . . this stern, grim, wind-tanned, rough,
> sea-salted, taciturn sailor of sixty-five was
> not only an artist, but a lover as well. In
> Haiphong, when they got there after a course of
> most unprofitable peregrinations (during which
> the ship was nearly lost twice), he got himself
> . . . "mixed up" with some woman. . . .
>   . . . A professional sorceress from the
> slums. (SL, 58-59)

On his return to the ship he appears to the mate Burns to
be dying, and is duly apprised of the fact. "If I had my
wish," he retorts, "neither the ship nor any of you would
ever reach a port" (SL, 61). In Burns's account, "He meant
to have gone wandering about the world till he lost her with
all hands" (SL, 62).

Unexceptionable as a replacement, the narrator is
further distanced from Oedipal rivalry by his failure to
seek a command; instead, Captain Giles, a "benevolent" (SL,
17) old meddler of Singapore, secured one for a youth on the
point of deserting the sea. Life as mate of a steamship had
lost its "glamour," had ceased to provide the "special
intensity of existence" he sought (SL, 5, 83). Kent, his
captain, conferred with Giles on a remedy; this paternal
convergence was augmented by Captain Ellis, the Harbour
Master, whose nearly last official act before retirement was
to hand the narrator his appointment.

In the circumstances, father-son rivalry would seem a
freak of the narrator's imagination. Even so, he reveals a
keen animosity to his busy elders. His principal target is
the chattery Giles, whose undoubted complacency is made
to epitomize the "menace of emptiness" in life, or the
"universal hollow conceit"; "everything was stupid and
overrated, even as [the famous] Captain Giles was" (SL, 23).
The choleric Ellis is seen as a self-appointed "divine
(pagan) emanation, the deputy-Neptune for the circumambient
seas" (SL, 29-30), with a pen for a trident. The captain
of the Melita, who ferries the new captain to his ship, is
found guilty of "jealous indignation" at his advancement,
and of poking "sly fun . . . in the manner some nasty,
cynical old men assume towards the dreams . . . of youth"
(SL, 47). The Chief Steward of the Sailors' Home, who
attempted to divert the vacant command to a guest with an
unpaid bill, was judged not "very fit to live" (SL, 39).
The steward's feeble ruse, easily set aside by Giles, evokes
echoes of Shakespearean regicide: ". . . as soon as I had
convinced myself that this stale, unprofitable world of my
discontent contained such a thing as a command to be seized,
I recovered my powers of locomotion" (SL, 28).[34]

In spite of the lack of any real contest, the narrator
suffers Oedipal guilt as intensely as if he had actively
striven with the father. As in Heyst on the death of
Morrison, the superego treats the parricidal wish as
tantamount to the deed. Guilt seems to surface in the
narrator's inordinate reaction to the loss of the ship's
quinine, which the dead captain apparently sold off in
Haiphong for a profit. "The seed of everlasting remorse was
sown in my breast"; "no confessed criminal had ever been so
oppressed by his sense of guilt" (SL, 95, 96). Objectively
the narrator's fault is limited to his faith in the kindly
legation doctor who inspected the ship's medicine chest in
Bangkok and found nothing to indicate the replacement of the
drug by a worthless powder. "Nothing should ever be taken
for granted" (SL, 95), laments a captain at sea without
quinine. Yet he excuses the doctor for having done exactly
that: "The fittings were in order and the medicine chest is
an officially arranged affair. There was nothing really to
arouse the slightest suspicion" (SL, 95). The application
of a rigorous standard to himself alone may signal the
existence of a repressed and displaced affect, as defined
by Freud: an affect seemingly "too great for the occasion" belongs to "some other content, which is unknown
(unconscious)."[35] Here the content appears to be a
parricidal wish accidentally gratified when the narrator
becomes "king in his country," a youth "brought there
to rule by an agency as remote from the people and as
inscrutable almost to them as the Grace of God" (SL, 62).

In The End of the Tether the paranoiac engineer Massy,
on winning a lottery prize that enabled him to buy a ship,
"swaggered and strutted . . . talking at the top of his
voice, and trembling like a leaf all the while" (ET,
205). In The Shadow-Line, the new captain responds to his
accession with a similar foreboding: "Seizing eagerly upon
the elation of the first command thrown into my lap, by the
agency of Captain Giles, I had yet an uneasy feeling that
such luck as this has got perhaps to be paid for in some
way" (SL, 83). The payment comes at sea, in delusions of
persecution. For Jule Nydes, who placed the origin of
paranoia in Oedipal conflict, the sufferer dreads "retaliation from the introjected paternal superego, which in
turn is projected onto surrogates."[36] In The Shadow-Line,
although there is no statement of a causal relationship,
the onset of delusion in two men is preceded by filial
rebellion. In the reduced assertiveness of the later
fiction, Burns, an overage mate who wanted the command,
never actually assumed it while a madman lived; but he
claims to have frightened him into rescinding an order to

proceed to Hong Kong in the monsoon season: "I believe I am the only man who ever stood up to him. . . . He thought I was going to twist his neck" (SL, 94). Burns later in a wasting fever combats the phantom of "the old dodging Devil" (SL, 119) whom he imagines lying in wait for the ship in a grave at latitude 8° 20' North. His superstition that the dead captain retains power over his former command communicates itself to the narrator, who can speak of a becalmed and fever-ridden ship as subject to an "evil spell," or a "purposeful malevolence" in violation of the "secular experience of seamen" (SL, 83, 87).

One wonders why the narrator accepts the sea as the test of manhood—of having crossed the shadow-line—and why he submits to Giles. A youth who once made up his mind to leave nautical drudgery—which Conrad sometimes eulogizes as "the true peace of God" (NN, 31) or "the test, the trial of life" (Y, 12) and sometimes stigmatizes as "ce métier de chien" (PR, 122)—has allowed Giles to return him to it. A motive may have been supplied by Jule Nydes, who surmised that both the paranoid and the masochist are motivated by unresolved Oedipal conflict, and assuage their guilt, at least temporarily, by incurring punishment.[37] For Nydes, these two character structures are related, as two possible strategies in a "futile and conflicted struggle for control with an 'omnipotent will.'"[38] But a distinction can be made between them: the masochist appears to submit, i.e., "to renounce 'power' for the sake of 'love,'" and the paranoid, demanding submission, appears "to renounce 'love' for the sake of 'power.'"[39] Not as far apart as they might seem, the "power" depends on the willingness of others to respond; and the "love" is manipulative, a means of insuring that someone else's strength will be used on the masochist's behalf.[40] The ease with which an individual can move between these two ways of confronting authority is noted by Nydes and demonstrated in The Shadow-Line. The narrating captain can speak, in paranoiac fashion, of seizing command and grappling with "supernatural evil" (SL, 85)—a phenomenon denied by Conrad in the Author's Note (SL, ix-x). But the captain's sense of power is contradicted by his masochistic claim of weakness, with its implicit need for love and protection, during the calm: "I always suspected that I might be no good" (SL, 107), he writes in the diary of his first command. He accepts protection from Burns, whose "awful laugh" on deck—a "provoking, mocking peal, with a hair-raising, screeching over-note of defiance"—he credits with having broken the spell of a vicious specter and allowed a saving wind to rise (SL, 119, 125). And the captain achieves punishment not in the paranoid's way, by provocative aggression, but in the masochist's, by submission[41]; he is self-identified with another Conradian Christ. On a motionless ship, when he finds himself just sane enough to command, he resembles "a mad carpenter making a box. Were he ever so convinced that he was King of Jerusalem, the box he would make would be a sane box" (SL, 101).

The concept of life at sea as a necessary punishment may have appeared in Conrad's work as early as The Nigger of the "Narcissus"; in that novel's imprecise rhetoric, a "weary succession of nights and days" is "redeemed at last by the vast silence of pain and labour, by the dumb fear and the dumb courage of men obscure, forgetful, and enduring" (NN, 90). What seems new in The Shadow-Line is the possibility that suffering may be the condition under which Conrad would permit a youthful narrator to take command.

Giles, who has "radiated benevolence" by a "'kind uncle' smile," may have a redemptive aspect, implied by his resemblance to a "church-warden" (SL, 12, 131). His "paternal fist" (SL, 27), which has closed on the narrator, yields an apt symbol of Freudian conscience: "The super-ego retains the character of the father."[42] In Conrad, however, that character remains ever suspect. Giles's interference may work to the narrator's advantage, by providing both a profession and an avenue for the expiation of guilt. But the older man's actual motive for a "mission" (SL, 43) to bestow a command on a stranger is unexplained, even when the narrator asks. Giles, an "expert in . . . intricate navigation" (SL, 12), knew of the calms in the Gulf of Siam. His protégé comes to mistrust both him and one of his analogs, God. In a sea diary kept by the novice captain: "There they are: stars, sun, sea, light, darkness, space, great waters; the formidable Work of the Seven Days, into which mankind seems to have blundered unbidden. Or else decoyed. Even as I have been decoyed into this awful, this death-haunted command" (SL, 97-98).

On his return to Singapore he may gain some insight into Giles's psychology. After a twenty-one-day passage from Bangkok, including seventeen days on deck and the last forty hours without sleep, steering all night, the initiate declares he must be off at dawn with a new crew: "There's no rest for me till she's out in the Indian Ocean and not much of it even then" (SL, 132). Without inquiry into this necessity Giles grunts approval: "That's the way. You'll do" (SL, 132). Unexpectedly he adds, "Precious little rest in life for anybody. Better not think of it" (SL, 132), and departs just as the younger man is beginning for the first time to take an interest in him. A shadow side of the

"insufferably exemplary" (SL, 131) benefactor may be that
legendary waster of lives, the Flying Dutchman, or the
homicidal violin captain. Conrad neglects to explain
whether Giles's attitude is part of the maritime code, an
evasion of it, or an extension of its severities. As in
Lord Jim, the code itself may be questioned. In either
case, Giles, a surrogate parent who at first seemed close to
Erik Erikson's ideal, by which an older generation fulfills
itself in the gift of protective assistance to a younger
one,[43] ends by raising a doubt--not to be dispelled by his
remark, ". . . a man should stand up . . . to his conscience" (SL, 131-32); one wonders what scruples Giles
may have combated in his entrapment of a novice. The
narrator's animosity toward this mentor, which at the
beginning of the novel may have appeared gratuitous or
disproportionate, was possibly justified.

A conjectural double for Giles, in ambivalence toward
youth, is Conrad himself in the role of Laius to his elder
son, stationed on the Western Front in the first World War.
His wife appears to have read correctly the intent of the
dedication of the novel of 1917: "To Borys and all others
who like himself have crossed in early youth the shadow-line
of their generation." To Jessie Conrad, it sounded as if
Borys were dead, but Conrad refused to alter it[44]; and he
insisted, with all the force of an unacknowledged desire,
that his son had indeed been killed in action; the father
"just knew it to be so--he had a presentiment."[45] A
parallel with Freud's wish-fulfilling dream of a son's
having been wounded at the front seems likely. In a rare
admission of paternal hostility, Freud generalized his own
reaction as "the envy which is felt for the young by those
who have grown old, but which they believe they have
completely stifled."[46] Perhaps not by coincidence,
Borys's survival was followed by a long estrangement between
father and son, lasting nearly to Conrad's death in 1924.
Meyer speculates that the existence of Borys was tolerable
to Conrad only so long as he had his offspring totally
subjugated.[47] But this thralldom waned with Borys's
army service and virtually ended in 1919 with the youth's
twenty-first birthday--the celebration for which Conrad
declined to attend.[48]

Yet for him the role of Laius could not have wholly
replaced that of Oedipus. His paternal dedication to The
Shadow-Line should not obscure his self-identification, in
the novel he labeled "personal experience" (SL, xi), with
the son who seeks maturity--the youth anxiously assuming
command, anxiously becoming a writer. The narrator
apologizes for having kept a diary during the voyage:

I don't remember how it came about or how the
pocket-book and the pencil came into my hands.
It's inconceivable that I should have looked
for them on purpose. . . .
        . . . I took to that sort of thing in
circumstances in which I did not expect,
in colloquial phrase, "to come out of it."
Neither could I expect the record to outlast
me. This shows that it was purely a personal
need for intimate relief and not a call of
egotism. (SL, 106)

A similar claim of inadvertence, and denial of egotism,
appear in A Personal Record (1912) to excuse the creation of
Conrad's first novel, Almayer's Folly.

The conception of a planned book was entirely
outside my mental range when I sat down to
write; the ambition of being an author had
never turned up amongst these gracious
imaginary existences one creates fondly for
oneself. (PR, 68)

Never had Rubicon been more blindly forded.
(PR, 69)

It was not the outcome of a need--the famous
need of self-expression which artists find in
their search for motives. The necessity which
impelled me was a . . . masked and unaccount-
able phenomenon. (PR, 68)

According to Zdzisław Najder, the adolescent Conrad "used to
say that he was very talented and planned to become a great
writer."[49] The later Conrad buried a boast allying him
with Marlow in Heart of Darkness: ". . . I have a voice,
too, and for good or evil mine is the speech that cannot be
silenced" (HD, 97).
        The Rover, Conrad's last completed novel, has been
called his Tempest[50]--his act of reconciliation. In
Peyrol, the hero, he is often said to have sentimental-
ized his own youthful apostasy. For Daniel Schwarz, his
fantasies of "a significant political act," "an heroic
return home" to Poland, "a significant death" are realized
in Peyrol.[51] Accused, like Conrad, of desertion, an exile
or prodigal son at the end of life demonstrates his patriotism by dying for France. But in his relationships with
others in the novel, the serenely authoritarian seaman

is a father figure--like the Emperor Napoleon, a touchstone
for the values of paternalism. If Conrad in a literary
testament sought to create an ideal son, he apparently also
intended an ideal father, puissant, uncomic, benign. An
ex-pirate based partly on the anarchistic, skillful Dominic
Cervoni of Conrad's youth, The Rover--like Lingard, another
Cervoni figure--is a nineteeth-century Ulysses. "On that
sea ruled by the gods of Olympus he might have been a pagan
mariner subject to Jupiter's caprices; but like a defiant
pagan he shook his fist vaguely at space which answered him
by a short and threatening mutter" (R, 237). In the account
of Peyrol's last voyage, Conrad may, as Schwarz says, have
deliberately evoked Tennyson's Ulysses, aged yet "strong in
will/To strive, to seek, to find, and not to yield."[52]
     Having assumed a mission to hoodwink the English who
track the French fleet in the Mediterranean, Peyrol draws an
enemy corvette after his tartane in a fast chase, and dies
in the gunfire his expert maneuvers have provoked. Fake
dispatches planted on the tartane convince Nelson that the
French fleet at Toulon will sail for Egypt instead of the
Atlantic. A minor French triumph, in which the victor dies,
is soon reversed at Trafalgar, in which a victorious Nelson
will die. The novel's epigraph from Spenser, "Sleep after
toyle, port after stormie seas . . . ," could refer to
either hero. In The Rover the English admiral draws a
parallel between himself and the French civilian as
patriots: "I aspire to repose somewhere in the country, in
the midst of fields, out of reach of the sea and . . .
responsibility. . . . But I am like that white-headed man
. . . I will stick to my task till perhaps some shot from
the enemy puts an end to everything" (R, 275-76).
     In Peyrol Conrad has labored to create a father figure
whose "mystery and power," which generate "awe," will be
seen to work in a beneficent manner; the novel abounds in
tributes to a reformed "skimmer of the seas" (R, 43, 218,
247). A member of the notorious "Brotherhood of the Coast,"
after nearly fifty years of "lawful and lawless sea-life,"
including desertion of both the royalist and the republican navies and the theft of a fortune in coins, enjoys a
"calmness of rectitude" and "the sleep of the just" (R, 4,
5, 8, 14). Conrad's usually acute moral sensitivity has
been blunted; unlike Nostromo's silver ingots, Peyrol's
treasure imposes no burden on the expropriator's conscience.
On the contrary, Jacobin gold is made to seem his just
reward for having abstained from the French revolution. As
Lt. Réal reflects in the novel: "The sincere lawlessness of
the ex-Brother of the Coast was refreshing. That one was
neither a hypocrite nor a fool. When he robbed or killed it

was not in the name of the sacred revolutionary principles
or for the love of humanity" (R, 209).

Peyrol scorns the movement by which "everything was
going to be changed. Everybody was going to tie up his dog
with a string of sausages for the sake of principles" (R,
95). Conrad's implication is that a cosmopolite like
his rover is proof against fixed ideas.[53] To give the
impression of a freer mind, he distanced Peyrol from
words. The seaman's patriotism, for example, is based on
an identification with individuals, not on abstractions.

> . . . any woman, lean and old enough, might have
> been his mother; he might have been any French-
> man of them all, even one of those he pitied,
> even one of those he despised. He felt the grip
> of his origins from the crown of his head to the
> soles of his feet. (R, 98)

Peyrol was probably designed as a corrective to a Conradian
line of obsessed father figures, including General T-- with
fidelity, Captain Beard with duty, Viola with liberty,
Avellanos with political purity, and Corbelàn with the
sacred rights of the church. In The Rover itself Peyrol
offsets a village abbé haunted by sin and, at the other end
of the religious and political spectrum, a somewhat younger
Scevola Bron bent on shedding blood for liberty, equality,
and fraternity. All these zealots serve, as did Conrad's
father, abstraction. They approximate a type of personality
discussed by Angus Fletcher, who, using Aeneas as his model,
links heroism to language and both to compulsion. The
compulsive, possessed by an idea over which he has no
control, is "always determined to get to some goal, to reach
home, to reach the Celestial City." He is characteristi-
cally aggressive, but contrives to make his hostility serve
the "'higher ends' of a cultural dream." Both his strengths
and his weaknesses derive from a kind of narrowing that "on
the one hand . . . enables him to work hard and long at single, difficult tasks, but on the other may prevent him from
discovering flexible paths, new short cuts." Perhaps most
important for Conrad, words possess magic for him: "He who
knows a word for a thing, masters the thing."[54]

Peyrol shows his flexibility when the English sailor
Symons, his former protégé in the Brotherhood of the Coast,
discovers the tartane in her hiding place. Peyrol takes him
prisoner but lets him escape with a trumped-up tale--the
tartane is a French courier boat--to pique the necessary
English interest in her last voyage. Loyalty to France has

been reconciled with loyalty to the Brotherhood. But the
most notable instance of Peyrol's adaptability is probably
his stance on religion. Though not an atheist--"I have
heard of and seen more gods than you could ever dream of in
a long night's sleep, in every corner of the earth. . . .
Figures, stones, sticks. There must be something in the
idea" (R, 76)--he is indifferent to dogma. ". . . you were
too hard on yourself" (R, 236), he advises an old woman who
has remained single for her youthful sin of loving a priest.
Priestly in appearance, Peyrol in effect supplants a rigid
abbé, whose sacerdotalism "lay in him like a cold passion"
(R, 148). The church's representative repulses the heroine
Arlette, an orphan of the Terror forced to join the mob that
had butchered her parents. He would deny her the right to
marry; what he considers her complicity in parricide must be
expiated by a withdrawal from the world. From a psychoanalytic standpoint, she may be guilty; in unknowingly shout-
ing the mob's slogans, she may have vented an unconscious
hostility to the dead. But the abbé by pejorative label-
ing has condemned her before he hears her story. Her
Escampobar farm, which eight years after the Terror still
harbors Scevola, signifies to a conservative churchman
"Jacobin," "republican," "impious"; moreover, her black
hair denotes something "provokingly pagan," "Saracen"
(R, 148, 149, 159). The priest exemplifies Fletcher's
description of compulsive thinking as not only abstract but
general, "directed toward systematization and categori-
zation; it is theoretical instead of real."[55] In contrast, Peyrol, struck by Arlette's "brilliance of life"
(R, 174), never questions her right to live.

He also, in a reversal of the Laius stereotype, removes
himself as a possible obstacle to her happiness. In a
virtual suicide he resigns to a surrogate son his claim on
a surrogate daughter. He was Lt. Réal's first friend, the
first to break through the naval officer's "schooled
reserve" (R, 71), which the dangers of the Revolution had
enjoined on another orphan. In an earlier restoration,
"Papa" (R, 174) had initiated Arlette's return to sanity
after the Terror. In a "miracle" the shattered girl learned
to talk again--as Peyrol says bitterly, "to--the old man"
(R, 169). In time she demands he step aside for her
marriage to a younger one. But her fear of his jealousy
triggers a dream in which Réal follows his aristocratic
parents to death because his rival has withheld aid. "She
had seen Réal set upon by a mob of men and women, all
dripping with blood . . . and going down in the midst of a
forest of raised arms brandishing sabres, clubs, knives,
axes" (R, 245-46). In the dream Peyrol appears with his

usual prop, a cudgel, but passes "unseeing and deaf" (R, 246). Reality, however, dissipates Arlette's fear; the claimant whose peace has been destroyed by a love "unexpected like an intruder and cruel like an enemy" (R, 268) abjures both love and life. On a "sudden impulse of scorn, of magnanimity, of a passion weary of itself" (R, 260) he saves Réal for Arlette by preempting the lieutenant's mission in the tartane.

Since his piracies have occurred long ago and far away, in Eastern waters, Conrad evidently meant him to be judged by his actions at the close of the novel. The verdict is one on a variant of paternity, Peyrol having served as a test case for the value of flexibility. The results are mixed. In choosing suicide, to gratify a personal death wish, he unhesitatingly chooses homicide as well; on the tartane he carries to death two other men, who had no choice. One is Scevola, the challenger who, eight years earlier, had effected the murder of Arlette's parents by denouncing them to a revolutionary tribunal. A rabid social parricide, and a personal one in inciting the slaughter of the Escampobar royalists, he remains in the Napoleonic era obsessed with purifying France of royalist and clerical "treachery" (R, 181).[56] Arlette affords him an excuse for bloodletting. Though he has never possessed his supposed wife, at the age of thirty-eight he mulls as a "fixed idea" (R, 187) the murder of a younger challenger, Réal. Scevola's jealousy, which may be a subordinate motive, is expressed in ideological terms. He believes that he would kill "in the cause of virtue and justice," not in a "personal contest"; he would simply rectify a political error: "We patriots held our hand too soon. All the children of the ci-devants and all the children of traitors should have been killed together with their fathers and mothers. . . . They grow up and trample on all the sacred principles. . . . The work of the Terror is undone!" (R, 166, 187).

Peyrol's elimination of Scevola might be taken as an act of purification, since the victim boarded the tartane in the hope of impaling Réal on a pitchfork. But the sacrifice of Michel, the simple-minded "last of men" (R, 82), who had attached himself to Peyrol as crew, is less easily condoned. Herbert Howarth has described the hero's disposal of a follower as the mercy killing of a friend "homeless, destitute, mindless"[57]; Michel after the death of his dog had nothing in life except Peyrol. His professed benefactor, calling him "camarade," tells him after the fatal voyage has commenced, "I could not have left you behind" (R, 263, 266). But Conrad's inveterate mistrust of

the father obtrudes in the statement that since Michel "had
become Peyrol's henchman he had lost the habit of thinking
altogether" (R, 252). He barely divines Peyrol's intent in
bringing the tartane under the guns of the corvette. In
"utter innocence," Michel's ". . . round and generally
staring eyes blinked as if dazzled. He . . . produced from
somewhere in the depths of his being a queer, misty smile
from which Peyrol averted his gaze" (R, 263). Quite
obviously, neither man needs to die; the success of the
French feint requires only that the vessel be captured, not
fired on. But Peyrol has at least two personal motives for
a suicide mission: the desire of a sexagenarian to expire
gloriously--not in a bed "like an old yard dog in his
kennel" (R, 174)--and the loss of Arlette. The first motive
reveals a craving for immortality at any cost. The second
may entail the wish of a suicide for the psychic death of
survivors; Peyrol's generosity to Réal and Arlette is
tempered by the burden his death imposes. Though initially,
in his lack of rigid ideology, more attractive than many
Conradian fathers, he proves not necessarily more humane.
Like all of them, he cannot be trusted.

A signal achievement for Peyrol might to some extent
have redeemed his selfishness. For W. R. Martin this hero,
through his sea victory and his sacrifice to secure the
marriage of a younger couple, becomes the symbolic restorer
of France from the sickness of revolution. Martin has
observed that the illegitimate patriot, who does not know
his true name and who "might have been any Frenchman of them
all" (R, 98), has a generic significance; that Eugene Réal's
surname means royal, or genuine money as distinct from the
paper assignats of the Revolution; that Arlette's father was
named Francois; that her change from a red-and-white striped
skirt to her mother's black-and-white Arlesian garb may
signify a return from revolutionary to conservative values.
Kindled to a vitality that lends even the stiff Réal a
"sense of triumphant life," she is "la belle France" renewed
(R, 207, 260).[58] Conrad, however, with characteristic
doubleness undercuts the symbolism of recovery by treating
Arlette as potentially deadly to Réal. The implications of
Réal's rescue of a distressed woman--Arlette with Scevola
and Peyrol, like Lena with Schomberg and Zangiacomo,
occupies an equivocal position--are parricidal. A guilt-
ridden lover contemplates suicide, feels himself "stabbed
to the heart" at Arlette's mention of their days to come,
and receives the sable figure of her Aunt Catherine as
a "sign from death" (R, 173, 223). Unexpectedly, Conrad
fails to repeat his motif of youthful suicide; instead,
Peyrol dies on Réal's mission. The younger man is then

exposed to survivor guilt, as well as increased Oedipal guilt for a parricidal wish granted.

The marriage of the surrogate son and daughter fails to demonstrate the renewed vitality of a nation (which was, in any case, soon to be defeated in the Napoleonic wars). Réal lives in retirement under the paternal sway of the Emperor, to whom he dutifully hands over Peyrol's hoard of treasure. More significantly, he lives also with the ghost of Peyrol, whose "white-headed, quiet, irresistible personality haunted every corner of the Escampobar fields. . . . they talked of him openly, as though he had come back to live again amongst them" (R, 284). As if paralyzed by a father-rival who has, in reality, never gone away, Réal remains childless. His alter ego is the cripple of the Madrague, rehabilitated as a useful citizen, but yet not a whole man; an absence of legs evokes the castration that afflicts Réal as well. The novel leaves us with a sense of diminution, as at the end of Lear: the elders pass; the young "shall never see so much, nor live so long."[59]

Still, the creation of an older man who would voluntarily resign his claim on a woman was unusual for Conrad; and he continued to experiment with the father-son theme in his final, unfinished novel, Suspense. Here a son becomes the sexual rival of his biological father; Cosmo loves his half sister Adèle, the daughter of Sir Charles Latham. As Cosmo tells her, ". . . when you were married my father could think of nothing for days but you" (S, 88). From this Oedipal extremity, and from the presence of Adèle's middle-aged husband, Count Helion de Montevesso, the hero escapes with a substitute father, the mariner Attilio. Attilio in a haunting glimpse of his own adoptive father, the hermit he met on a voyage to South America, provides an Edenic view of surrogate parenthood. "The wisdom of a great plain as level almost as the sea" (S, 6) becomes incarnate.

> "The evening shadows had closed about me just after I had seen to the west, on the edge of the world as it were, a lion miss his spring on a bounding deer. They went away right into the glow and vanished. It was as though I had dreamed. When I turned round there was the old man behind me no farther away than half the width of this platform. He only smiled at my startled looks. His long silver locks stirred in the breeze. He had been watching me, it seems, from folds of ground and from amongst reed beds for nearly half a day, wondering what I might be at. I had come ashore to wander on the plain. I like to be alone sometimes. My

ship was anchored in a bight of this deserted
coast a good many miles away, too many to walk
back in the dark for a stranger like me. So I
spent the night in that old man's ranch, a hut
of grass and reeds, near a little piece of water
peopled by a multitude of birds. He treated me
as if I had been his son. We talked till dawn
and when the sun rose I did not go back to my
ship. What I had on board of my own was not of
much value, and there was certainly no one there
to address me as 'My son' in that particular
tone--you know what I mean, signore."

    "I don't know--but I think I can guess," was
[Cosmo's] answer. (S, 6)

This vision is Conrad's nearest fictional approach to the
apotheosis of a father figure. The passage may signify that
an ideal father-son relation--possibly the one Attilio and
Cosmo would have had if Conrad had finished--is superior to
any tie with women. Or, if one looks at the setting sun,
the dream may only foreshadow that peace which is death, and
a return to the God in whom Conrad did not believe. Or,
since the renunciation of women is a kind of death, both
meanings may have been intended. In any event, the Oedipal
problem is not solved in any life-giving way.

    At the end of the fragment Cosmo, having left Adèle and
drifted into the service of the exiled Napoleon, has an
experience of darkness and silence like Decoud's in the
Golfo Placido. The outcome is nearly the same; although
Cosmo does not succumb to a death wish, he issues in a state
that could be called death in life--"disembodied," "neither
sleepy nor tired, nor hungry, nor even curious, as if
altogether freed from the weaknesses of the body, and not
indifferent but without apprehensions or speculations of any
sort to disturb his composure as if of a fully informed
wisdom" (S, 272). A last hero all but buried links two
repeated failures of Conrad's fiction, the youth without
sufficient assertiveness to captivate a reader and the
abrupt youthful suicide.

    Both lapses in artistry might be traced to an
irrepressible Oedipal conflict in the author. Aside from
Cosmo's appearance in a work of Conrad's decline, this hero
exemplifies a statement by Frederick Crews:

    No moral or formal commentary can account for
    the fact that Conrad's best work . . . produces
    an effect of "obstruction and deadlock, an
    opposition of matched and mutually paralyzed
    energies." Conrad's most significant level of

discourse is the unconscious level, where
inadmissible wishes are entertained, blocked,
and allowed a choked and guarded expression.[60]

Crews's analysis is applicable to much of Conrad's weaker
fiction, and to more forms of Oedipal conflict than the
sexual, on which the critique is mainly based. But in the
work after 1910 the expression allowed positive Oedipal
wishes has been so curtailed that what Crews termed Conrad's
"real agon . . . the struggle against inhibition"[61] often
loses the look of a contest; the chief indication that any
"opposition of matched and mutually paralyzed energies" is
occurring in a hero may be the fact of his exhaustion.

A comparison of two dissidents may indicate the
distance Conrad has traveled from an early audacity. In
Suspense the reader must remind himself that the flaccid
hero is a recruit--albeit by an act of the stars (S, 273),
not his own volition--in the cause of liberty, against
political reaction. Cosmo passively throwing in his lot
with Napoleon is not "even curious . . . and not indifferent
but without apprehensions or speculations of any sort" (S,
272). Attilio tells him:

"Cantelucci's an experienced conspirator.
He thinks that the force of the people is such
that it would be like an uprising of the ground
itself. May be, but where is the man that would
know how to use it?"
     Cosmo let it go by like a problem that could
await solution or as a matter of mere vain
words. (S, 272)

He contrasts sharply with Conrad's Professor, who has
recruited himself for pure destruction and who utters his
battle cry--"Madness and despair! Give me that for a lever,
and I'll move the world" (SA, 309)--in the face of fear that
nothing can move it. The earlier son shows an overweening
self-assertion and a desperate engagement, the later
prostration and apathy.

Epilogue

Enough has perhaps been said to indicate the utility of a
psychoanalytic approach to the ambivalent relations of
fathers and sons in Conrad. The method provides an
explanation for the inability of both to know their
own motives; for their mutual hostility; for the son-
protagonist's often remarkable passivity, a form of submission almost unbroken in the later works; and for what
seems his choice between asceticism and an early death.
Conrad's fiction reveals an affinity with concepts generally
called "Freudian" (whether or not they originated with
Freud); these include the unconscious with its burden of
guilt, repression, pregenital sexuality, the Oedipus complex
in its positive and negative forms and sexual and asexual
manifestations, and the punitive superego as a legacy from
the father. For both Conrad and Freud, in determining the
adult's attitude toward the authority of the state and
toward belief in God, ". . . the father-relation is the
decisive factor."[1] Both writers saw suicide as an act
that could be parricidal in its implications. Even one of
Freud's most dubious notions, that a primal human horde once
existed under paternal tyranny, finds a parallel in Conrad's
sense of an exclusively paternal sexual prerogative.

Some aspects of the novelist's work, however, suggest
the conclusions of other psychoanalysts. His intimations of
a complex suicidal motivation resemble the theory that Karl
Menninger built on Freud's foundation. Conrad's assumption,
especially in Heart of Darkness, of a sadistic orality that
vitiates both paternal and paternalistic relationships
suggests Karl Abraham's division of Freud's single, relatively benign oral stage. In regard to the Oedipus
complex, part of Conrad's thought not only lies outside

Freud's theory but opposes it. There is, first of all, a
difference in the range assumed for the complex. Freud
concluded from self-analysis that he himself had one, and
universalized this facet of his psyche. In The Interpretation of Dreams he wrote, "It is the fate of all of us,
perhaps, to direct our first sexual impulse towards our
mother and our first hatred and our first murderous wish
against our father."[2] Five years later, in Three Essays
on the Theory of Sexuality, he declared flatly, "Every new
arrival on this planet is faced by the task of mastering the
Oedipus complex."[3] The confidence of his generalization
is surprising, if only because his own life experience had
been quite special. Indeed, the atypicality of his childhood could be compared at several points with the atypicality of Conrad's. Freud was the favorite child of a
woman much younger than her husband, Conrad the only child
of one who had died when he was seven. Each had a dis-
advantaged father--Freud's as a Jew in the Austro-Hungarian
Empire, Conrad's as a Pole and a rebel in the Russian
Empire--who must have roused in his son (among other emotions) both pity and contempt.[4] Moreover, both Freud
and Conrad began as sons struggling for power, independence, and recognition in a particular milieu, the patriarchal and (at least in its ethos) sexually repressive
society of late-nineteenth-century Europe. Like Erich
Fromm, but unlike Freud, Conrad apparently entertained
the idea that the Oedipus complex might be a product of
authoritarian society.[5] In his fiction men from outside
Europe are generally exempt from Oedipal conflict. Such
nonwhite youths as Dain Maroola in Almayer's Folly, Tamb'
Itam in Lord Jim, and Wang in Victory are foils to guilt-
ridden white protagonists in the same works.

        Differences between Conrad and Freud also appear in the
ramifications assigned to the Oedipus complex. In place
of Freud's view, now widely discredited, that paranoia
originates in homosexuality, Conrad's The End of the Tether
and The Shadow-Line assert the position later affirmed by
the post-Freudian Jule Nydes, that it stems from Oedipal
conflict. A second difference from Freud's theories, and
one central to Conrad's fiction, lies in the latter's
assumption of the Oedipal father's hostility to the son, as
a complement to the son's hatred and fear of him; Oedipus
and Laius interact. Here Conrad's position is that assumed
by Neil Friedman and Richard Jones, or by John Munder Ross,
who posited a potential "heart of darkness" in fatherhood--a
paternal animus Freud imputed to himself and others but
omitted from his theory. The lacuna was possibly a concession to the father-dominated society in which he sought

acceptance. A further difference from Freud, or an extension of his thought, lies in Conrad's notion of Oedipal
compromise, a concept later to be formulated by Jule Nydes
as an aspect of paranoid or masochistic psychology: "Success
may be tolerated in one area, if defeat is endured in
another."[6] Freud himself noted the possibility of a
defensive renunciation when he diagnosed a son's flight from
women and work as motivated by fear of the father, to whom
these pursuits seemed rightfully to belong.[7] Freud's
formulation, however, does not indicate any necessary benefit, apart from decreased guilt or anxiety, to the son.
Conrad, on the other hand--like Nydes--seems to have
envisioned a positive gain, a success; his fictional
celibates, left free of guilt in the pursuit of nonsexual
goals, are often substantial achievers.

    Nydes's formula--victory in one area, defeat in
another--does not specify the kind of accommodation to be
reached. In his reinterpretation of Freud's Schreber
case,[8] the wish to overthrow the God-father is relinquished for the "voluptuousness" of sexual union with
God and the opportunity to mother a new race of superior
human beings; instead of God's Oedipal rival Schreber
became God's wife.[9] The bargain that Conrad strikes for
his characters is virtually the opposite: a resignation of
sexual privileges (in this case, with women) to insure
survival and a wide latitude in nonsexual self-assertion.
My analysis of his fiction has been structured on his use
of this compromise, his general adherence to it in his best
fiction, and his abandonment of it in later and weaker
works.

    Conrad's inability to sustain the bargain, and thus to
allow his later heroes an interesting scope in self-
assertion, was seemingly due, at least in part, to conflicts attendant on his writing of an overtly parricidal
novel, Under Western Eyes, in 1910. I doubt that his
post-1910 heroes' quiescence can be attributed to a weak-
ening, as he grew older, of his own urge to rebel. In
the late fiction his trenchant portraits of such fathers
as the elder Heyst, Giles and the violin captain, and the
Ulyssean Peyrol--a man-god no less autocratic than Lingard--
would suggest, on the contrary, that his Oedipal hostility
remained undiminished. His fiction reaches no reconciliation with the father; rather, the son--caught, as Marvin
Mudrick has said, in a "deadlock, an opposition of matched
and mutually paralyzed energies"[10]--ceases to struggle.

    A hypothesis that Conrad himself suffered from Oedipal
conflict is consonant with many biographical facts--in

particular, his desertion of his father's cause in Poland, his single brief tenure--terminated by his resignation--as a ship's captain, his frequent experience of blockage in writing, and the coincidence of a parricidal novel and a mental breakdown in 1910. The same hypothesis accords with such characteristics of his fiction as the splitting of the father figure; the need for an Oedipal compromise before he would allow his young European heroes to survive the ends of his works; the continual repetition, as if by compulsion, of Oedipal themes; and the selection from his triad of paternal traits--benevolence, comedy, and menace--of the third as predominant. Even so, Conrad's fictional treatment of Oedipal conflict might represent merely a problem transcended, that is, sublimated into art, were it not that the sublimation sometimes appears to break down. I have tried to indicate two such points of possible collapse: a failure to transmute suicidal motivation fully into art, and a shift after 1910 to heroes so passive as to be inadequate for fiction. Nothing here can be said to prove that Conrad was an adult victim of Oedipal conflict. However, the interest of a psychoanalytic approach to an author, as well as to his characters, lies in the unifying explanation it can offer for a range of otherwise disparate phenomena.

Notes

Chapter 1. INTRODUCTION

1. The Ego and the Id, in vol. 19 of The Standard Edition of the Complete Psychological Works of Sigmund Freud, ed. and trans. James Strachey, 24 vols. (London: Hogarth Press, 1953-73), 33. This edition is cited hereafter as SE.

2. Irving Howe, "Conrad: Order and Anarchy," in Politics and the Novel (London: Stevens & Sons, 1961), 81.

3. Thomas Parkinson, "'When Lilacs Last in the Door-Yard Bloom'd' and the American Civil Religion," Southern Review 19 (1983): 6.

4. Conrad to Marguerite Poradowska, 4 September 1892, The Collected Letters of Joseph Conrad, ed. Frederick R. Karl and Laurence Davies, vol. 1, 1861-1897 (Cambridge: Cambridge University Press, 1983), 113-14.

5. Joseph Conrad, "Well Done," NLL, 183.

6. In his Familiar Preface to A Personal Record, Conrad wrote: "Those who read me know my conviction that the world, the temporal world, rests on a few very simple ideas; so simple that they must be as old as the hills. It rests notably, among others, on the idea of Fidelity" (PR, xxi).

7. Erik H. Erikson, "The Problem of Ego Identity," Journal of the American Psychoanalytic Association 4 (1956): 110.

8. Conrad's assumption of a sexual basis for Oedipal rivalry differentiates him from Carl Jung, Erich Fromm, and other post-Freudians who have endeavored to supersede Freud's insistence on infantile sexuality. Fromm, for example, found that the child's tie to his mother is not

essentially erotic; the conflict between father and son is merely a product of authoritarian, patriarchal society, in which the son, having been treated as his father's property, has a compelling need to assert his freedom and independence (Patrick Mullahy, Oedipus Myth and Complex: A Review of Psychoanalytic Theory [New York: Hermitage Press, 1948], 277-78).

9. Jacqueline Rose, Introduction 2, Feminine Sexuality: Jacques Lacan and the école freudienne, ed. Juliet Mitchell and Jacqueline Rose, trans. Jacqueline Rose (London: Macmillan, 1982), 30.

10. Freud paid tribute to Schopenhauer as a precursor of psychoanalysis. In the essay titled "A Difficulty in the Path of Psycho-Analysis" he proposed Copernicus, Darwin, and Schopenhauer as three great foes--"cosmological," "biological," and "psychological"--of the "universal narcissism of men." The first of these iconoclasts displaced man's habitat, the earth, from the center of the universe; the second established his affinity with animals, and his descent from them; the third anticipated Freud in denying man's mastery of his life by the exercise of conscious will. Schopenhauer's unconscious Will Freud declared to be "equivalent to the mental instincts of psycho-analysis" (SE 17:139, 140, 141, 143-44). For Schopenhauer the adjective "unconscious" described mental contents latent but capable of becoming conscious at any time. Freud added to this meaning the concept that some unconscious contents were repressed, that is, barred from consciousness by a resistance. He had encountered repression--the theory of which he termed "the cornerstone on which the whole structure of psycho-analysis rests" (On the History of the Psycho-Analytic Movement, SE 14:16)--in his work with patients. Ernest Jones has speculated that he also, through his teacher Theodor Meynert, knew it from J. F. Herbart, a philosopher who had actually used the word Verdrängung as early as 1806. Herbart had "expounded the notion of one idea driving another out of consciousness (without supplying any motive for its doing so) and taught that the expelled idea could then influence the conscious mood" (The Life and Work of Sigmund Freud, vol. 1, The Formative Years and the Great Discoveries, 1856-1900 [New York: Basic Books, 1953], 281).

11. John E. Saveson, Joseph Conrad: The Making of a Moralist (Amsterdam: Rodopi NV, 1972), 12-13, 54-63.

12. H. R. Lenormand, "Note on a Sojourn of Conrad in Corsica," trans. Charles Owen, in The Art of Joseph Conrad: A Critical Symposium, ed. Robert W. Stallman (1960; rpt. Athens: Ohio University Press, 1982), 6, 7.

13. Sigmund Freud, "Splitting of the Ego in the Process of Defence," SE 23:278. The castration was actually said to have been performed by Kronos on his father Uranus. In The Psychopathology of Everyday Life, SE 6:218-20, Freud attributed the error to his own Oedipus complex. In age resembling a grandson (Zeus) more than a son (Kronos) of his elderly father, he made himself the castrator.

14. Norman N. Holland, "Style as Character: The Secret Agent," Modern Fiction Studies 12 (1966): 222. Holland uses the terms "ego" and "id" in their usual psychoanalytic sense: the rational and instinctual agencies of the psyche.

15. Ernest Jones, Hamlet and Oedipus (New York: Doubleday, Anchor Books, 1954), 138, 140, 153-55. Jones amplifies Freud's discussion of Hamlet in The Interpretation of Dreams, SE 4:264-66.

16. Jones, Hamlet and Oedipus, 161-62.

17. Sigmund Freud, Totem and Taboo, SE 13:145.

18. Sigmund Freud, "A Seventeenth-Century Demonological Neurosis," SE 19:85-86.

19. Sigmund Freud, Ego and Id, 34.

20. Sigmund Freud, Totem and Taboo, 141.

21. Steven Marcus, The Other Victorians: A Study of Sexuality and Pornography in Mid-Nineteenth-Century England (New York: New American Library, Meridian, 1977), 22-26.

22. Sigmund Freud, "The Psychogenesis of a Case of Homosexuality in a Woman," SE 18:159n.

23. Jule Nydes, "The Paranoid-Masochistic Character," Psychoanalytic Review 50 (1963): 228-29, 234.

24. Conrad's practice of doubling corresponds to the description given by C. F. Keppler in The Literature of the Second Self (Tucson: University of Arizona Press, 1972), 9-13: the second self is externally real, independent of the first; the two exist in "combined affinity and opposition" (12). Together they comprise "a being sometimes suggesting the total human personality, sometimes a very narrow segment of it" (12).

25. Jessie Conrad to David S. Meldrum, 6 February 1910, Joseph Conrad: Letters to William Blackwood and David S. Meldrum, ed. William Blackburn (Durham, N. C.: Duke University Press, 1958), 192.

26. Thomas Moser, Joseph Conrad: Achievement and Decline (1957; rpt. Hamden, Conn.: Archon Books, 1966), 178; Albert J. Guerard, Conrad the Novelist (Cambridge: Harvard University Press, 1958), 256-58.

27. Bernard C. Meyer, Joseph Conrad: A Psychoanalytic Biography (Princeton, N. J.: Princeton University Press, 1967), 221-22. Hereafter cited as Psychoanalytic Biography.

28. Richard F. Sterba, "Remarks on Joseph Conrad's Heart of Darkness," Journal of the American Psychoanalytic Association 13 (1965): 574-75; Frederick Crews, "Conrad's Uneasiness--and Ours," in Out of My System: Psychoanalysis, Ideology, and Critical Method (New York: Oxford University Press, 1975), 56.

29. Meyer, Psychoanalytic Biography, 112.

30. Sigmund Freud, "Dostoevsky and Parricide," SE 21:187.

31. Gustav Morf, The Polish Heritage of Joseph Conrad (London: Sampson, Low, Marston & Company, 1930), 127-41, 149-66, 198-202. Conrad's own explanation of this act appears in PR, 35-36. A typically enigmatic sentence is the following: "It would take too long to explain the intimate alliance of contradictions in human nature which makes love itself wear at times the desperate shape of betrayal" (36).

32. Robert R. Hodges, The Dual Heritage of Joseph Conrad (The Hague: Mouton & Company, 1967), 63-79, gives an excellent account of the Bobrowski-Korzeniowski opposition.

33. Zdzisław Najder, Joseph Conrad: A Chronicle, trans. Halina Carroll-Najder (New Brunswick, N. J.: Rutgers University Press, 1983), 35.

34. Robert M. Armstrong, "Joseph Conrad: The Conflict of Command," Psychoanalytic Study of the Child 26 (1971): 494-500. Hereafter cited as "Conflict of Command."

35. Sigmund Freud, "The Paths to the Formation of Symptoms," SE 16:376.

36. Ernst Kris, "Prince Hal's Conflict," Psychoanalytic Quarterly 17 (1948): 506; Psychoanalytic Explorations in Art (New York: International Universities Press, 1952), 29.

37. T. S. Eliot, "Hamlet," in Selected Essays, 1917-1932 (New York: Harcourt, Brace & Company, 1932), 124.

38. Sigmund Freud, Civilization and Its Discontents, SE 21:69.

39. Meyer, Psychoanalytic Biography, 345-46.

40. Ibid., 182.

41. The phrase was coined by Moser, Joseph Conrad, 50. What seems a conscious authorial intent to idealize women is undercut by a relentless subterranean misogyny. A reluctant Freudian, Moser tentatively diagnoses Conrad's attitude to women as one of sexual fear (5).

42. Armstrong, "Conflict of Command," 532. Conrad's stereotyped portraits of women suggest that his creative imagination was not deeply engaged with the dead mother and her fictional derivatives. Frederick Karl, despite a strong interest in psychobiography, has offered literature

as the source of many Conradian heroines. Such androgynes
as Rita in The Arrow of Gold closely resemble the women of
fin de siècle and decadent art, as analyzed by Mario Praz
in The Romantic Agony (Karl, Joseph Conrad: The Three Lives
[New York: Farrar, Straus & Giroux, 1979], 163-68).

    43. Eliot, "Hamlet," 125.

    44. During his lifetime Conrad passed off the injury
as the result of a duel, fictionalized in The Arrow of
Gold. Bernard Meyer's account, based on a letter written
by Bobrowski 24 March 1879 and discovered in 1937, stresses
Conrad's adherence to the psychology of the unsuccessful
suicide, who commonly thwarts his own act. Granted that
Conrad's bullet could have been fatal, the incompleteness
of his will to die at twenty was shown by his precau-
tions: the shot fired shortly before the arrival of a
creditor, invited to tea, who could summon aid; the family
addresses left in a conspicuous place so that the rescuer
could notify Bobrowski--the source of cash urgently needed
for his nephew's debts (Meyer, Psychoanalytic Biography,
35-39).

    45. Karl A. Menninger, Man against Himself (New York:
Harcourt, Brace & Company, 1938), 24-80.

    46. Norman L. Farberow and Edwin S. Shneidman,
"Suicide and Age," in Clues to Suicide, ed. Edwin S.
Shneidman and Norman L. Farberow (New York: McGraw-Hill
Book Company, Blakiston, 1957), 42. The terms are taken
from Menninger's description of the three wishes in Man
against Himself.

    47. Sigmund Freud, Beyond the Pleasure Principle, SE
18:38.

    48. Sigmund Freud, "Homosexuality in a Woman," 162-63.

    49. Sigmund Freud, Ego and Id, 34.

    50. Meyer, Psychoanalytic Biography, 356.

    51. Sigmund Freud, Civilization and Its Discontents,
137.

    52. Clarence P. Oberndorf, "Psychoanalysis in
Literature and Its Therapeutic Value," Psychoanalysis and
the Social Sciences 1 (1947): 301, 310.

Chapter 2. THE PROTOTYPE OF THE FATHER: LINGARD IN
ALMAYER'S FOLLY AND AN OUTCAST OF THE ISLANDS

    1. I have omitted the Lingard of a late novel, The
Rescue, an inverse sequel that purports to show the same
philanthropist at the age of about thirty-five. But
Almayer's Folly (1895), An Outcast of the Islands (1896),
and The Rescue (begun 1896, published 1920) do not appear

to constitute a trilogy in the life of a single adventurer.
In accord with the simplifying and normalizing effort of
Conrad's fiction after 1910, Lingard in The Rescue has been
reduced from the power-hungry egotist of the first two
novels to an innocent, and less interesting, victim of
circumstance; the issue of moral responsibility has been
lost. See Thomas Moser, "The Later Affirmation," in his
Joseph Conrad, 131-78.
    2. For a discussion of the god-man in late-Victorian
fiction, see Bruce Johnson, "'Heart of Darkness' and the
Problem of Emptiness," Studies in Short Fiction 9 (1972):
387-400. For Conrad the archetype was to be found in the
career of Rajah James Brooke of Sarawak, who was worshipped
as a god by Malays. In an occasional touch of deification
by natives, Lingard foreshadows the more fully developed
Conradian white gods of Heart of Darkness and Lord Jim:
". . . the Rajah Laut could make himself invisible. Also,
he could be in two places at once, as everybody knew" (OI,
317).
    3. Sigmund Freud, Totem and Taboo, 125, 141.
    4. John Munder Ross, "Oedipus Revisited: Laius and the
'Laius Complex,'" Psychoanalytic Study of the Child 37
(1982): 170.
    5. Conrad's seeming reluctance to confront Lingard
would be difficult to trace to any single source for this
character. He resembles Apollo Korzeniowski as a widely
destructive idealist and egotist, Tadeusz Bobrowski as a
substitute father to a circle of dependents, and Conrad's
Corsican sea mentor Dominic Cervoni as a rover making his
own laws. From Conrad's reading, as noted above, there
emerged the model of Rajah Brooke, an equivocal benefactor
discussed by Avrom Fleishman in Conrad's Politics: Community and Anarchy in the Fiction of Joseph Conrad (Baltimore: Johns Hopkins Press, 1967), 99-105. According to
Norman Sherry in Conrad's Eastern World (Cambridge: Cambridge University Press, 1966), 89-135, the principal
source, known to Conrad only by hearsay, was a Captain
William Lingard, called Rajah Laut by the natives, who
traded in the Malay Archipelago as early as the 1860s and
discovered a navigable channel for ships in the Berau River
of Borneo. His partner in a trading post he established at
Berau was Olmeijer, the original of Almayer. Like the
fictional Lingard, the historical Rajah Laut was a Ulyssean
sea hero famed for recklessness, wealth, generosity, and
the desire to collect protégés. Nevertheless, for reasons
unstated by Sherry, the friends of William Lingard
considered Conrad's portrayal a libel on his memory.
    6. R. A. Gekoski, "An Outcast of the Islands: A New
Reading," Conradiana 2, no. 3 (1969-70): 50-51.

7. Ibid, 52.

8. Sigmund Freud, "Instincts and Their Vicissitudes," SE 14:138-39.

9. "A Short Study of the Development of the Libido, Viewed in the Light of Mental Disorders," trans. Douglas Bryan and Alix Strachey, in Selected Papers of Karl Abraham, M. D. (London: Hogarth Press, 1927), 450, 451.

10. Allan O. McIntyre, "Conrad on Conscience and the Passions," University Review 31 (1964): 72. McIntyre quotes from Conrad to R. B. Cunninghame Graham, 1 May 1898 and Sunday February 1898, in G. Jean-Aubry, Joseph Conrad: Life and Letters, vol. 1 (New York: Doubleday, Page & Company, 1927), 229, 236.

11. Royal Roussel, The Metaphysics of Darkness: A Study in the Unity and Development of Conrad's Fiction (Baltimore: Johns Hopkins Press, 1971), 1-6. Roussel quotes from Joseph Conrad's Letters to R. B. Cunnninghame Graham, ed. C. T. Watts (Cambridge: Cambridge University Press, 1969), 56.

12. Gekoski, "Outcast," 49.

13. After Almayer's refusal to let him share in the trade of Sambir, Willems, backed by the Arabs, humiliates this antagonist by sewing him into his hammock like a corpse (OI, 183-86). Almayer reciprocates by sending Joanna to remove Willems from Lingard's captivity. To the junior partner, the possibility of the traitor's reinstatement is a definite threat. "In view of the absurd softness of Lingard's heart, every one in whom Lingard manifested the slightest interest was to Almayer a natural enemy" (OI, 302). His intrigue produces the death of Willems at the hands of Aïssa, who declines to release him to the wife and child she did not know he had.

14. This dry phrase is Babalatchi's.

15. Sigmund Freud, "Instincts," 138, 139.

16. Ross, "Oedipus Revisited," 171, 196. Nothing in his article would indicate that the tragic process, described in a phrase from Sandor Ferenczi, is inevitable.

17. Ibid., 181-82. The first quotation is from Erik Erikson, a pioneer in interpersonal psychology.

18. Ibid., 190.

19. Sigmund Freud, The Interpretation of Dreams, SE 5:560. The passage should be compared with Freud's summary of the Oedipus myth in Interpretation of Dreams, SE 4:261-64, in which no word of blame attaches to Laius.

20. Ross, "Oedipus Revisited," 175.

21. Neil Friedman and Richard M. Jones, "On the Mutuality of the Oedipus Complex," American Imago 20 (1963): 125, 127.

22. Not only Aïssa but all of the four women courted by sons in Conrad's first two novels are more notable for motherly than for romantic qualities. Malevolent and protective by turns, they easily overpower their men--for good or ill. The union of a witchlike Mrs. Almayer and Nina destroys Almayer, but Nina expects to make her slave and future spouse a great Malay chieftain. Joanna in a reversal of Aïssa's decisions--first for the son and later for the father--originally aligns herself with the father, in evicting Willems after he has robbed Hudig, but later goes over to the son and even attempts to rescue him from bondage to Lingard. The vacillations of the latter two women suggest an ambivalence in the Oedipal mother.

23. Meyer, Psychoanalytic Biography, 114. Noting Conrad's freedom in writing of some patterns of incest, such as that between father and daughter (in, for example, the first two novels, "Freya of the Seven Isles," and Chance), or between cousins (The Arrow of Gold), or between brother and half sister (Suspense), Meyer considers the omission of the mother-son pattern, between blood relatives, indicative of a suppressed fascination with it.

24. The theme of male rivalry for Nina is carried back into An Outcast, in which a "radiant" Almayer and Lingard admire an erotically described child, with bare shoulders and long black hair in "luxuriant profusion . . . like a close-meshed and delicate net of silken threads" (OI, 192, 193). When the prophetic house of cards Lingard has built for her collapses under the child's light breath, the old seaman is nettled but Almayer laughs.

25. John Dozier Gordan, in Joseph Conrad: The Making of a Novelist (1940; rpt. New York: Russell & Russell, 1963), remarks that Conrad completely disregarded a normal Dutch tolerance for Malay blood, thus laying himself open to the charge by Sir Hugh Clifford, a regional authority, that he did not understand Malayan life (39). It is possible, however, that the racial barrier was a substitute in Conrad's imagination for another obstacle, an Oedipal one.

26. The conclusions of Sterba and Crews will be discussed in ch. 3 below.

27. Meyer, Psychoanalytic Biography, 116n-117n. Meyer (116n) cites a second example of the erotic meaning, for Conrad, of steering a vessel through narrows: Falk, a river tugboat captain, is characterized as a "centaur"--"not a man-horse . . . but a man-boat" (F, 162).

28. The three wishes are listed by Menninger in Man against Himself, 24-80.

29. Robert Wälder, "The Principle of Multiple

Function: Observations on Over-Determination," trans.
Marjorie Haeberlin Milde, Psychoanalytic Quarterly 5
(1936): 45-62.

30. Robert R. Hodges, "Deep Fellowship: Homosexuality
and Male Bonding in the Life and Fiction of Joseph Conrad,"
Journal of Homosexuality 4 (1979): 379-93. Male friendship
in Conrad's fiction may or may not possess sexual overtones; it does strongly for Hodges in the attraction of
Denver and Marlow to Jim, of the "Secret Sharer" captain to
Leggatt, of Jones to Ricardo in Victory, and of the
Shadow-Line captain to Ransome, a young sailor. In Victory
Jones shoots his paramour Ricardo for infidelity with a
woman. For works less explicit than Victory, two of
Hodges's criteria of homosexuality are the intense
preoccupation of one man with another, and an ecstasy or
awkwardness on slight physical contact, as in the captain's
parting from Ransome: "'Won't you shake hands, Ransome?' I
said gently. He exclaimed, flushed up dusky red, gave my
hand a hard wrench--and next moment, left alone . . . I
listened to him going up the companion stairs" (SL, 133).

31. Nydes, "Paranoid-Masochistic Character," 228-29.

Chapter 3. THE JEOPARDY OF THE SON ON LAND: FROM "THE
IDIOTS" TO LORD JIM

1. The two warnings are noted by Meyer, Psychoanalytic
Biography, 117, 125.

2. In progress were two novels, The Sisters, abandoned
as a fragment, and The Rescuer, finally published as The
Rescue in 1920.

3. The chief aim of a Laiuslike marquis and priest is
to hold on to whatever prerogatives the nineteenth century
has left them. Two comic social fathers, relics of an
ancien régime, joyfully read Jean-Pierre's afflictions as
signs of God's wrath against an infidel. When he makes a
temporary conversion, to try what God can do for him, the
curé scents a "triumph for the Church and for the good
cause" (I, 65), and the conservative marquis becomes
certain of re-election as mayor.

4. Stephen A. Reid, "The 'Unspeakable Rites' in Heart
of Darkness," in Conrad: A Collection of Critical Essays,
ed. Marvin Mudrick (Englewood Cliffs, N. J.: Prentice-Hall,
1966), suggests "that Kurtz's unspeakable rites and secrets
concern (with whatever attendant bestiality) human sacrifice and Kurtz's consuming a portion of the sacrificial
victim" (45). According to Reid's argument, derived from
Sir James Frazer's The Golden Bough, these ceremonies

were demanded by anxious natives intent on preserving the
life of a man-god obviously dying but thought to be capable
of rejuvenation if he ate part of a younger and more vigor-
ous man (48).

5. Sterba, "Conrad's Heart of Darkness," 574-82;
Crews, "Conrad's Uneasiness," 56-57.

6. Joseph Conrad, "Geography and Some Explorers," LE,
16. The incident also appears in PR, 13.

7. Freud wrote, "To represent castration symbolically, the dream-work makes use of baldness, hair-cutting,
falling out of teeth and decapitation" (Interpretation of
Dreams, SE 5:357). The blinding of Oedipus, as a punishment for sexual impulses toward the mother, suggests the
same symbolism. But as J. Laplanche and J.-B. Pontalis
have pointed out in The Language of Psycho-Analysis, trans.
Donald Nicholson-Smith (New York: W. W. Norton & Company,
1973), 56, the act of castration may be "distorted or
replaced by other types of attack upon the wholeness of the
body (accidents, syphilis, surgical operations) or even of
the mind (madness)." By implication, any injury might
assume the significance of castration.

8. Crews might have noted that this parallel is
explicit in the text: the Intended putting out her arms to
the retreating image of the dead Kurtz is "a tragic and
familiar Shade, resembling in this gesture another one,
tragic also, and bedecked with powerless charms, stretching
bare brown arms over the glitter of the infernal stream,
the stream of darkness" (HD, 160-61) as the steamer takes
away the dying Kurtz.

9. Crews, "Conrad's Uneasiness," 57.

10. Joseph Dobrinsky, The Artist in Conrad's Fiction:
A Psychocritical Study (Ann Arbor, Mich.: UMI Research
Press, 1989), 9. For Dobrinsky (15), the silver of
Nostromo and the coal as "potential diamond" in Victory
have the same significance as the ivory of Heart of
Darkness.

11. Dobrinsky, Artist in Conrad's Fiction, 15. The
quotations are from NN, x; "Henry James: An Appreciation,"
NLL, 13; and Arthur Symons, Notes on Joseph Conrad: With
Some Unpublished Letters (London: Myers & Company, 1925),
17. Dobrinksy (5, 48) also cites Conrad's statement in the
preface to The Nigger of the "Narcissus": the artist
"descends within himself" (NN, viii).

12. Dobrinsky, Artist in Conrad's Fiction, 4, 7-11.

13. Ibid., 8.

14. Ibid., 17-20. In citing Freud's view that
artistic regression is dangerous, Dobrinsky apparently
refers to the theory that a tendency to mental illness,

stemming from "a certain degree of laxity in the repressions" ("Paths to Symptoms," 376), may be inherent in the artist. In Three Essays on the Theory of Sexuality sublimation is described as a process which "enables excessively strong excitations arising from particular sources of sexuality to find an outlet and use in other fields, so that a not inconsiderable increase in psychical efficiency results from a disposition which in itself is perilous" (SE 7:238).

15. Crews, "Conrad's Uneasiness," 193–94. The ways in which Apollo differs from Kurtz, a self-accused horror, are also striking. The ivory collector's blend of extreme idealism and extreme depravity owes something to a nineteenth-century stereotype of European deterioration in the tropics. Among possible sources Norman Sherry, in Conrad's Western World (Cambridge: Cambridge University Press, 1971), 95–118, has singled out one Arthur Hodister, who, like Kurtz, was a professed humanitarian and who was finally, for his cruelty, killed and eaten by Congo Arabs. However, as Ian Watt has remarked, in Conrad in the Nineteenth Century (Berkeley: University of California Press paperback, 1981), 145, ". . . to create a character who revealed the brutal discrepancy between the colonising ideal and the reality, Conrad needed no other historical model than the two founders of the Congo Free State," the explorer Henry Morton Stanley and King Leopold II of Belgium. Perhaps an official policy of exploitation would have been necessary to create the Congo that Conrad visited in 1890 and described as "the vilest scramble for loot that ever disfigured the history of human conscience and geographical exploration" ("Geography and Some Explorers," LE, 17).

16. Zdzisław Najder, ed., Conrad's Polish Background: Letters to and from Polish Friends, trans. Halina Carroll (London: Oxford University Press, 1964), 11. The particular form (admiration plus pity) of Conrad's ambivalence may have been conditioned by the character of Apollo; but if one accepts Freud's view, some mixture in any son's feelings toward his father would be inevitable.

17. Conrad to Edward Garnett, 23 February 1914, Letters from Joseph Conrad, 1895-1924, ed. Edward Garnett (Indianapolis: Bobbs-Merrill Company, 1928), 245.

18. Sigmund Freud, Civilization and Its Discontents, 110; "'Civilized' Sexual Morality and Modern Nervous Illness," SE 9:191.

19. Conrad to Edward Garnett, 23 February 1914, 244. Paradoxically, the sexual restrictions imposed by Conrad on fictional youths often exceed in severity those imposed by

society on real ones. Society allowed marriage and pro-
creation; Conrad, in response to what may have been
unconscious guilt, denied them to whites.

20. Sigmund Freud, "Paths to Symptoms," 376.

21. Sigmund Freud, "Creative Writers and Day-
Dreaming," SE 9:152.

22. See, for example, Holland, "Style as Character,"
222, and Marshall Bush, "The Problem of Form in the
Psychoanalytic Theory of Art," Psychoanalytic Review 54
(1967): 5-35.

23. Jan Verleun, "Marlow and the Harlequin,"
Conradiana 13 (1981): 198-99.

24. Otto Fenichel, The Psychoanalytic Theory of
Neurosis (New York: W. W. Norton & Company, 1945), 155,
157.

25. Fenichel, Theory of Neurosis, 153.

26. Sigmund Freud, "A Special Type of Choice of Object
Made by Men," SE 11:172-73.

27. Richard F. Sterba, "Aggression in the Rescue
Fantasy," Psychoanalytic Quarterly 9 (1940): 505-8.

28. C. T. Watts, "Heart of Darkness: The Covert
Murder-Plot and the Darwinian Theme," Conradiana 7 (1975):
138.

29. Fenichel, Theory of Neurosis, 157.

30. Sigmund Freud, Psychopathology of Everyday Life,
207.

31. According to Najder, in Joseph Conrad: A Chronicle, 35-36, this goal preceded Conrad's departure for
Marseilles, at the age of sixteen, to go to sea.

32. Conrad to Edward Garnett, 29 March 1898, Letters,
Garnett, 134.

33. Armstrong, "Conflict of Command," 507.

34. Moser, Joseph Conrad, 50, 69.

35. Armstrong, "Conflict of Command," 512.

36. For the symbolism of decapitation see Sigmund
Freud, Interpretation of Dreams, SE 5:357.

37. Ross, "Oedipus Revisited," 190. Ross's theories
have been discussed in ch. 2 above.

38. Armstrong, "Conflict of Command," 514.
Menninger's clinical experience with actual suicides
supports the hypothesis of an erotic significance in the
particular method by which self-destruction is achieved
(Man against Himself, 60-66).

39. Armstrong, "Conflict of Command," 514. Since
Morf's Polish Heritage of Joseph Conrad, critics have
generally agreed that Jim succumbs to Brown under the
"paralysing influence" of some identification with this
canny pirate; identification, according to Morf, "is

characterized always by an extraordinary indulgence for the second self" (157, 158). There is more than one point of similarity; in addition to the id tie noted by Armstrong, Brown, as will be seen, makes a superego appeal.

40. "The respectable Cornelius (Inchi 'Nelyus the Malays called him, with a grimace that meant many things) was a much-disappointed man. I don't know what he had expected would be done for him in consideration of his marriage; but evidently the liberty to steal, and embezzle, and appropriate to himself for many years and in any way that suited him best, the goods of Stein's Trading Company (Stein kept the supply up unfalteringly as long as he could get his skippers to take it there) did not seem to him a fair equivalent for the sacrifice of his honourable name" (LJ, 289).

41. Roussel, Metaphysics of Darkness, 92–93.

42. Edwin S. Shneidman, "Prologue: Fifty-eight Years," in On the Nature of Suicide, ed. Edwin S. Shneidman (San Francisco: Jossey-Bass, 1969), 18–19.

43. Sigmund Freud, Ego and Id, 34.

44. H. M. Daleski, Joseph Conrad: The Way of Dispossession (New York: Holmes & Meier Publishers, 1977), 92; Giles Mitchell, "Lord Jim's Death Fear, Narcissism, and Suicide," Conradiana 18 (1986): 166.

45. Sigmund Freud, "Mourning and Melancholia," SE 14:247.

46. Jeffrey Berman, "Conrad's Lord Jim and the Enigma of Sublimation," American Imago 33 (1976): 397.

47. Guerard, Conrad the Novelist, 148–49.

48. Charles C. Clark, "The Brierly Suicide: A New Look at an Old Ambiguity," Arlington Quarterly 1, no. 2 (1967–68): 263–65.

49. The theme of Oedipal rivalry is supported by the names of two ships--or Greek mountains--the Pelion and the Ossa. In the futile campaign of older gods, the Titans, to reach and conquer their Olympian supplanters, the second mountain was piled on the first (J. E. Zimmerman, Dictionary of Classical Mythology [New York: Bantam Books, 1966], 197).

50. Sigmund Freud, Beyond the Pleasure Principle, 21.

51. Sigmund Freud, Fragment of an Analysis of a Case of Hysteria, SE 7:80.

52. Sigmund Freud, "Special Choice," 173.

53. Conrad appears to have agreed with Ruskin, who defined the grotesque as "in almost all cases composed of two elements, one ludicrous, the other fearful" (quoted by Elsa Nettels, "The Grotesque in Conrad's Fiction," Nineteenth-Century Fiction 29 [1974]: 148).

54. In John Phillipson's Freudian analysis of this passage, the engineer's hallucination comes from his unconscious guilt for a breach of duty; the repulsive toads represent the pilgrims, made hideous by their death throes on a sinking ship. Although the traditional animal for such visions is the snake, Conrad consciously or unconsciously supplied a reptile with legs, symbolic of the escape denied the 800 hapless passengers; besides, toads are akin to frogs, which croak, and "croak" is slang for "to die" ("Conrad's Pink Toads: The Working of the Unconscious," Western Humanities Review 14 [1960]: 437-38). Phillipson's remarks are compatible with Freud's description of two important mechanisms, displacement and condensation, in the formation of dreams. By the first, ". . . the essence of the dream-thoughts need not be represented in the dream at all" (Interpretation of Dreams, SE 4:305); sinking ships and corpses are omitted from the engineer's vision. By the second, each element in the dream's manifest content "turns out to have been 'overdetermined'--to have been represented in the dream-thoughts many times over" (SE 4:283); here, at least three different ideas, ugliness, flight, and death, converge on the image of the toads.

55. The phrasing of Stein's advice--"to follow the dream--and so--ewig" (LJ, 215)--may echo Goethe's con-clusion to Faust: "Das Ewig-Weibliche/Zieht uns hinan." If so, Conrad's version is ironic; the woman who draws Jim on to higher things lures him to death--in a secular universe, the end of striving. His dream of heroism can bring him to his "Eastern bride" (LJ, 416), but no further.

56. Guerard, Conrad the Novelist, 147.

57. Jacques Lacan, "The Function and Field of Speech and Language in Psychoanalysis," in Écrits: A Selection, trans. Alan Sheridan (New York: W. W. Norton & Company, 1977), 42.

Chapter 4. THE IMMUNITY OF THE SON AT SEA

1. A related sea story, in which the captain's incompetence is merely conjectural, is "The Secret Sharer" (1909), to be discussed in ch. 5.

2. The progression is from "they" to "we" to "I."

3. See Conrad's essay "Confidence": "The seamen hold up the Edifice. . . . the British Empire rests on trans-portation." In his day on the high seas the sight of any flag other than the ubiquitous Red Ensign produced "a slight shock" (NLL, 202).

4. Conrad to Spiridion Kliszczewski, 25 November 1885, Letters, Karl, 15.

5. Sigmund Freud, Ego and Id, 37.

6. The Writings of Anna Freud, vol. 2, The Ego and the Mechanisms of Defense, rev. ed. (New York: International Universities Press, 1966), 109, 113, 118, 119.

7. Sigmund Freud, "Dostoevsky and Parricide," 190.

8. Dying on the Narcissus, Wait endeavors to convince himself that he extends a history of apparently genuine shirking: "Last ship--yes. I was out of sorts on the passage. . . . It was easy. They paid me off in Calcutta, and the skipper made no bones about it either. . . . I got my money all right. Laid up fifty-eight days! The fools! O Lord! The fools! Paid right off" (NN, 111).

9. John A. Palmer, Joseph Conrad's Fiction: A Study in Literary Growth (Ithaca, N. Y.: Cornell University Press, 1968), 72.

10. Charles Dickens, Hard Times, ed. George Ford and Sylvère Monod, Norton Critical Edition (New York: W. W. Norton & Company, 1966), 54.

11. Dickens, Hard Times, 106.

12. Ross, "Oedipus Revisited," 182.

13. William W. Bonney, "Christmas on the Nan-Shan: Joseph Conrad and 'The New Seamanship,'" Conradiana 10 (1978): 27.

14. Henri Bergson, "Laughter," in Comedy, ed. Wylie Sypher (New York: Doubleday, Anchor Books, 1956), 84, 111, 112.

15. Sigmund Freud, Jokes and Their Relation to the Unconscious, SE 8:209.

16. Charles I. Schuster, "Comedy and the Limits of Language in Conrad's 'Typhoon,'" Conradiana 16 (1984): 57.

17. Sigmund Freud, Civilization and Its Discontents, 72, 74.

18. Conrad to R. B. Cunninghame Graham, 6 December 1897, Letters, Karl, 1:418.

19. Conrad in "The Fine Art" lamented the reduced responsibilities of the master of a steamship, who has not the same "intimacy with nature" (MS, 30) as the sailing captain. Modern seagoing "has not the artistic quality of a single-handed struggle with something much greater than yourself"; it is "simply the skilled use of a captured force, merely another step forward upon the way of universal conquest" (MS, 31).

20. Charles Schuster has suggested that MacWhirr's principle of equal shares relates him to the Jewish king who proposed to divide a child equally between its two mothers, and also pairs him with the wisest character of

"Typhoon," the engineer Solomon Rout--"a King Solomon figure in his own circle," famous for bon mots (Schuster, "Comedy in 'Typhoon,'" 60). But the tie between MacWhirr and wisdom surely is ironic, and implies no more than Conrad's recognition that the limited mind is sometimes convenient. The captain, proceeding from the fact that the coolies have all worked in the same place for the same length of time, reaches a solution that excludes what he does not know, and has no way of learning: their possible differences in value as employees.

21. Sigmund Freud, "A Seventeenth-Century Demonological Neurosis," 85.

22. See, for example, Conrad's references to "secular trees" and "secular inviolable shade" (ET, 257, 265).

23. Sigmund Freud, "Some Neurotic Mechanisms in Jealousy, Paranoia, and Homosexuality," SE 18:226. As an instance of projection, Massy on the ship shoulders others aside as his inferiors, but flares up when Whalley--whose failing sight he has noted--accidentally forces him back: "I--am--not--dirt. . . . As you seem to think" (ET, 216, 218). A further characteristic of paranoia is the inability to "regard anything in other people as indifferent," the habit of using in "delusions of reference" the most "minute indications" which these others offer ("Some Neurotic Mechanisms," 226). When Whalley and the Malay serang are attempting to traverse a bar, Conrad shows minutiae fueling Massy's rage: "Very busy looking forward at the land, they had not a glance to spare; and Massy, glaring at them from behind, seemed to resent their attention to their duty like a personal slight upon himself" (ET, 221).

24. Sigmund Freud, Psycho-Analytic Notes on an Autobiographical Account of a Case of Paranoia (Dementia Paranoides), SE 12:59, 63.

25. The absence in Conrad's mind of any necessary connection between paranoia and homosexuality is indicated by his portrayal of Whalley's friend Van Wyk. For the bachelor white man of Batu Beru, his magnificent visitor can seem without warning to grow "an inch taller and broader, as if the girth of his chest had suddenly expanded under his beard" (ET, 284-85). ". . . the very physical traits of the old captain of the Sofala . . . made up a seductive personality. Mr. Van Wyk disliked littleness of every kind, but there was nothing small about that man" (ET, 290-91). For Van Wyk as for Massy, an intense admiration of Whalley's physique suggests homosexuality; but Van Wyk displays no sign of paranoia.

26. Nydes, "Paranoid-Masochistic Character," 226, 229.

27. Sigmund Freud, "Dostoevsky and Parricide," 191, 193, 194.

28. Nydes, "Paranoid-Masochistic Character," 228-29.

29. "He had never before allowed anybody to remain under any sort of false impression as to himself. Well, let that go--for [Ivy's] sake. After all, he had never said anything misleading--and Captain Whalley felt himself corrupt to the marrow of his bones" (ET, 214).

30. William Moynihan, "Conrad's 'The End of the Tether': A New Reading," in The Art of Joseph Conrad: A Critical Symposium, 189. Unfortunately, Moynihan fails to present evidence that Conrad was aware of the Sofala region and took from it the name of Whalley's ship.

31. Sigmund Freud, Totem and Taboo, 50-51.

32. Ibid., 50.

Chapter 5. THE FAILURE OF A COMPROMISE

1. Karl, Joseph Conrad: Three Lives, 626. The question of primacy of the personal or the political has been extensively debated. The view that these works are properly treated as political is represented by Fleishman in Conrad's Politics, Howe in "Conrad: Order and Anarchy," and Eloise Knapp Hay in The Political Novels of Joseph Conrad (Chicago: University of Chicago Press, 1963). On the other hand, Helen Funk Rieselbach has recently concluded, in Conrad's Rebels: The Psychology of Revolution in the Novels from Nostromo to Victory (Ann Arbor, Mich.: UMI Research Press, 1985), 2, that Nostromo, The Secret Agent, and Under Western Eyes are chiefly concerned "with the breakdown of human relationships--sexual and familial--rather than with a threatened social order. . . . Politics are essentially a backdrop."

2. Joseph Frank, "Spatial Form in Modern Literature," in The Widening Gyre: Crisis and Mastery in Modern Literature (New Brunswick, N. J.: Rutgers University Press, 1963), 3-62.

3. Daniel R. Schwarz, Conrad: Almayer's Folly to Under Western Eyes (London: Macmillan Press, 1980), 143.

4. According to the text (N, 43), a mispronunciation by Captain Mitchell--apparently of the Italian for "our man."

5. Hodges, Dual Heritage, 116, 117.

6. According to the Author's Note (xii), the powerful original of Nostromo, with his scorn for hombres finos like Conrad, was Conrad's sea mentor, the Corsican Dominic Cervoni. He may have been mastered by his demotion, in fiction, to a son.

7. Dobrinsky, <u>Artist in Conrad's Fiction</u>, 47–48.

8. Harry Marten, "Conrad's Skeptic Reconsidered: A Study of Martin Decoud," <u>Nineteenth-Century Fiction</u> 27 (1972): 83.

9. Jeffrey Berman, <u>Joseph Conrad: Writing as Rescue</u> (New York: Astra Books, 1977), 100–101.

10. Ibid., 100.

11. Evidence that Costaguana is a disguised Poland, periodically engaged in revolution against Russia, is summarized by Meyer, <u>Psychoanalytic Biography</u>, 282–85.   In <u>Nostromo</u> Apollo the patriot has at least three possible avatars—Viola, Avellanos, and Garibaldi; Teresa Viola and the wife of Garibaldi, both of whom die of revolution, reenact the fate of Ewa Korzeniowska.   And Conrad himself, in his Author's Note, identifies the original of Antonia Avellanos as his own "first love" as a schoolboy in Cracow: ". . . she was an uncompromising Puritan of patriotism with no taint of the slightest worldliness in her thoughts.   I was not the only one in love with her; but it was I who had to hear oftenest her scathing criticism of my levities— very much like poor Decoud—or stand the brunt of her austere, unanswerable invective" (xiv).   Martin Ray in "Conrad and Decoud," <u>Polish Review</u> 29, no. 3 (1984): 53–64, summarizes the similarities of these two exiles, and the differences; Conrad may have depicted "the tragic failure of Decoud's return in order to justify his own refusal to return to his homeland" (55)—i.e., to assume the burden of his father's revolutionary legacy.

12. Hodges, <u>Dual Heritage</u>, 47.

13. Sigmund Freud, "Dostoevsky and Parricide," 183.

14. Farberow and Shneidman, "Suicide and Age," 42.

15. Hodges, <u>Dual Heritage</u>, 47.

16. Claire Rosenfield, <u>Paradise of Snakes: An Archetypal Analysis of Conrad's Political Novels</u> (Chicago: University of Chicago Press, 1967), 53.

17. The feminine aspects of the urn—womb shape, flowers—belie Vincent P. Tartella's assertion, in "Symbolism in Four Scenes in <u>Nostromo</u>," <u>Conradiana</u> 4, no. 1 (1972): 65, that it stands for the ruin of Charles's father by the silver mine.

18. Roussel, <u>Metaphysics of Darkness</u>, 130.

19. Michael Wilding, "The Politics of <u>Nostromo</u>," <u>Essays in Criticism</u> 16 (1966): 451.   Wilding cites <u>HD</u>, 66: Natives "were dying slowly—it was very clear. They were not enemies, they were not criminals, they were nothing earthly now,—nothing but black shadows of disease and starvation, lying confusedly in the greenish gloom."

20. Najder, <u>Conrad's Polish Background</u>, 11.

21. Sigmund Freud, "Dostoevsky and Parricide," 187.

22. Sigmund Freud, Notes upon a Case of Obsessional Neurosis, SE 10:175, 176.

23. Ibid., 206.

24. Sigmund Freud, "Repression," SE 14:154.

25. Stevie's habitual stutter is cited by Meyer as evidence of an unconscious aggressive impulse (Psychoanalytic Biography, 174-75, 175n).

26. Sigmund Freud, Obsessional Neurosis, 239.

27. The hat as a mark of sexual privilege will also distinguish the paternal Peter Ivanovitch in Under Western Eyes. In "A Connection between a Symbol and a Symptom," SE 14:339-40, Freud treated both hat and head as symbols of the genitals, and suggested that the first had taken its meaning from close proximity to the second.

28. Meyer has seen autobiographical significance in a novel in which a father kills the child beloved by his wife: begun in the second or third month of Mrs. Conrad's second pregnancy and finished about three months after the birth of the baby, The Secret Agent reflects Conrad-Verloc's hostility to a second son, John (Psychoanalytic Biography, 188). Perhaps, but Stevie, who has the same first name as the lonely Slavic émigré of The Sisters, is equally credible as a self of the author. Although Conrad as he aged doubtless acquired affinities with the Oedipal father, his earlier identification with the son was retained. St. Stephen's, the church Stevie passes in the "Cab of Death" (SA, 145), is named for the first Christian martyr.

29. Joseph I. Fradin, "Anarchist, Detective, and Saint: The Possibilities of Action in The Secret Agent," PMLA 83 (1968): 1415.

30. James W. Hamilton, "Joseph Conrad: His Development as an Artist, 1889-1910," Psychoanalytic Study of Society 8 (1979): 320.

31. Robert D. Wyatt in "Joseph Conrad's 'The Secret Sharer': Point of View and Mistaken Identities," Conradiana 5, no. 1 (1973): 12-26, offers a useful analysis of the narrator's unreliability; however, Wyatt's conclusion, that maturation does not occur, differs from mine.

32. Captain Wallace of the Cutty Sark, the original of the young "Secret Sharer" captain, let a murderer go free but atoned for his breach of duty by committing suicide. See Guerard, Conrad the Novelist, 27-29.

33. Sigmund Freud, "Repression," 151.

34. Josiane Paccaud, "The Name-of-the-Father in Conrad's Under Western Eyes," Conradiana 18 (1986): 205, 211.

35. Anna Freud, Ego and Mechanisms of Defense, 109, 113, 118, 119. See ch. 4 above.

36. That he has not, after all, paid for Haldin, whose phantom has tormented him, is revealed by his actions as "the puppet of his past" (UWE, 362); he goes to his fatal confession at midnight, the hour at which he sent Haldin into a police trap.

37. Conrad to John Galsworthy, 6 January 1908, quoted by Karl, Joseph Conrad: Three Lives, 636.

38. Nothing in the novel has prepared us for Razumov's claim of diabolism: "I was given up to evil" (UWE, 359). The design on Natalia may, in an unconscious return to the plan put forward to Galsworthy, represent simply the violation, by marriage to her brother's betrayer, of her trust in Razumov.

39. Quoted by George Goodin, in "The Personal and the Political in Under Western Eyes," Nineteenth-Century Fiction 25 (1970): 337, from the First American edition (New York, 1911), 336. Goodin's explanation of the removal of this passage is a desire on Conrad's part to make his hero appear sexually normal, in order to focus the reader's attention on political rather than personal issues: "Apparently, Conrad had been trying to motivate Razumov by a general feeling toward women as a group rather than through romantic love. Unfortunately, a strong suggestion of sexual inadequacy results, which endangers the political theme" (336). For Goodin, the deletion works with another textual change, an addition to the last entries of Razumov's diary: "I felt that I must tell you that I had ended by loving you" (UWE, 361). "This passage," writes Goodin, "is the only one in the novel which authorizes us to say definitely that Razumov loved Natalia" (336). Razumov was not, however, to be normalized by a single pair of emendations.

40. Rieselbach, Conrad's Rebels, 69.

41. Meyer, Psychoanalytic Biography, 205.

42. Armstrong, "Conflict of Command," 516.

43. Menninger, Man against Himself, 60-66.

44. Lenormand, "Conrad in Corsica," 7. Conrad's refusal to read Freud has a parallel in his rejection of Dostoevsky, with whose Crime and Punishment Under Western Eyes has often been compared (see, for example, Karl, Joseph Conrad: Three Lives, 678-80), and whom he tried to dismiss as a "grimacing haunted creature" (Conrad to Edward Garnett, May 1917, Letters, Garnett, 249).

45. Jessie Conrad to David S. Meldrum, 6 February 1910, Letters, Blackburn, 192.

46. Meyer, Psychoanalytic Biography, 207.

Chapter 6. QUIETUS

1. Meyer, _Psychoanalytic Biography_, 144–45, 148.
Ford's search for a substitute parent extended to the
fabrication that Violet Hunt had been at school with his
mother (145).

2. Quoted by Meyer, 149, from a letter of Conrad's to
Perceval Gibbon (dated "Sunday"), the Berg Collection, New
York Public Library. For Meyer, however, the "indulged
child reveling in popularity" (_Psychoanalytic Biography_,
148) enjoyed a preoedipal rather than an Oedipal relationship with the new mother.

3. Meyer, _Psychoanalytic Biography_, 167.

4. Ibid., 133; quoted by Meyer, 134.

5. Ibid., 167. The quotation is from _LJ_, 93.

6. Ibid., 135–37.

7. Ibid., 167, 243. The quotation is from _T_, 4.

8. Ibid., 221–22. The quotation is from Moser, _Joseph
Conrad_, 140.

9. Ibid., 221.

10. Lenormand, "Conrad in Corsica," 7.

11. The effect of an isolated and disappointed father
on an impressionable son suggests Apollo's stamp on Conrad
as a boy.

12. Morrison, like the later Charles Gould, is
"perfect" (_N_, 521) in materialism.

13. Janet Butler Haugaard, "Conrad's _Victory_: Another
Look at Axel Heyst," _Literature and Psychology_ 31, no. 3
(1981): 36–38.

14. Dobrinsky, _Artist in Conrad's Fiction_, 9. See ch.
3 above.

15. Sigmund Freud, "Special Choice," 173. That Heyst
never knew his dead mother would not, in Otto Fenichel's
view, prevent him from having an Oedipus complex; rather,
the complex, which Fenichel considered to have a phylogenetic root, might be fostered by deprivation: "In
general one may say that when the parent of the child's
own sex dies, this is perceived as a fulfillment of the
oedipus wish and specially strong feelings of guilt are
therefore aroused. If the other parent dies, the oedipus
longing which remains unsatisfied leads to the fantastic
idealization of the dead parent and to an increase of the
longing" ("Specific Forms of the Oedipus Complex," in
Collected Papers, First Series [New York: W. W. Norton &
Company, 1953], 213).

16. Sigmund Freud, "Special Choice," 166.

17. Ibid., 166.

18. Ibid., 168.

19. Ibid., 167–68.

20. Ibid., 168–69.

21. Ibid., 169–72.

22. Donald A. Dike, "The Tempest of Axel Heyst," Nineteenth-Century Fiction 17 (1962): 108.

23. The correspondence between Jones and Heyst, Sr., as Satanic figures was noted by Gerard A. Pilecki, "Conrad's Victory," Explicator 23, no. 5 (1965): item 36, and was doubtless intentional; as Pilecki may have been the first to observe, each man sports a blue dressing gown (V, 91, 376, 411).

24. Wilfred S. Dowden, Joseph Conrad: The Imaged Style (Nashville, Tenn.: Vanderbilt University Press, 1970), 164.

25. Sigmund Freud, "Special Choice," 174.

26. Sigmund Freud, "On the Universal Tendency to Debasement in the Sphere of Love," SE 11:180, 185.

27. Ibid., 182–83.

28. In Sons and Lovers, published two years before Victory, both the "lower" and the "higher" sexual objects are depicted. Simon O. Lesser in Fiction and the Unconscious (New York: Random House, Vintage Books, 1962), 175–78, has analyzed Lawrence's novel in the light of "On the Universal Tendency to Debasement."

29. Menninger, Man against Himself, 60–66.

30. Berman, "Lord Jim and Sublimation," 399.

31. Hodges, "Deep Fellowship," 389.

32. Sigmund Freud, "Homosexuality in a Woman," 159n.

33. Nydes, "Paranoid-Masochistic Character," 226.

34. Hamlet 1.2.133–34, Richard III 1.1.1–2, in The Complete Works of Shakespeare, ed. Hardin Craig (Chicago: Scott, Foresman & Company, 1961).

35. Sigmund Freud, Obsessional Neurosis, 175–76.

36. Nydes, "Paranoid-Masochistic Character," 229.

37. Ibid., 229.

38. Ibid., 215.

39. Ibid., 216.

40. Ibid., 216.

41. Ibid., 229: the masochist "openly submits to punishment," whereas the paranoid "in the name of avoiding unjust punishment unconsciously provokes punishment."

42. Sigmund Freud, Ego and Id, 34.

43. Erikson, "Problem of Ego Identity," 110.

44. Meyer, Psychoanalytic Biography, 250n.

45. Ibid., 250. Meyer quotes from Jessie Conrad, Joseph Conrad As I Knew Him (New York: Doubleday, Page & Company, 1926), 15.

46. Sigmund Freud, Interpretation of Dreams, SE 5:560. The correlation of this dream with the theory of John

Munder Ross has been discussed in ch. 2 above.

47. Meyer, Psychoanalytic Biography, 248.

48. Conrad apparently feigned illness as an excuse; see Meyer, Psychoanalytic Biography, 247-48.

49. Najder, Joseph Conrad: A Chronicle, 35.

50. M. C. Bradbrook, quoted by Moser, Joseph Conrad, 131.

51. Daniel R. Schwarz, Conrad: The Later Fiction (London: Macmillan, 1982), 141, 142.

52. Ibid., 141.

53. Lloyd Fernando in "Conrad's Eastern Expatriates: A New Version of His Outcasts," PMLA 91 (1976): 78-90, has summarized the liberalizing (or unsettling) effect of Conrad's own "discovery of new values in life" (OI, vii) as he traveled: "Truth in Conrad has no face" (89).

54. Angus Fletcher, "Psychoanalytic Analogues: Obsession and Compulsion," in Allegory: The Theory of a Symbolic Mode (Ithaca, N. Y.: Cornell University Press, 1964), 287, 288, 289, 295. He quotes from Fenichel, Theory of Neurosis, 295.

55. Ibid., 296. Fletcher quotes from Fenichel, Theory of Neurosis, 297.

56. In Scevola, who thinks conspiracy everywhere, Conrad once more links parricide with paranoia. The Jacobin resembles Massy in The End of the Tether, and Burns and the narrator in The Shadow-Line.

57. Herbert Howarth, "The Meaning of Conrad's The Rover," Southern Review, n.s., 6 (1970): 687.

58. W. R. Martin, "Allegory in Conrad's The Rover," English Studies in Africa 10 (1967): 186-91.

59. King Lear 5.3.326, Complete Shakespeare.

60. Crews, "Conrad's Uneasiness," 46. Crews quotes from Marvin Mudrick, Introduction, Conrad: A Collection of Critical Essays, 2.

61. Crews, "Conrad's Uneasiness," 49.

EPILOGUE

1. Sigmund Freud, "Dostoevsky and Parricide," 187.

2. Sigmund Freud, Interpretation of Dreams, SE 4:262.

3. Sigmund Freud, Three Essays on Sexuality, 226, n. 1.

4. In The Interpretation of Dreams Freud records his sensitivity to the small incident in which a Christian knocked the elder Freud's cap into the mud and the father failed to resist (SE 4:197). Conrad's father was inclined to resist but proved, as a revolutionary, wholly ineffec-

tual.

5. A possible alternative to the view that the Oedipus complex derives entirely from experience is the supposition that it has a phylogenetic root but that some contact with authoritarian, patriarchal society is requisite to its development.

6. Nydes, "Paranoid-Masochistic Character," 234.

7. Sigmund Freud, "Homosexuality in a Woman," 159n.

8. Sigmund Freud, Autobiographical Account of Paranoia, 3-82.

9. Nydes, "Paranoid-Masochistic Character," 223-24. Among other possible compromises he mentions one similar to Conrad's: ". . . a man who becomes successful in his career may avoid jeopardy by finding himself almost completely devoid of sexual interest in his wife" (234).

10. Mudrick, Introduction, 2.

Bibliography

Abraham, Karl. "A Short Study of the Development of the
     Libido, Viewed in the Light of Mental Disorders." In
     Selected Papers of Karl Abraham, M. D., 418-501.
     Trans. Douglas Bryan and Alix Strachey. London:
     Hogarth Press, 1927.
Armstrong, Robert M. "Joseph Conrad: The Conflict of
     Command." Psychoanalytic Study of the Child 26 (1971):
     485-534.
Bergson, Henri. "Laughter." In Comedy, ed. Wylie Sypher,
     61-190. New York: Doubleday, Anchor Books, 1956.
Berman, Jeffrey. "Conrad's Lord Jim and the Enigma of
     Sublimation." American Imago 33 (1976): 380-402.
___. Joseph Conrad: Writing as Rescue. New York: Astra
     Books, 1977.
Bonney, William W. "Christmas on the Nan-Shan: Joseph
     Conrad and 'The New Seamanship.'" Conradiana 10
     (1978): 17-39.
Bush, Marshall. "The Problem of Form in the Psychoanalytic
     Theory of Art." Psychoanalytic Review 54 (1967): 5-35.
Clark, Charles C. "The Brierly Suicide: A New Look at an
     Old Ambiguity." Arlington Quarterly 1, no. 2
     (1967-68): 259-65.
Conrad, Jessie, to David S. Meldrum. 6 February 1910.
     Letters to William Blackwood and David S. Meldrum, ed.
     William Blackburn. Durham, N. C.: Duke University
     Press, 1958.
Conrad, Joseph. "Geography and Some Explorers." In Last
     Essays, 1-21. New York: Doubleday, Page & Company,
     1926.
___. Works. Uniform Edition. 22 vols. London: J. M. Dent
     & Sons, 1923-28.
Crews, Frederick. "Conrad's Uneasiness--and Ours." In Out

of My System: Psychoanalysis, Ideology, and Critical
Method, 42-62. New York: Oxford University Press,
1975.

Daleski, H. M. Joseph Conrad: The Way of Dispossession.
New York: Holmes & Meier Publishers, 1977.

Dickens, Charles. Hard Times, ed. George Ford and Sylvère
Monod. Norton Critical Edition. New York: W. W.
Norton & Company, 1966.

Dike, Donald A. "The Tempest of Axel Heyst." Nineteenth-
Century Fiction 17 (1962): 95-113.

Dobrinsky, Joseph. The Artist in Conrad's Fiction: A
Psychocritical Study. Studies in Modern Literature,
no. 92. Ann Arbor, Mich.: UMI Research Press, 1989.

___. "The Son and Lover Theme in Lord Jim." Cahiers
d'etudes et de recherches victoriennes et edouardiennes
2 (1975): 161-66.

Dowden, Wilfred S. Joseph Conrad: The Imaged Style. Nashville, Tenn.: Vanderbilt University Press, 1970.

Eliot, T. S. "Hamlet." In Selected Essays, 1917-1932,
121-26. New York: Harcourt, Brace & Company, 1932.

Erikson, Erik H. "The Problem of Ego Identity." Journal of
the American Psychoanalytic Association 4 (1956):
56-121.

Farberow, Norman L., and Edwin S. Shneidman. "Suicide and
Age." In Clues to Suicide, ed. Edwin S. Shneidman and
Norman L. Farberow, 41-49. New York: McGraw-Hill Book
Company, Blakiston, 1957.

Fenichel, Otto. The Psychoanalytic Theory of Neurosis. New
York: W. W. Norton & Company, 1945.

___. "Specific Forms of the Oedipus Complex." In Collected
Papers, First Series, 204-20. New York: W. W. Norton &
Company, 1953.

Fernando, Lloyd. "Conrad's Eastern Expatriates: A New
Version of His Outcasts." PMLA 91 (1976): 78-90.

Fleishman, Avrom. Conrad's Politics: Community and Anarchy
in the Fiction of Joseph Conrad. Baltimore: Johns
Hopkins Press, 1967.

Fletcher, Angus. "Psychoanalytic Analogues: Obsession and
Compulsion." In Allegory: The Theory of a Symbolic
Mode, 279-303. Ithaca, N. Y.: Cornell University
Press, 1964.

Fradin, Joseph I. "Anarchist, Detective, and Saint: The
Possibilities of Action in The Secret Agent." PMLA 83
(1968): 1414-22.

Frank, Joseph. "Spatial Form in Modern Literature." In The
Widening Gyre: Crisis and Mastery in Modern Literature,
3-62. New Brunswick, N. J.: Rutgers University Press,
1963.

Freud, Anna. The Writings of Anna Freud. Vol. 2, The Ego

and the Mechanisms of Defense, rev. ed. New York:
     International Universities Press, 1966.
Freud, Sigmund. The Standard Edition of the Complete
     Psychological Works of Sigmund Freud, ed. and trans.
     James Strachey. 24 vols. London: Hogarth Press,
     1953-73.
Friedman, Neil, and Richard M. Jones. "On the Mutuality of
     the Oedipus Complex" and "Notes on the Hamlet Case."
     American Imago 20 (1963): 107-31.
Garnett, Edward, ed. Letters from Joseph Conrad, 1895-1924.
     Indianapolis: Bobbs-Merrill Company, 1928.
Gekoski, R. A. "An Outcast of the Islands: A New Reading."
     Conradiana 2, no. 3 (1969-70): 47-58.
Goodin, George. "The Personal and the Political in Under
     Western Eyes." Nineteenth-Century Fiction 25 (1970):
     327-42.
Gordan, John Dozier. Joseph Conrad: The Making of a
     Novelist. 1940; rpt. New York: Russell & Russell,
     1963.
Guerard, Albert J. Conrad the Novelist. Cambridge: Harvard
     University Press, 1958.
Gutierrez, Donald. "Fathers and Son: Conrad's The Shadow
     Line as an Initiation Rite of Passage." University of
     Dayton Review 12, no. 3 (1976): 101-6.
Hamilton, James W. "Joseph Conrad: His Development as an
     Artist, 1889-1910." Psychoanalytic Study of Society 8
     (1979): 277-329.
Haugaard, Janet Butler. "Conrad's Victory: Another Look at
     Axel Heyst." Literature and Psychology 31, no. 3
     (1981): 33-46.
Hay, Eloise Knapp. The Political Novels of Joseph Conrad.
     Chicago: University of Chicago Press, 1963.
Hodges, Robert R. "Deep Fellowship: Homosexuality and Male
     Bonding in the Life and Fiction of Joseph Conrad."
     Journal of Homosexuality 4 (1979): 379-93.
___. The Dual Heritage of Joseph Conrad. The Hague: Mouton
     & Company, 1967.
___. "The Four Fathers of Lord Jim." University Review 31
     (1964): 103-10.
Holland, Norman N. "Style as Character: The Secret Agent."
     Modern Fiction Studies 12 (1966): 221-31.
Howarth, Herbert. "The Meaning of Conrad's The Rover."
     Southern Review, n.s., 6 (1970): 682-97.
Howe, Irving. "Conrad: Order and Anarchy." In Politics and
     the Novel, 76-113. London: Stevens & Sons, 1961.
Johnson, Bruce. "'Heart of Darkness' and the Problem of
     Emptiness." Studies in Short Fiction 9 (1972): 387-
     400.
Jones, Ernest. Hamlet and Oedipus. New York: Doubleday,

Anchor Books, 1954.

___. The Life and Work of Sigmund Freud. Vol. 1, The Form-
    ative Years and the Great Discoveries, 1856-1900. New
    York: Basic Books, 1953.

Karl, Frederick R. Joseph Conrad: The Three Lives, A Biog-
    raphy. New York: Farrar, Straus & Giroux, 1979.

Karl, Frederick R., and Laurence Davies, eds. The Collected
    Letters of Joseph Conrad. Vol. 1, 1861-1897.
    Cambridge: Cambridge University Press, 1983.

Keppler, C. F. The Literature of the Second Self. Tucson:
    University of Arizona Press, 1972.

Kris, Ernst. "Prince Hal's Conflict." Psychoanalytic Quar-
    terly 17 (1948): 487-506.

___. Psychoanalytic Explorations in Art. New York: Inter-
    national Universities Press, 1952.

Lacan, Jacques. Écrits: A Selection. Trans. Alan Sheridan.
    New York: W. W. Norton & Company, 1977.

Laplanche, J., and J.-B. Pontalis. The Language of Psycho-
    Analysis. Trans. Donald Nicholson-Smith. New York:
    W. W. Norton & Company, 1973.

Lesser, Simon O. Fiction and the Unconscious. New York:
    Random House, Vintage Books, 1962.

Lincoln, Kenneth R. "Conrad's Mythic Humor." Texas Studies
    in Literature and Language 17 (1975): 635-51.

Low, Anthony. "Heart of Darkness: The Search for an Occu-
    pation." English Literature in Transition, 1880-1920
    12 (1969): 1-9.

McIntyre, Allan O. "Conrad on Conscience and the Passions."
    University Review 31 (1964): 69-74.

Marcus, Steven. The Other Victorians: A Study of Sexuality
    and Pornography in Mid-Nineteenth-Century England. New
    York: New American Library, Meridian, 1977.

Marten, Harry. "Conrad's Skeptic Reconsidered: A Study of
    Martin Decoud." Nineteenth-Century Fiction 27 (1972):
    81-94.

Martin, W. R. "Allegory in Conrad's The Rover." English
    Studies in Africa 10 (1967): 186-94.

Menninger, Karl A. Man against Himself. New York: Harcourt,
    Brace & Company, 1938.

Meyer, Bernard C. Joseph Conrad: A Psychoanalytic Biog-
    raphy. Princeton, N. J.: Princeton University
    Press, 1967.

Mitchell, Giles. "Lord Jim's Death Fear, Narcissism, and
    Suicide." Conradiana 18 (1986): 163-79.

Morf, Gustav. "Conrad versus Apollo." Conradiana 11
    (1979): 281-87.

___. The Polish Heritage of Joseph Conrad. London:
    Sampson, Low, Marston & Company, 1930.

Moser, Thomas. Joseph Conrad: Achievement and Decline.

1957; rpt. Hamden, Conn.: Archon Books, 1966.

Mudrick, Marvin, ed. Conrad: A Collection of Critical Essays. Englewood Cliffs, N. J.: Prentice-Hall, 1966.

Mullahy, Patrick. Oedipus Myth and Complex: A Review of Psychoanalytic Theory. New York: Hermitage Press, 1948.

Najder, Zdzisław. Joseph Conrad: A Chronicle. Trans. Halina Carroll-Najder. New Brunswick, N. J.: Rutgers University Press, 1983.

____. ed. Conrad's Polish Background: Letters to and from Polish Friends. Trans. Halina Carroll. London: Oxford University Press, 1964.

Nettels, Elsa. "The Grotesque in Conrad's Fiction." Nineteenth-Century Fiction 29 (1974): 144-63.

Nydes, Jule. "The Paranoid-Masochistic Character." Psychoanalytic Review 50 (1963): 215-51.

Oberndorf, Clarence P. "Psychoanalysis in Literature and Its Therapeutic Value." Psychoanalysis and the Social Sciences 1 (1947): 297-310.

Paccaud, Josiane. "The Name-of-the-Father in Conrad's Under Western Eyes." Conradiana 18 (1986): 204-18.

Palmer, John A. Joseph Conrad's Fiction: A Study in Literary Growth. Ithaca, N. Y.: Cornell University Press, 1968.

Parkinson, Thomas. "'When Lilacs Last in the Door-Yard Bloom'd' and the American Civil Religion." Southern Review 19 (1983): 1-16.

Phillipson, John. "Conrad's Pink Toads: The Working of the Unconscious." Western Humanities Review 14 (1960): 437-38.

Pilecki, Gerard A. "Conrad's Victory." Explicator 23, no. 5 (1965): item 36.

Ray, Martin. "Conrad and Decoud." Polish Review 29, no. 3 (1984): 53-64.

Rieselbach, Helen Funk. Conrad's Rebels: The Psychology of Revolution in the Novels from Nostromo to Victory. Studies in Modern Literature, no. 42. Ann Arbor, Mich.: UMI Research Press, 1985.

Rose, Jacqueline. Introduction 2. Feminine Sexuality: Jacques Lacan and the école freudienne, ed. Juliet Mitchell and Jacqueline Rose, 27-57. Trans. Jacqueline Rose. London: Macmillan, 1982.

Rosenfield, Claire. Paradise of Snakes: An Archetypal Analysis of Conrad's Political Novels. Chicago: University of Chicago Press, 1967.

Ross, John Munder. "Oedipus Revisited: Laius and the 'Laius Complex.'" Psychoanalytic Study of the Child 37 (1982): 169-200.

Roussel, Royal. The Metaphysics of Darkness: A Study in the

Unity and Development of Conrad's Fiction. Baltimore: Johns Hopkins Press, 1971.

Saveson, John E. Joseph Conrad: The Making of a Moralist. Amsterdam: Rodopi NV, 1972.

Schuster, Charles I. "Comedy and the Limits of Language in Conrad's 'Typhoon.'" Conradiana 16 (1984): 55-71.

Schwarz, Daniel R. Conrad: Almayer's Folly to Under Western Eyes. London: Macmillan, 1980.

___. Conrad: The Later Fiction. London: Macmillan, 1982.

Shakespeare, William. The Complete Works of Shakespeare, ed. Hardin Craig. Chicago: Scott, Foresman & Company, 1961.

Sherry, Norman. Conrad's Eastern World. Cambridge: Cambridge University Press, 1966.

___. Conrad's Western World. Cambridge: Cambridge University Press, 1971.

Shneidman, Edwin S. "Prologue: Fifty-eight Years." In On the Nature of Suicide, ed. Edwin S. Shneidman, 1-32. San Francisco: Jossey-Bass, 1969.

Stallman, Robert W., ed. The Art of Joseph Conrad: A Critical Symposium. 1960; rpt. Athens: Ohio University Press, 1982.

Sterba, Richard F. "Aggression in the Rescue Fantasy." Psychoanalytic Quarterly 9 (1940): 505-8.

___. "Remarks on Joseph Conrad's Heart of Darkness." Journal of the American Psychoanalytic Association 13 (1965): 570-83.

Sullivan, Sister Mary. "Conrad's Paralipses in the Narration of Lord Jim." Conradiana 10 (1978): 123-40.

Tartella, Vincent P. "Symbolism in Four Scenes in Nostromo." Conradiana 4, no. 1 (1972): 63-70.

Verleun, Jan. "Marlow and the Harlequin." Conradiana 13 (1981): 195-220.

Wälder, Robert. "The Principle of Multiple Function: Observations on Over-Determination." Trans. Marjorie Haeberlin Milde. Psychoanalytic Quarterly 5 (1936): 45-62.

Watt, Ian. Conrad in the Nineteenth Century. Berkeley: University of California Press paperback, 1981.

Watts, C. T. "Heart of Darkness: The Covert Murder-Plot and the Darwinian Theme." Conradiana 7 (1975): 137-43.

Wilding, Michael. "The Politics of Nostromo." Essays in Criticism 16 (1966): 441-56.

Wyatt, Robert D. "Joseph Conrad's 'The Secret Sharer': Point of View and Mistaken Identities." Conradiana 5, no. 1 (1973): 12-26.

Yoder, Albert C. "Oral Artistry in Conrad's 'Heart of Darkness': A Study of Oral Aggression." Conradiana 2, no. 2 (1969-70): 65-78.

Zimmerman, J. E. Dictionary of Classical Mythology. New
    York: Bantam Books, 1966.

Index

About the Author

CATHARINE RISING was born in Berkeley and earned her Ph.D. at the University of California, Berkeley. Now free-lancing, she has written for *Conradiana* and is working on an interpretation of Conrad's major fiction from the standpoint of Kohut's self psychology.

Rising, Catherine

Darkness at heart.

DATE DUE			
JUL 3 0 2001			

Germanna Community College